WRITING INSTRUCTION AND ASSESSMENT FOR ENGLISH LANGUAGE LEARNERS K–8

Writing Instruction
and Assessment for
English Language Learners
K–8

SUSAN LENSKI
FRANCES VERBRUGGEN

THE GUILFORD PRESS
New York   London

© 2010 The Guilford Press
A Division of Guilford Publications, Inc.
72 Spring Street, New York, NY 10012
www.guilford.com

Printed in the United States of America

This book is printed on acid-free paper.

Last digit is print number: 9   8   7   6   5   4   3   2   1

Library of Congress Cataloging-in-Publication Data

Lenski, Susan Davis, 1951–
    Writing instruction and assessment for English language learners K–8 /
Susan Lenski, Frances Verbruggen.
        p. cm.
    Includes bibliographical references and index.
    ISBN 978-1-60623-666-6 (pbk.: alk. paper)
    ISBN 978-1-60623-667-3 (cloth : alk. paper)
    1. English language—Composition and exercises—Study and teaching.
2. English language—Study and teaching (Elementary)—Foreign speakers.
3. English language—Study and teaching (Middle school)—Foreign speakers.
4. Language arts—Ability testing.   5. Literacy—Evaluation.   I. Verbruggen,
Frances.   II. Title.
    LB1576.L418 2010
    372.62'3—dc22
                                                                    2010001133

To the many teachers in Illinois and Oregon
who have inspired me to continue learning new ways
to instruct English language learners
S. L.

In loving memory of my mom, Hazel DeSilva Ramos,
who was an extraordinary teacher
F. V.

About the Authors

Susan Lenski, EdD, is Professor at Portland State University in Portland, Oregon, where she teaches graduate reading and language arts courses. Before joining the faculty at Portland State, she taught in public schools for 20 years and at Illinois State University for 11 years. Her teaching experiences include working with children from kindergarten through high school. Dr. Lenski has been recognized by several organizations for her commitment to education. She is a recipient of the Nila Banton Smith Award from the International Reading Association; was instrumental in her school receiving an Exemplary Reading Program Award from the International Reading Association; and was inducted into the Illinois Reading Hall of Fame. She also served as a member of the International Reading Association Board of Directors (2004–2007). Dr. Lenski has conducted numerous presentations and has published over 60 articles and 15 books. Her research interests focus on strategic reading, English language learners, and adolescent literacy.

Frances Verbruggen, MA, is a student in the Doctor of Education program at Portland State University. She earned a BA in Spanish from the University of Maryland and an MA in teaching French from the University of Illinois at Urbana–Champaign. She became fluent in Dutch while living for 7 years in Belgium. Ms. Verbruggen has worked as an elementary-level classroom teacher and a reading specialist in the Portland area since 2003. Her areas of research interest include struggling readers and writers and English language learners.

Acknowledgments

We would like to thank the teacher candidates in the Portland State University Bilingual Teacher Pathway program, who brainstormed the first draft of the poem "B Is for *Bilingual*," and Anna Tachouet and McCale Ashenbrenner, who edited the final version (Figure 3.2). We also thank students who contributed writing samples for this book.

The teacher candidates who contributed to the poem include:

Jaimie Angeles	Monica P. Kennedy
Adrianne H. Bee	Hong Y. Liu
David W. Brallier	Cynthia Lozornio
Maria C. De Valdenebro	Kimberly J. McCoy
Ana H. Estrada	Patrick S. Milligan
Angelica N. Fuentes	Ian A. Niktab
Ritsuko Fujiwara	Grace Rodgers
Sylvanna M. Gallegos	Peter J. Sincliar
Liliane A. Gerwing	Calvin A. Smith
Dora A. Godinez	Donelle R. Sokolov
Rana S. Hakkoum	Renee Sutter
Silke Howell	Andreina Velasco
Jaclynn J. Hughes	Olga Volnyoheva

Preface

Writing Instruction and Assessment for English Language Learners K–8 was written for educators who are interested in supporting the writing development of English language learners (ELLs), including mainstream classroom teachers, English as a second language/English language development (ESL/ELD) teachers, literacy coaches, administrators, and teacher educators. The book concentrates on the research and proven practices of teaching writing. We decided to address the topic of writing because we found it is the most neglected area of the language arts. We have found that the majority of ELL teachers focus on language development, speaking, listening, and reading and spend little time instructing ELLs in writing. As a result, many of the ELLs whom we see in schools are sadly behind their classmates in their ability to write organized, coherent pieces using Standard English.

The ideas presented in this book are a combination of research that we conducted, our personal experiences as teachers and literacy coaches, and practices that we observed from other teachers. Our combined 50-plus years of experience as language researchers and learners form the basis for the anecdotes and many of the instructional practices.

In the course of our careers, we have found many teachers who are successfully teaching ELLs how to write, but we have not found an entire school with such a focus. So we decided to organize *Writing Instruction and Assessment for English Language Learners K–8* as if it were an entire school with classroom teachers who are interested in improving their ELLs' writing and with a literacy coach who helps them as they learn. These individual teachers and the literacy coach, Ms. Ramos, are a compilation of our experiences and observations, and as such do not exist in real life. We included a literacy coach because we believe that classroom and ESL/ELD teachers often get much of their information and ideas from colleagues, whether they are ESL/ELD specialists, literacy coaches, reading specialists, other classroom teachers, or school administrators.

We were both actively engaged in working with ELLs in different capacities while writing this book. Sue was teaching and supervising ELL paraprofessionals and teachers at Portland State University, and Fran was the ELL mentor coach in Molalla, Oregon. We tried to obtain authentic student writing samples to use as illustrations and were successful in many instances. But we were unable to get parental permissions for some types of writing because most of the schools in our areas were preparing their students for the state writing test. So we developed some of the student writing samples from the many examples of student writing that we had on file. Since our samples were not taken directly from any one student, we believe they represent the type of writing we commonly see from students to illustrate a specific point. Each chapter also features a list of useful web resources.

Writing Instruction and Assessment for English Language Learners K–8 is divided into seven chapters. Chapter 1, "English Language Learners and Writing Research," outlines the diversity that exists among ELL students in elementary and secondary schools in the United States. Characteristics that influence how quickly and how well an ELL will become proficient in academic English include place of origin, previous educational achievement, generation in the United States, and attitude toward education. The chapter also presents a framework for instructing ELLs in academic English writing across the curriculum. Chapter 2, "From Theory to Practice: Writing with English Language Learners," draws on current best practices in English language instruction, such as Susana Dutro's Systematic English Language Development, Jane Echevarria's Sheltered Instruction Observation Protocol, and Marcia Brechtel's Guided Language Acquisition Design, to describe elements of effective writing instruction for ELLs at each different stage of the writing process. To help teachers set high and appropriate expectations for ELLs in their classrooms, we also discuss standards for ELL writing development at various grade and language proficiency levels. Chapter 3, "Facilitating Writing Fluency," discusses the kinds of ELL instruction that facilitate writing fluency, which is the ability to compose text with minimal cognitive effort. To achieve fluency, many ELLs need basic instruction in the English alphabet and some might need to learn the directionality of English writing. All ELLs, from beginning to advanced writers, need practice in writing connected text, and this chapter provides instructional examples that increase writing fluency, such as writing in journals, responding to writing, and writing to learn. Chapter 4, "Teaching Narrative Writing," explains how narrative texts in English are organized in a linear fashion, using a series of events to portray a conflict between characters, and that the way we tell stories could be different from the stories ELLs have experienced in their native language. This chapter provides instructional practices that teach ELLs the structure of both personal experience and fictional stories. Chapter 5, "Academic Writing Genres: Description, Exposition, and Persuasion," tackles the very difficult topic of teaching ELLs how to communicate clearly in academic writing. Similar to narrative writing, academic writing in English is much more linear and direct than the academic writing of other languages. This chapter examines academic writing patterns, the transition words that are commonly used in them, and instructional strategies that teach ELLs how to compose academic genres. Chapter 6, "How Language Works: Grammar and Usage," explains how to teach ELLs to write in Standard English. Many ELLs have different instructional needs from native English speakers and need more explicit instruction on the unique features of English grammar, such as contractions, idioms, and homonyms. This chapter presents helpful games and activities that teach and reinforce grammatical rules so that ELLs learn how to incorporate them into their writing. Finally, Chapter 7, "Assessing Writing," describes various purposes for writing assessments and outlines how to develop effective writing assessments for ELLs. Issues of validity, reliability, and practicality, as well as suggestions for how to base assessments on state and national standards for ELD and how to interpret assessment results, are discussed. In addition, this chapter provides a wide variety of ideas for writing assessments that teachers can implement with ELLs.

Contents

CHAPTER 1

English Language Learners and Writing Research

Ms. Bowden sighed as she closed Pedro's journal and set it back on the pile on her desk. Of all the students in her third-grade class, Pedro was the one who struggled the most with writing. His journal entries did not show the intelligence that she knew he possessed, nor the expressiveness that she tried to bring out in her students during writer's workshop. Certainly, Pedro's poor writing skills were not due to a lack of opportunities to practice writing. In addition to the writer's workshop, Ms. Bowden worked hard to incorporate writing across the curriculum, and she actively encouraged her students to write on topics of their own choice. Furthermore, Esperanza, Huong, and Oleg also struggled with writing. Ms. Bowden knew that all four students spoke a language other than English at home. She could understand why Esperanza, Huong, and Oleg had difficulty with English. After all, Huong and Oleg had come to the United States when they were in second grade, and Esperanza had arrived from Mexico just a couple of months ago. But Pedro was born in the United States, and had gone to the same school since kindergarten.

Ms. Bowden knew she needed to learn more about her English language learners (ELLs). She wanted to understand the thinking processes that they experienced as they tried to compose their journal entries. She also wanted to find out what parts of the writing task posed unique challenges for her ELLs. If she understood what prevented them from fluent and expressive writing, Ms. Bowden reasoned, she could design lessons to address their needs.

As she thought about who she might be able to ask for practical help and insight, her mind instantly turned to Ms. Ramos. Ms. Ramos was the literacy coach at her school. A thoughtful, reflective educational leader with a warm, friendly smile, Ms. Ramos was a trusted resource to the entire faculty. Not only did she have expertise in reading and writing instructional strategies, she had also spent 2 years in Guatemala, learning the language and culture of that country. Ms. Bowden was confident that Ms. Ramos could help her.

An increasing number of teachers in classrooms throughout the United States, like Ms. Bowden, are teaching students who are ELLs. Many teachers feel overwhelmed with the responsibility of presenting grade-appropriate content information to students with limited English proficiency in a way that students from multiple language backgrounds can understand. Teachers are wondering how they can capitalize on students' linguistic and cultural backgrounds, as well as their personal family stories, to help students learn.

Indeed, in our current climate of educational accountability, effectively teaching a rapidly increasing population of students from diverse language backgrounds is an ever-growing challenge. While ELLs all hold in common a need to become proficient and literate in English, many different factors affect how successful they will be at achieving this goal. As Ms. Bowden realized, understanding and learning to appreciate who the ELLs are, where they come from and why, the educational levels that they have already achieved, and expectations for schooling in America, are the first steps in succeeding with this growing segment of students. In this chapter we sketch a profile of ELL students in the United States, and we discuss some of the factors that affect how quickly and how well ELLs acquire the English language.

WHO ARE THE ELLs IN U.S. SCHOOLS?

Ms. Bowden wanted to learn more about the students in her classroom and also about the ELLs that she would teach in the future. She decided to talk with Ms. Ramos, the literacy coach, on a regular basis to learn what she could about the background of her ELLs and how she could teach them more effectively. Before she met with Ms. Ramos, Ms. Bowden decided to read *The Lotus Seed* (Garland, 1997), a story about a young Vietnamese refugee's journey from her homeland to America. As she returned the book to its place on the chalkboard ledge, she wondered how the story related to each one of her ELLs. Many of these students, or their parents, had, like the young girl in the story, come to the United States from such faraway places as Mexico, Laos, Vietnam, Russia, the Ukraine, or Somalia.

Ms. Ramos, the literacy coach, shared some interesting data on ELLs in U.S. schools with Ms. Bowden. According to data from the National Clearinghouse for English Language Acquisition and Language Instruction Educational Programs (National Clearinghouse for English Language Acquisition [NCELA], 2006), approximately 5.1 million ELLs (almost 11% of the entire U.S. public school population) attended school in the United States, in grades pre-K to 12 during the 2004–2005 school year. Public school enrollment of ELLs increased by over 56% between the 1994–1995 and the 2005–2006 school years (NCELA, 2006). The National Council of Teachers of English estimates that there were nearly 47 million ELLs, or 18% of the total population, in the United States by 2000. It is projected that by the year 2030, the number of ELLs in the United States will increase to 40% of the total population (National Council of Teachers of English [NCTE], 2008). Greater enrollment of ELLs means that more and more teachers will be teaching students who are not yet proficient in English.

Ms. Ramos explained that from a global perspective, it is not unusual to find so many ELLs and bilingual students in schools. There are more bilingual or multilingual people in the world than there are monolingual people (Tucker, 1999; Valdés, n.d.), and more of the world's students receive at least a part of their education in a second language than receive it exclusively in their mother tongue (Tucker, 1999). The school in which Ms. Bowden taught encouraged students to become bilingual by teaching after-school classes in both Spanish and Chinese and expecting teachers to be conversational in at least one other language. Ms. Ramos was multilingual, being fluent in English, Spanish, and Portuguese, and Ms. Bowden was learning Spanish and made it a point to learn a few phrases from the native languages of her students.

Where Do ELLs in U.S. Schools Come From?

Ms. Bowden continued to gather information about ELLs and was surprised to learn that a large proportion of ELLs in the United States are actually U.S. born. During the 2001–2002 school year, close to half of all ELLs in the United States were born in this country. This statistic mirrors what Ms. Bowden found in her classroom. First generation immigrants compose only slightly more than half of the ELL population on a national level. Long-term U.S. residents (those who had been in the United States for at least 5 years) make up nearly 15% of ELLs. Twenty-two percent of ELLs had been in the country between 1 and 4 years, and 17% were recent immigrants (in the United States for less than 1 year) (Zehler et al., 2003).

Spanish speakers make up the largest group of ELLs in the United States. During the 2001–2002 school year, half of the ELLs whose first language was Spanish were U.S. born, almost one-third were born in Mexico, and the rest were born in other Spanish-speaking countries (Zehler et al., 2003). While the majority of immigrants to the United States are Spanish speakers from Mexico, immigrants and their school-age children also come from Central and South America, the Caribbean, Europe, Asia and the Pacific Islands, Africa, Oceania, and North America (Shields & Behrman, 2004).

The school in which Ms. Bowden taught had students who spoke 27 different native languages. Some U.S. schools have only 1 or 2 different languages represented and others may have as many as 60 or more. According to Kindler (2002), most ELLs in the United States are Spanish speakers. Next to Spanish, the largest minority language groups are Vietnamese, Hmong, Chinese, Korean, Haitian Creole, Arabic, and Russian. There are literally hundreds of additional languages that are spoken as first languages by students in U.S. elementary and secondary schools. Table 1.1 provides more details about the regions from which students of immigrants to the United States have their origins.

What Does It Mean to Be an Immigrant?

Ms. Ramos knew that the teachers in her school had many misconceptions about immigrants so she gathered information to share with the faculty. The term *immigrant* often conjures up mental images of huddled masses of poor people on ships headed to New York's Ellis Island. However, Ms. Ramos learned that many immi-

TABLE 1.1. **Origins of Children of Immigrants to the United States in 2000**

Region of origin	Percentage of children of immigrants from regions of origin who were present in the United States in 2000
Mexico	40%
Asia and Pacific Islands	23%
Central America and Caribbean	16%
Europe	11%
South America	5%
Africa	3%
North America	2%

Note. Based on U.S. Census 2000: Table 1-1 Nativity, Place of Birth of the Native Population, and Region of Birth of the Foreign-Born Population: 2000. *www.census.gov/population/socdemo/foreign/ppl-145/tab01-1.pdf.*

grants come from middle-income nations, and most immigrants do not represent the poorest among the people in their native country. It takes a certain amount of money to emigrate, whether the emigration is legal or not. The families that make the journey to the United States usually have at least some financial resources. The notion that immigrants are uneducated is also largely inaccurate. Most immigrants in the United States come from cities, where education is more available than it is in rural areas, and where they received at least some education. From some countries, immigrants' level of education and skill is comparable to that of native-born Americans (Portes & Rumbaut, 2006).

While few would disagree that immigrants need to learn English to competently interact with mainstream American society and succeed in the U.S. educational system, the philosophy of Ms. Ramos's school was not to *replace* the home language with English. She knew that to do so would have serious negative implications for immigrants and their families, as well as for society as a whole. Students of immigrants who quickly become English dominant tend to identify more with their peer group than with their families, abandoning the language and culture of their parents, which can result in the breakdown of strong family ties and the rejection of family values. When this happens, parents have more difficulty guiding their students through the turbulent years of adolescence because of both the language and values differences within the family (Portes & Rumbaut, 2006). Furthermore, research on dominant languages of immigrants and their children indicates that it takes as little as three generations for immigrant families to become English dominant (Alba, Logan, Lutz, & Stults, 2002). Table 1.2 provides information about the percentages of fluent speakers of language of origin by generations.

TABLE 1.2. Percentage of Fluent Speakers of Language of Origin by Generations

Generation	Percentage of fluent speakers of language of origin	
	Mexicans	White Europeans
Arrived in the United States before age 13 (gen. 1.5)	60%	50%
Born in the United States to two foreign-born parents (gen. 2.0)	62%	22%
Born in the United States to one foreign-born parent and one U.S.-born parent (gen. 2.5)	35%	3%
Born in the United States to two U.S-born parents and three or four foreign-born grandparents (gen. 3.0)	17%	1%
Born in the United States to two U.S.-born parents and one or two foreign-born grandparents (gen. 3.5)	7%	1%
All parents and grandparents born in the United States (gen. 4.0)	5%	1%

Note. Based on Rumbaut, R. G., Massey, D. S., & Bean, F. D. (2006). Linguistic life expectancies: Immigrant language retention in Southern California. *Population and Development Review, 32*(3), 447–460.

Bilingualism, far from being a disadvantage for immigrant students, has many advantages. Students who are bilingual often have more developed cognitive abilities than monolingual students (Portes & Rumbaut, 2006). In one study that examined dropout rates among monolingual and bilingual students from certain ethnic backgrounds, bilingual students from all the language groups who had not fully developed both of their languages were more likely to drop out of school than were fluent bilinguals. Among fluent Asian bilinguals, the dropout rate was even lower than it was for monolingual English students from Asian backgrounds (Rumbaut, 1995). This would imply that it is important to help bilingual students to develop their academic language skills in both English and in their home language.

Given these facts, Ms. Bowden and Ms. Ramos believed that ELLs have a better chance of success in school when they are supported in the academic development of their home language while learning English (Crawford, 2004). Their school did not have a bilingual program but they knew that native language support can come from home, school, churches, and the community at large. The teachers at Ms. Bowden's school believed that students improve when teachers help parents to understand the importance of home language development and suggest strategies that parents and students can use at home to strengthen the students's home language abilities. Therefore, the teachers all made sure that they fostered this learning.

Educational Backgrounds of Immigrants from Different Regions of the World

Ms. Ramos shared what she had learned about immigrant students with the teachers in order to help them understand the wide diversity that exists among immigrant students. Immigrants arrive in the United States with a wide spectrum of educational backgrounds. At one end of the spectrum are those whom the U.S. government encourages to emigrate; people who are highly educated and highly skilled in fields where Americans may be lacking. At the other end of the spectrum are those with little formal schooling who cross our borders. The kind of education that immigrants received before coming to the United States depends largely on the educational opportunities available to people of their social and income status in the home countries.

Mexicans comprise by far the largest group of immigrants in the United States, and Ms. Bowden found this to be the case in her classroom as well. Most years at least one-half of her ELLs were immigrants from Mexico. She knew that another school in her district had an even higher percentage. As a result, the teachers in the school employed a number of strategies to help the Mexican immigrant students to achieve to their academic potential and graduate from high school and college. As stated earlier, they offered after-school Spanish classes to all of the students in the school; the teachers conducted action research to find out what worked for their particular ELL population; a group of teachers, including Ms. Bowden, took Spanish classes at the local community college; and the district sponsored language immersion classes in Mexico. All of these efforts targeted ways to help the Spanish-speaking ELLs and especially those who had recently arrived from Mexico. Table 1.3 shows the percentage of high school and college completion of immigrants ages 25 years or older who had come to the United States between 1990 and 2000 and who were present in the United States in 2000 (U.S. Census Bureau, 2000).

Immigrants' Attitudes toward Education

Research indicates that immigrants and their children usually arrive in the United States with very positive attitudes toward education and high expectations about education as the key to success in American society, and Ms. Bowden found this to be true for her students as well (Suárez-Orozco & Suárez-Orozco, 2001). Compared with opportunities "back home," the United States appears to have more opportunities for good jobs for immigrants and their families who get a good education (Ogbu & Simons, 1998). The anticipation of a bright future and societal values promising that future motivate many immigrant students and their parents to invest substantial effort in education. It is not enough, however, to continue hoping and believing that schooling will make a positive difference in their lives. Immigrant students need to see that their efforts and the efforts of those who have gone before them actually do lead to success (Ogbu & Matute-Bianchi, 1986).

TABLE 1.3. Percentage of High School and College Completion of Immigrants Ages 25 Years or Older

Place of origin	Percentage of college completion	Percentage of high school completion
All	28.1%	62.5%
Asia	43.1%	78.9%
Africa	42.8%	86.4%
Europe	29.2%	76.5%
Canada	33.3%	82.4%
Oceania	28.6%	80.2%
Latin America	9.6%	43.9%

Note. Based on U.S. Census Bureau. (2000). *Profile of selected demographic and social characteristics for the foreign-born population who entered the United States 1990–2000: 2000. www.census.gov/population/cen2000/stp-159/1990-2000.pdf.*

While the majority of students from some immigrant groups do well in school, and some members of all immigrant groups go on to become successful high school and college graduates, there is a connection between a student's region of origin and educational success in the United States. In other words, some immigrant groups tend to achieve more academic success than others. Racism and job discrimination against some immigrant groups affect attitudes toward education and result in the immigrants losing faith in the American dream of upward mobility. Students may react by resigning themselves to the notion that they cannot achieve, or they may resist, either in positive ways, by hard work and a persistent hope for a better future, showing the world that they can succeed, or in negative ways, channeling their anger through gang membership and other undesirable behaviors (Suárez-Orozco & Suárez-Orozco, 2001). Ms. Bowden wondered whether this might be the case with some of her struggling ELLs.

When immigrant parents perceive that their efforts will not lead to success, this attitude may subtly, or not so subtly, be passed on to their children. High hopes and expectations of some immigrant groups in the United States can crumble in the face of the realities of earning a living. As a result, some parents place less emphasis on education and make less of a personal investment in education, even as their English language skills improve. Ogbu and Matute-Bianchi (1986) call this the "low academic effort syndrome" (p. 127). So it is not that some immigrant families do not value education. The problem lies, rather, in the perception that they cannot get ahead in American society, no matter how hard they try.

Ms. Bowden knew that the parents of some of the ELLs in her classroom were on the verge of becoming discouraged with the realities of earning a living in the United States. She knew that teachers can help to change immigrant families' negative attitudes toward schooling by bringing guest speakers, successful professionals who represent the students' ethnic groups, into the classroom to talk about their work. She believed that if students are to believe that they can be rewarded for their hard work, they need role models who they can perceive themselves emulating and who they can look up to, so she made every effort to provide those role models for her students.

Immigrants and School Achievement

The school success of immigrant students is dependent upon a variety of factors. One factor, as we have seen, is the belief, passed down from parents to their children, that education is the key to success. Socioeconomic status also influences much in a student's life. Poorer immigrants tend to settle in urban ethnic communities, where they can find affordable housing, but where they are segregated from the middle-class American society (Portes & Rumbaut, 2006). Income levels determine which neighborhood a family can afford to live in. The student's neighborhood, along with the socioeconomic status of the school that the student attends, has a greater influence on the student's success than the family's income status (Sirin, 2005).

A third factor that affects students' academic achievement is culture; that is to say, orientation toward group or individual activities, cognitive patterns, values, beliefs, and goals. The kinds of culturally related experiences that students from different groups bring to school with them helps to shape their classroom experiences (August & Shanahan, 2006). Classroom culture and the teacher's ability to validate student home cultures in the classroom will also affect students' academic performance.

As Ms. Bowden and Ms. Ramos talked about issues affecting immigrant students' school success, Ms. Bowden understood how these factors related to her immigrant students. She agreed that when she provided instruction to meet the unique needs of each student, he or she has a better chance of succeeding (August & Shanahan, 2006).

TEACHING WRITING TO ELLs

Ms. Bowden knew that in the classroom, writing activities offer students not only the opportunity to showcase their knowledge, understanding, and creativity but also a means through which they acquire knowledge, process and organize their thinking to find and fill in holes in their understanding, and build their creative skills. She knew that her students would become better learners as they became more proficient writers. In fact, the National Commission on Writing in America's Schools and Colleges charged in its 2003 report, *The Neglected "R": The Need for a Writing Revolution,* "If students are to make knowledge their own, they must struggle with the details, wrestle with the facts, and rework raw information and dimly understood concepts into language they can communicate to someone else.

In short, if students are to learn, they must write" (National Commission on Writing, 2003, p. 9). To write is to engage in a complex process interaction of ideas and language that compels the writer to articulate, in clear and precise terms, thoughts that may previously have been only vague in the writer's mind.

The Challenge of Effective Writing Instruction for ELLs

As discussed earlier in the chapter, the past several years have seen a rapid influx of school-age immigrant students, who speak little or no English, into the United States. In addition, there is a large population of U.S.-born students who speak a language other than English at home and who have difficulty with English at school. The National Commission on Writing (2003) observed that writing instruction in public schools in the United States is not as strong as it should be. Students are indeed learning basic writing skills, but they are not learning how to write deeply and proficiently. With regard to ELLs, the report states:

> All of these issues resonate with a special force when English-language learners and immigrant students enter the classroom. Teachers confront growing linguistic diversity; English-language learners are one of the fastest growing student populations in the United States. Too frequently, teachers are forced to confront these new challenges without the support and training required to respond to the special needs of these students. Outside the regular classroom, poorly designed English as a Second Language programs can oversimplify communication in English and provide little interaction between English–language learners and other students. (National Commission on Writing, 2003, pp. 23–24)

In addition the National Assessment of Educational Progress (NAEP, 2007) published in *The Nation's Report Card: Writing* found that while writing assessment scores for ELLs at grades 8 and 12 were higher in 2007 than in the previous two assessments (2002 and 1998), they are still well below the scores for English-speaking students.

Like the students in Ms. Bowden's class, the majority of ELLs enrolled in U.S. public schools fail to achieve literacy levels that allow them to compete with their native English-speaking peers in school and in the workforce. Teachers across the nation are challenged to find effective ways of bringing their ELLs to a proficient level in English reading and writing. While a relatively large amount of research has been done on speaking and reading development with ELLs, there is very little research that informs our understanding of second-language writing development. The *National Literacy Panel on Language-Minority Children and Youth* (August & Shanahan, 2006) reports that the literature that exists today suggests some connections among various aspects of language development in the student's first and second language and writing proficiency, as well as what practices are effective in teaching writing skills to ELLs. As we seek to understand the complex task of writing for elementary and middle school ELLs and the development of writing skills in the second language, we briefly review the research that is available on the topic.

Skills Students Need for Proficient Writing

Learning to write is a complex process involving lower-level transcription skills and higher-level organizational skills as well as the ability to express oneself with the written word. Transcription skills, such as handwriting and spelling, are important to the writing task because they allow students to express their thinking in a fluent manner, minimizing interruptions in the thinking process in order to find out how a word is spelled or how to form an unfamiliar letter, as frequently happens when students are beginning to learn cursive writing. Learning to write coherently also involves the ability to use a rich vocabulary, apply grammatical rules, and present one's thinking in an organized and logical manner.

Handwriting

As Ms. Bowden knew, students who read fluently often comprehend what they read better than nonfluent readers because they do not lose track of the ideas in reading passages while they are attempting to decode. She was surprised to learn that handwriting fluency is important in the same way for ELLs who are developing writing skills. If a student must stop composing in order to figure out how to form difficult or unfamiliar letters, the student's train of thought can be easily disrupted. Mildred Donoghue (2009) writes;

> Handwriting can be taught as easily to most English learners as to native speakers of English. For students whose native language carries roughly the same alphabet as English, how to form the letters in manuscript or cursive would be taught the same way to both groups. When teaching handwriting, teachers need to be aware of students whose native language has no written alphabet or in which the alphabet is significantly different from English. (p. 323)

In addition, handwriting characteristics vary from one country to another, even among students who learn the Latin alphabet! Figure 1.1 shows characteristic differences in how the Latin alphabet is taught in different world regions.

While it was good news for Ms. Bowden that many ELLs will be able to learn handwriting as easily as native English-speaking students, she did not want to underestimate the importance of fluent and automatic handwriting on the composition skills of ELLs in later grades, such as her third graders. For beginning writers (not just ELLs) effective writing depends on fluency in lower-level transcription skills, such as letter production. This allows the writer to focus on the more cognitive aspects of the writing process (Torrance & Galbraith, 2008). Handwriting interventions involving brief, explicit instruction on a frequent basis improve both handwriting and writing fluency (Berninger et al., 1997; Jones & Christensen, 1999). In primary level writers, handwriting is related to written expression. Interventions for students with handwriting difficulties focus on developing more legible and automatic handwriting (Jones & Christensen, 1999). For young ELLs, handwriting skills are an essential part of the process of learning to write effectively. Because they are working with two languages, the cognitive demands

FIGURE 1.1. Examples of handwriting from different world regions.

West Africa

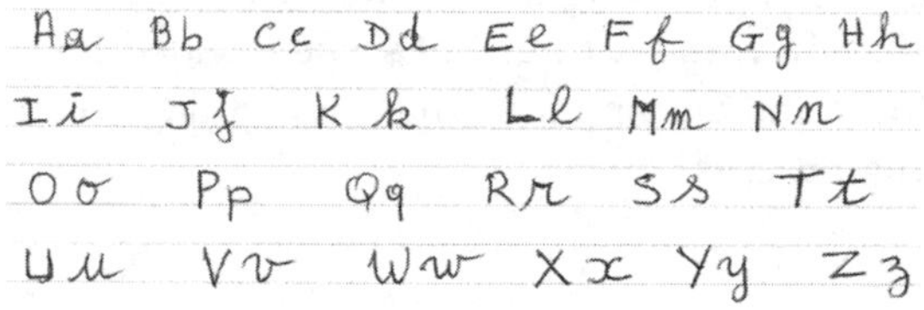

Aa Bb Cc Dd Ee Ff Gg Hh
Ii Jj Kk Ll Mm Nn
Oo Pp Qq Rr Ss Tt
Uu Vv Ww Xx Yy Zz

Romania

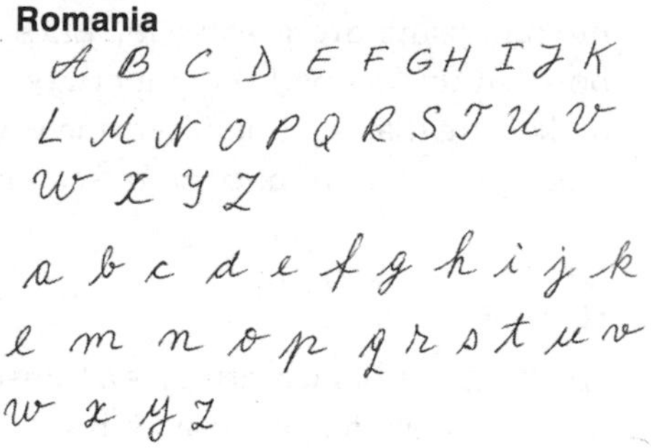

A B C D E F G H I J K
L M N O P Q R S T U V
W X Y Z
a b c d e f g h i j k
l m n o p q r s t u v
w x y z

Romania

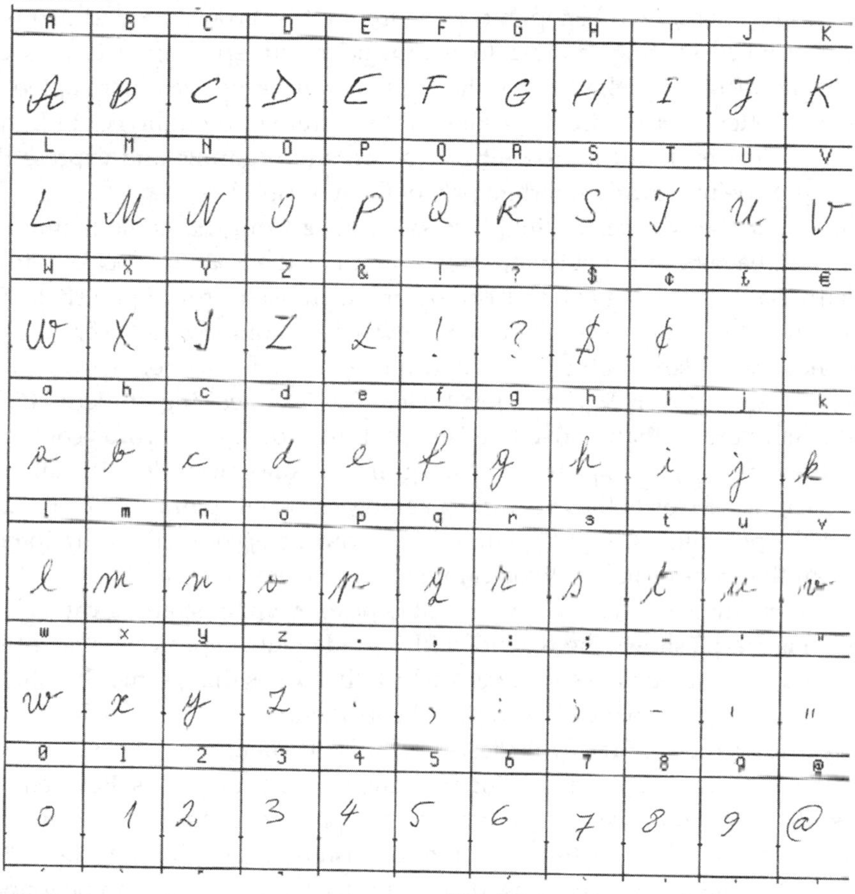

A	B	C	D	E	F	G	H	I	J	K
A	B	C	D	E	F	G	H	I	J	K
L	M	N	O	P	Q	R	S	T	U	V
L	M	N	O	P	Q	R	S	T	U	V
W	X	Y	Z	&	!	?	$	¢	£	€
W	X	Y	Z	&	!	?	$	¢		
a	b	c	d	e	f	g	h	I	j	k
a	b	c	d	e	f	g	h	i	j	k
l	m	n	o	p	q	r	s	t	u	v
l	m	n	o	p	q	r	s	t	u	v
w	x	y	z	.	,	:	;	-	'	"
w	x	y	z	.	,	:	;	-	'	"
0	1	2	3	4	5	6	7	8	9	@
0	1	2	3	4	5	6	7	8	9	@

United States

Aa Bb Cc Dd Ee Ff Gg
Hh Ii Jj Kk Ll Mm
Nn Oo Pp Qq Rr Ss
Tt Uu Vv Ww Xx Yy
Zz

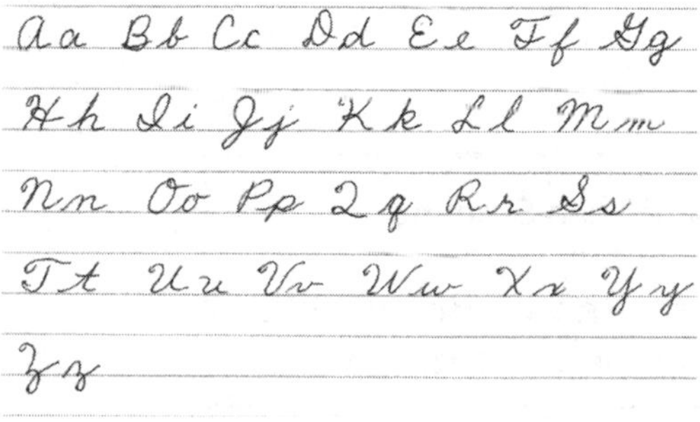

Belgium

Aa Bb Cc Dd Ee Ff Gg Hh
Ii Jj Kk Ll Mm Nn Oo Pp
Qq Rr Ss Tt Uu Vv Ww
Xx Yy Zz

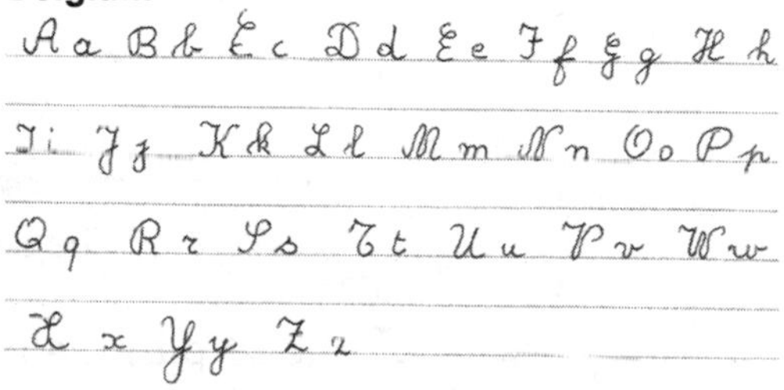

in composing are greater for ELLs than for native English speakers. Once Ms. Bowden understood the importance of handwriting for her ELLs, she decided to make sure that their handwriting was fluent and automatic so that they could give more cognitive attention to the composing process.

Spelling

Spelling, like handwriting, is a transcription skill that helps students to write with fluency. (Chapter 3 presents instructional strategies for facilitating writing fluency.) During writing workshop in her classroom, Ms. Bowden found that when students stopped writing in order to ask for help with spelling or to look up a word in the dictionary, the flow of the students' thinking was interrupted and they would often have difficulty picking up their train of thought. For ELLs, who need to use the bulk of their cognitive resources to organize and express their ideas, fluent spelling is an important part of fluent writing.

For ELLs, the transfer of linguistic knowledge from the home language to English can have both benefits and drawbacks. For the Spanish speakers in Ms. Bowden's class, phonological and orthographic transfer from Spanish to English accounted for many spelling errors in words containing /k/, /b/, and /h/ allophones, /sk/ blends, all clusters, and phonemes, such as /e/, /pr/, and /u/ (Fashola, Drum, Mayer, & Kang, 1996). Her Spanish-speaking students tended to make more errors than native English-speaking students in words containing these phonemes. There appears to be a significant amount of Spanish influence in the spelling of words that Spanish-speaking students spell incorrectly. Much of Spanish-speaking students' spelling errors can be accounted for by interference from the transfer of phonological knowledge from Spanish (Dressler, 2002). Spanish-speaking students are not the only ones for whom spelling can be challenging. Figure 1.2 shows the work of a fifth-grade Dutch-speaking student who had been in the United States for 1 year, which illustrates that point. This student, like many ELLs, spells words the way she hears them.

Because of the challenges for teaching ELLs to spell, Ms. Ramos suggested that a phonetically organized spelling program would provide Ms. Bowden's students with explicit practice in the organizational patterns of the English language, and could improve their writing and other English language skills (Wright, 2001). (Additional research and recommendations for teaching spelling can be found in Chapter 6.)

FIGURE 1.2. The story of Brian Swimmer.

lots of thees picturs represen wat Brian's like.
But one of them shows wat he ones did.

Vocabulary

For ELLs, having academic vocabulary knowledge is a crucial part of being able to express their understanding of content material in English. While this seemed obvious to Ms. Bowden, she was surprised that she actually spent minimal time explicitly teaching vocabulary to her students. She often assumed that her students already knew basic academic vocabulary. Another reason that Ms. Bowden did not explicitly teach the words related to content topics was because she was not sure how to effectively provide students with contexts for learning new vocabulary. Ms. Ramos recommended that Ms. Bowden use vocabulary games such as word plays, scavenger hunts, and word riddles (Brassell & Furtado, 2008) to give her ELLs opportunities to practice using academic vocabulary in ways that are fun and engaging.

One strategy that Ms. Bowden found to be effective in teaching academic vocabulary to her ELLs was to have her students use specific vocabulary in compositions after using the words in reading. When teachers elicit specific words in compositions and explicitly explain the words, when students are exposed to vocabulary in multimodal contexts (speaking, listening, reading, and writing), and when there is opportunity to discuss and negotiate word meanings, teachers provide the scaffolding that students need in order to use targeted vocabulary more frequently in their compositions. The use of writing frames, interactive elicitation of vocabulary words, and explicit instructions to use the vocabulary all contribute to students' use of targeted words in compositions (Lee & Muncie, 2006).

ELLs need to learn vocabulary in meaningful texts, have access to the text's meaning in their home language, encounter words in a variety of contexts, and include spelling, pronunciation, morphology, and syntax when they learn word meanings. Word analysis and vocabulary learning strategies can improve comprehension and literacy outcomes for both ELLs and native English speakers (Carlo et al., 2004).

Grammar

No matter what a student's home language, English grammar is bound to differ from that language in some significant ways. Students who are learning English need to know standard grammatical structures of the English language in order to write effectively in English. Native English-speaking students and ELLs do not necessarily learn grammatical features of English in the same sequence. ELLs from different language backgrounds may have different sequences of English grammar acquisition, reflecting an influence from the student's first language (Shin & Milroy, 1999).

Like many other teachers, Ms. Bowden had believed that students easily pick up new languages just by being immersed in an environment where the new language is used. Ms. Ramos explained to her that while this myth, like most, is based on some element of truth, the fact is that merely exposing ELL students to a new language does not seem sufficient to help them acquire the more sophisticated language patterns they need to be successful in school. ELLs usually need explicit instruction in more complex language patterns to help them develop the ability to use them (Morris, 2001; Spada & Lightbrown, 1999). Explicit grammar instruction combined with a process approach to writing can benefit ELLs (Cahyono, 2002). In addition, when teachers are explicit in the forms of the English language, student usage of more appropriate forms may continue beyond the period of instruction (Herman & Flanigan, 1995).

the need for targeted instruct-

Many of the grammatical errors in ELLs' writing are not random. In one study, errors in syntax in the English writing samples of Spanish-speaking students appeared to be influenced by speech patterns from a transitional form of Spanish, known as "interlanguage" (the language usage that forms the bridge between first language and fluent second language), and/or Chicano English, as well as Spanish spelling (Cronnell, 1985). Because written expression needs to be more precise than spoken expression (you don't get a second chance to make your meaning clear to the reader), writing requires a greater control over the syntactical forms of English than does speaking. As students add new structures to their grammatical repertoires, they gain the ability to add interest to their compositions by varying their sentence structures. But learning English grammar for academic writing takes time and practice. (Chapter 6 addresses instructional strategies for teaching grammar and usage.)

Organization

Ms. Bowden found that when her students were composing text, they were able to use what they knew about story organization in one language to organize their story writing in English. The complexity and sophistication of students' writing in their first language seems to influence how much complexity and sophistication they are able to put into their writing in the second language. Incidentally, students are able to develop writing skills in a second language before they develop them in their first language when they are first taught to read and write in the second language (Francis, 2000), as in the case of students who live in places where an indigenous language is spoken in homes, but where schools, businesses, and government operate in an "official" language. Research also indicates that ELLs' writing instruction in their first language strongly influences writing performance in their second language (Phung, 2006). Therefore, writing instruction in the students' first language has significant benefits for second-language writing. Many skills involved in the writing task can transfer from the first to the second language if students are given first-language writing instruction (Lanauze & Snow, 1989).

Ms. Ramos also pointed out that different cultures may have different styles of organizing writing. For example, while the five-paragraph composition with an introduction, the main ideas with supporting details, and a conclusion tends to be a standard way of teaching school writing organization in the United States, other cultures may use more circular reasoning in their writing layout. (Chapters 4 and 5 provide a variety of instructional strategies for teaching narrative and expository writing, respectively.)

FACTORS AFFECTING SECOND-LANGUAGE ACQUISITION

Learning to write is, in many ways, like learning to drive a car. A student driver must simultaneously attend to multiple tasks, such as operating the automobile's machinery, knowing where he or she is going and how to get there, and keeping everybody safe along the way. In a similar way, a student learning to write must attend to multiple cognitive tasks such as expressing knowledge and understanding, organizing the writing piece, and attending to appropriate transcription and conventions. Continuing the metaphor, learning how to write in a second language is a lot like learning to drive in the dark and the rain. It takes more cognitive energy as well an additional set of strategies in order for ELLs to learn to write effectively.

There are a number of factors that affect how quickly and how well an ELL student will develop the strategies to communicate in English, and that specifically affect the development of the student's skills in using written English to express an understanding of content topics and concepts. The level of oral proficiency and of reading skills in the student's first language, his or her English reading proficiency, and the kind of writing instruction that the student receives all influence the development of English writing skills.

First-Language Proficiency

Research suggests that students who are proficient in their first language tend to perform significantly better on writing tasks in the second language than students who do not have proficient first-language skills (Dweik & Abu Al Hommos, 2007). When students have developed strategies for manipulating language and for expressing themselves in an articulate manner, those skills tend to transfer from the first language to English. Studies have shown that writing performance in English reflects writing performance in the first language of students who are literate in their first language (Davis, Carlisle, & Beeman, 1999). Therefore, older students and those who have received an education in their home country will often develop English writing proficiency more quickly than younger students or those who have had few opportunities to go to school.

On a related note, parents and teachers sometimes express concern about native English-speaking students in two-way immersion bilingual programs. A study conducted by Bae (2007) suggests that students in two-way immersion programs do not suffer in terms of their English language development while they are gaining proficiency in a second language. The writing sample in Figure 1.3

was created by a bilingual sixth grader who had been in the United States for just over 2 years.

It is essential to help ELLs in schools master oral English, but researchers also found that ELLs' oral proficiency does not necessarily develop before writing proficiency (Edelsky & Jilbert, 1985). Writing performance in English does not always reflect oral English skills, and writing skills may exceed oral language skills. Some research has attempted to identify skills that predict students' writing proficiency. Native language listening comprehension and literacy skills as well as phonological memory have been found to be predictors of second-language writing proficiency. Instruction in first-language literacy and second-language phonology can help primary level students' literacy achievement in the second language (Dufva & Voeten, 1999).

What all this means for teachers is that if opportunities exist for ELLs to receive literacy instruction in their first language, either through school, church, or community organizations, teachers will increase their students' chances of success in school by encouraging them and their parents to take advantage of them.

FIGURE 1.3. "My Penney Book."

The first friend I ever had is also my best. Her name is Maya. I met her when I was really young. I must have been, because she's been my friend as long as i can remember. We did all kinds of things together. From playing cats to going to school together. But now we've moved and we haven't seen each other since 2000. She might be able to come over the summer. I'm really looking forward to that!

One thing that has really changed my life is when we moved to America. I guess I never realized how hard it would be on me. I used to say "oh I will miss my friends but I'll make more." It was not nearly close to as easy. Sometimes when I am having a bad day my friend pops into my head and makes my day even worse.

My first friend in America is one of my best. Her name is Pennilynn. We usually call her Penn for short. I'm lucky she's my friend because she lives across the street. So I get to see her a lot. I met her not long after I came to America. I'm glad I did because you get lonely if you have no one to be with. So that's my friend from America.

One of the most exciting things in my life, was my first sleepover. I was at Penn's house. I was 8 years old when this happened. We started out by dressing up and playing that we were going to a royal ball. We then set out our blankets and watched a movie. I can't remmber which one it was. That was one of the best nights I ever had.

One thing that I struggled with at first was playing the piano. Its really fun at first but then there's this very frustrating part were a lot of people drop out. I know my sister did. Once you get past that part though, it all becomes really fun because you get to play all kinds of beautiful music. I'm really glad I didn't quit piano.

Reading and Listening Proficiency and Writing

It stands to reason that students who are good readers tend to be good writers, and students who are good writers are also good readers. Research has shown the connection between reading ability, writing proficiency, and the other language modalities. A study conducted by Davis et al. (1999) suggests that English writing proficiency in ELLs is related to the students' reading comprehension in English and that English writing proficiency also correlates closely with English listening comprehension. Studies that connect reading skills and writing proficiency in the first language have taught us that instruction in reading improves writing and instruction in writing can improve reading (Shanahan, 2006). Research on the relationship between reading proficiency and writing in the second language, however, is scarcer. Studies suggest that reading proficiency transfers from the first language to the second language more readily than does writing proficiency (Abu-Akel, 1997; Carson, Carrell, Silberstein, Kroll, & Kuehn, 1990).

Reading and writing involve many similar cognitive processes in that students activate background knowledge and past experiences, construct meaning, apply complex linguistic and cognitive skills, and engage in problem solving (Ferris & Hedgcock, 1998). Krashen (1993) asserts that free, voluntary reading is a powerfully effective way for second-language learners to develop language skills, including reading comprehension, writing, grammar, vocabulary, and spelling. While reading is important for developing language skills in second-language learners, it is not, in itself, sufficient for the development of writing proficiency in ELLs (Hedgcock & Atkinson, 1993). Recommendations include writing to read, text analysis, and write-before-you-read activities (Ferris & Hedgcock, 1998).

Many strategies enable ELLs to learn how to compose successfully in English. One study found that ELLs were able to elaborate on their ideas significantly better in writing when given the opportunity to brainstorm before and after reading and when they clustered their ideas to use as a basis for writing assignments (Bermudez & Prater, 1990).

Ms. Ramos also introduced Ms. Bowden to the use of a cognitive strategies approach to reading and writing with ELLs that she found beneficial. This approach makes explicit the thinking processes that good readers and writers use to construct meaning. Ms. Ramos modeled important aspects of the approach including having high expectations for ELLs, providing them with a rigorous English language arts curriculum, explicitly teaching and modeling the strategies, providing guided practice in the use of strategies that help them to be successful readers and writers of challenging text, and involving students in communities of learners. In a study by Olson and Land (2007), teachers and students used a wide variety of cognitive strategies, such as planning and goal setting, tapping prior knowledge, asking questions and making predictions, constructing the gist, monitoring, revising meaning, reconstructing the draft, reflecting and relating, and evaluating, in ways that cultivated a deep knowledge and application of the strategies in reading and writing.

Quality Writing Instruction

The quality of writing instruction that students are exposed to has a significant influence on their composition performance. In a debriefing meeting following Ms. Ramos's visit to Ms. Bowden's class, Ms. Ramos reinforced the idea that explicit instruction in writing for ELLs is more beneficial than merely giving them opportunities to write. She showed Ms. Bowden how having a balance of transcription- and composition-oriented writing activities may be useful (Kim, 2007). Explicit grammar instruction, she explained, is important to support the academic success of students who may not acquire Standard English outside of school, even if they have spent their whole lives in the United States. Without English language instruction, U.S.-born ELLs do not always acquire the levels of academic English that they need to be successful in high school. Acquisition of inaccurate grammar forms can limit students' ability to write proficiently at levels expected of students in high school. Ms. Ramos cautioned Ms. Bowden that when teachers do not expect grammatical accuracy and language proficiency, students may not acquire them (Besser, 2006). She encouraged Ms. Bowden to set high expectations for her students in those areas.

Structured writing seems to be more beneficial to ELLs than freewriting (Gómez, Parker, & Lara-Alecio, 1996). Having students write nonfiction as a model for teaching them to write, minimizing freewriting until they have mastered elements of the writing process, giving them plenty of opportunity to prewrite, and keeping conferences teacher-controlled are some effective alterations for ELLs to the traditional writing process (Haynes, 2006). Sentence-combining activities can help students learn to comprehend different types of phrases and clauses, which helps to improve student writing (Sjolie, 2006).

Other aspects of the writing process are also important for ELLs. Students who have regular opportunities to write and revise with peers show improvement in voice, audience, and a sense of power in language. Just as native English speakers do, ELLs benefited from regular opportunities to practice writing, the expectation that they would revise their writing and from peer response and confidence in themselves as writers (Urzua, 1987). When ELLs reach the grades in which the coverage of content material increases and the expectation that students write competently in the content areas becomes greater, the achievement gap between native English speakers and ELLs widens (Aguierrez-Muñoz & Boscardin, 2008). When ELLs write in the content areas, they need scaffolding to be able to express themselves through the words and unique language structures of each particular content area. Many instructional strategies that support ELL writing are discussed in the following chapters.

SUMMARY

We began this chapter with a vignette about Ms. Bowden, the third-grade teacher who was perplexed about how to give her ELLs effective instruction that would help them to become proficient writers in the English language. As in so many classes in schools across the country, Ms. Bowden's class included ELLs, who are a vastly diverse and rapidly growing group of students in U.S. classrooms. They and/or their parents or grandparents come from all parts of the globe and have hundreds of different home languages. Many already speak two or more languages. Immigrant ELLs come from all sectors of society in their home countries and have a vast array of educational backgrounds and experiences.

The majority of ELLs do not achieve the level of writing proficiency that is needed in order to succeed in school and the workplace. Teachers can help ELLs improve their English writing skills by giving them more opportunities to write across the curriculum and by providing explicit instruction in lower-level transcription skills, such as handwriting and spelling, as well as higher-level cognitive skills such as grammar and organization. Explicitly teaching students effective writing strategies helps ELLs become more effective writers.

Learning to write is a complex process that requires additional cognitive resources of ELL students. Many factors affect how quickly and how well an ELL student will learn English and how easily the student will develop skills in written English in order to express an understanding of content topics and concepts. These factors include the level of oral proficiency in the student's first language, his or her reading skills in the first language, his or her English reading proficiency, and the kind of writing instruction that the student receives in the English-speaking classroom.

WEB RESOURCES

Colorín Colorado: Fostering Literacy Development in English Language Learners
www.colorincolorado.org/article/12924

Article discusses the role of alphabet knowledge and phonological awareness in ELL literacy, and links to other resources on ELLs.

Doing What Works: English Language Learners
dww.ed.gov/priority_area/priority_landing.cfm?PA_ID=6

Recommended practices for teaching ELLs in grades K–5, and links to research and planning templates.

Elementary Websites for English Language Learners
www.everythingesl.net/inservices/elementary_sites ells_71638.php

Links to websites that give ELLs practice in using the English language to speak, listen, read, and write, categorized by grade level.

English Language Learners: A Policy Research Brief Produced by the National Council of Teachers of English
www.ncte.org/library/NCTEFiles/Resources/PolicyResearch/ELLResearchBrief.pdf

Information on ELL diversity, myths about ELLs, tips for teaching, and policy recommendations.

English Language Learners Network: National Writing Project
www.nwp.org/cs/public/print/programs/ell

Professional development, networking, ELL-related events, and grant resources.

National Center for Education Statistics: Fast Facts
nces.ed.gov/fastfacts/display.asp?id=96

Information on ELL students in U.S. public schools.

Tapestry for Teacher of English language learners
www.tesol.org/s_tesol/cat_tapestry.asp?CID=1585&DID=8732

Research and teaching resources for teachers of ELLs in grades pre- K to 12.

CHAPTER 2

From Theory to Practice

Writing with English Language Learners

Mrs. Littleford thought about her sixth-grade students as she finished an assignment on writing for an English as a second-language (ESL) class that she was taking. She had learned a great deal about the sources of ELLs' writing difficulties. She realized that when they tried to spell, they often used phonological patterns from their first language, which caused errors in English. She now understood that even abundant, high-quality exposure to academic vocabulary and the structures of Standard English, without explicit grammar and vocabulary instruction, was not sufficient to help her students develop academic writing skills. She knew that there were instructional techniques that would enhance her ELLs' learning, as well as writing strategies that she could teach them to use. But how would she be able to weave all this new knowledge into her daily teaching?

The four ELLs in Mrs. Littleford's class were at very different levels of English proficiency. Juana and Miguel, whose parents were migrant farm workers from Mexico, knew very little English and had little exposure to either reading or writing. Marina, whose parents spoke Russian, had several older brothers and sisters who preferred to speak English at home. She had learned a lot from them. Truc's parents were refugees from Laos and were learning English themselves. They wanted their daughter to learn English very much, and she was making good progress, but had not yet mastered many of the basic structures of the language.

Mrs. Littleford wanted to know how to prevent the achievement gap between her four ELLs and the rest of her class of 21 native English speakers. She knew that Ms. Ramos, the literacy coach, was developing a framework for helping ELLs be successful writers, and she decided to talk with her about implementing the ideas in her classroom.

Like Mrs. Littleford in the vignette above, many teachers of ELLs recognize the need to provide their students with the kind of instruction that will close or even prevent an achievement gap. Mrs. Littleford and other teachers in her school felt competent with some aspects of teaching ELLs, including language development and reading. However, they felt overwhelmed with the idea of teaching ELLs writing skills. So the teachers contacted Ms. Ramos, who said they could use additional knowledge about the structures of the English language and how and why language is used in the classroom. The teachers were excited to learn more about language to help their students acquire higher levels of English language proficiency and improve their writing. They agreed to form an ELL study group and to meet weekly with Ms. Ramos as their facilitator.

In this chapter, we describe the differences between social and academic language and explain why ELLs need to become proficient users of academic English. We then present a framework for how English language instruction can be incorporated into any classroom and show how to apply the framework in order to teach writing to ELLs and support them at each stage of the writing process. We also discuss English language development (ELD) standards and show how the standards can be used to help teachers set high expectations for ELL students.

ACADEMIC LANGUAGE AND ELLs

The first thing Ms. Ramos discussed with the teachers in the study group was the distinction between Basic Interpersonal Communication Skills (BICS) and Cognitive Academic Language Proficiency (CALP) (Cummins, 1979a). BICS can be understood as the language that students use in their everyday communication with classmates and teachers, primarily in social contexts. It is often referred to as "playground language." CALP, on the other hand, is the language proficiency that students must have to communicate clearly about academic content. This includes not only academic vocabulary, but also the varieties of discourse that are specific to each content area. This academic language of CALP is more complex and often more abstract than the social language of BICS and is the language in which students communicate higher-order thinking in the academic content areas.

Ms. Ramos told the teachers that academic language is the basis for most of the writing that students are asked to do in school. It includes figurative expressions, explicit wording that can be understood without additional clarification, language that people use to provide supporting evidence, language in which the author detaches him- or herself from the text, and language that emphasizes or qualifies specific ideas or that conveys nuances of meaning. Academic grammar often involves longer sentences than social grammar. The passive voice and nominalization are often used, and complex messages are condensed into concise sentences or phrases (Zwiers, 2008). In addition, academic language occurs in writing much more frequently than does "playground language."

Ms. Ramos explained that ELLs need to learn academic English. Academic language is not the same as speech. It is the language that students encounter in their textbooks and discussions of content material, and the language that is used to communicate content concepts in formal writing tasks. In order to interact proficiently with academic English, students must have the ability to "interpret and infer meaning from oral and written language, discern precise meaning and information from text, relate ideas and information, recognize the conventions of various genres, and enlist a variety of linguistic strategies on behalf of a wide range of communicative purposes" (Dutro & Moran, 2003, pp. 230–231). For ELLs, this is a significant challenge indeed.

Models for Teaching CALP

Effective models of English language instruction take into account the aspects of language with which ELLs are likely to have difficulty and present a set of instructional strategies that teachers can readily apply to their teaching repertoire. Many of the teachers in the ELL study group already had training in some of the popular CALP models, and some teachers had training in Guided Language Acquisition Design (GLAD), developed by Marcia Brechtel (1992) and Linnea Haley. Many others had training in Sheltered Instruction Observation Protocol (SIOP), designed by Jane Echevarria, MaryEllenVogt, and Deborah Short (2010). These teaching models were implemented in the classrooms and helped the teachers ensure that their ELLs achieved at grade level in the content areas while at the same time learning academic English. Ms. Ramos decided to introduce a third CALP model, one that she believed would complement what the teachers knew and would help the teachers understand how to better teach ELLs to write.

The Brick and Mortar of English Language Instruction

Ms. Ramos had learned in an ELL course about Systematic English Language Development (Systematic ELD), proposed by Dutro and Moran (2003), a research-based model that focuses on the development of academic speaking, listening, reading, and writing skills for ELLs. The Systematic ELD approach uses an architectural metaphor to illustrate an effective framework of English language instruction. A key feature of Systematic ELD is the explicitness of language instruction throughout the instructional day. "Through instruction that makes explicit the tools needed for different academic language functions, students learn the vocabulary and sentence structures needed for a range of cognitive tasks and uses of language" (Dutro & Moran, 2003, p. 234).

Ms. Ramos explained that academic language is made up of two kinds of words: "brick" words and "mortar" words. Brick words are the vocabulary items that are specific to the content concepts of a particular lesson. For example, in a geometry lesson on polygons, brick words that students use in their math journals might include words such as *line segment, equilateral, acute angle,* and *closed plane figure.* In a science lesson on thunderstorms students might include the following brick words: *lightning, electric current, unstable air, cumulus cloud, ice particles,* and *frontal system* in a report.

Mortar words, on the other hand, are those words and phrases that "determine the relation between and among words" (Dutro & Moran, 2003, p. 239). They include vocabulary such as "connecting words required to construct complex sentences, prepositions and prepositional phrases, basic regular and irregular verbs, pronouns and pronominal phrases, general academic vocabulary . . ." (pp. 239–240). For example, in a geometry lesson on polygons, *meet, intersect, determine, extend, measure, is formed by, closed figure, through a polygon,* and *by two adjacent sides* are all words or phrases that show the connections among the elements represented by the brick words. Similarly, in a science lesson on thunderstorms, *strike, flash, clap, is heated by the sun, rises, in a thundercloud, to the upper levels of the atmosphere,* and *above the earth's surface,* are some mortar words and phrases that might be taught.

Some of the teachers had difficulty understanding the concept of brick and mortar words. Ms. Ramos helped by explaining that an easy way to figure out the basic discourse patterns of a particular content area is to look at sentences that provide directions or explanations and other expository texts from the curriculum area. When the specific academic vocabulary items are taken out of the text, what's left is the mortar.

The teachers tried it. They examined pieces of texts from the books they used and discovered content-specific patterns in the discourse. Ms. Ramos stated that these patterns, as well as the specific vocabulary words, need to be explicitly taught to ELLs. Verbs and prepositions are often some of the most difficult words for ELLs to learn how to use correctly, because they are the words that frame the context and explain the relationships among nouns in academic language. Ms. Ramos emphasized that the teachers would need to explicitly teach not only the brick words, but also the mortar words and phrases. Attending to the mortar of the language would help their students construct meaning with and understand relationships among content words and concepts.

Ms. Ramos had tried several strategies using the brick and mortar approach with the ELLs she taught. One method that she used was to "front-load" language; that is, she pretaught the brick and mortar words demanded by a particular content concept, so that *all* students could access the content. Ms. Ramos found that the front-loading of a particular lesson is determined by the vocabulary and sentence structures needed for students to be able to understand and communicate content skills and concepts. The next section explains how teachers can decide which brick and mortar words to teach in any given lesson.

Determining the Purposes for Academic Language Use in the Classroom

Planning for explicit teaching of academic language requires teachers to think purposefully about how and why language is used in the classroom. To prepare lessons that develop students' academic language proficiency, Ms. Ramos told the teachers to think about the academic language that their students would need in order to engage with the content material, and prepare front-loading activities that effectively conveyed the meaning of the vocabulary words and showed students how to use the structures. She explained that understanding both the functions of language (what we are using language to accomplish) and the forms of academic language (vocabulary and discourse styles that are specific to various content areas) make it possible for teachers to analyze the language that they need to teach.

Key uses-

purpose   grammar

The linguistic terms *language functions* and *language forms* refer to the purposes that language is used to accomplish and to the structures used to accomplish those purposes. Language forms "include parts of speech, verb tenses and subject/verb agreement, the use of pronouns and conjunctions, and sentence structure or syntax (complex and compound sentences and word order)" (Dutro & Moran, 2003, p. 237). Language functions, on the other hand, are the tasks that language is used for.

> Functions are essentially the purposes that we accomplish with language, e.g., stating, requesting, responding, greeting, parting, etc. Functions cannot be accomplished, of course, without the forms of language: morphemes, words, grammar rules, discourse rules, and other organizational competencies. While forms are the outward manifestation of language, functions are the realization of those forms. (Brown, 2000, p. 248, 250)

Incorporating Language Instruction into Daily Lessons

Ms. Ramos asked some of the teachers to bring in lessons they had taught that identified the language focus and the structures that could be highlighted. Mrs. Littleford brought in a lesson in which the goal for her students was to write a paragraph describing the Big Bad Wolf from *Little Red Riding Hood*. Ms. Ramos explained that *describing* is the communicative *purpose* that the students would use language to achieve. Students would, in other words, use language to communicate by *describing* someone, who happens to be the Big Bad Wolf. *Writing* is not in itself the goal of the assignment, but is the *modality* in which the communication is accomplished. (The other three language modalities are reading, speaking, and listening.) Ms. Ramos asked the teachers what kinds of words they use when describing. One teacher responded that she uses adjectives. Another teacher added that adverbs help to describe as well. Ms. Ramos agreed and illustrated how, in the Big Bad Wolf description activity, teachers could explicitly teach about adjectives and adverbs, their role in grammar, where they are placed in sentences, and so on. They could help students think of adjectives such as *clever, cunning, ferocious, big, gray, hungry,* and others, and adverbs such as *very, boldly, hungrily, fast,* and *stealthily,* and make sure that students are able to write these words.

Another teacher had students compare two fairytales. The goal of the lesson was to compare *Little Red Riding Hood* with *The Three Little Pigs*. In this lesson, the communicative purpose of the language use became *comparing,* and the accompanying structures to be taught include adjectives (e.g., *little, big, hungry, wise, foolish*), conjunctions (e.g., *and, but, however*), comparatives (e.g., *littler, bigger, hungrier, wiser, more foolish*), superlatives (e.g., *littlest, biggest, hungriest, wisest, most foolish*), and adverbs (e.g., *quickly, loudly, happily, frightfully*). Again, teachers cannot assume that ELLs know and are able to use features of language such as these. It is important to explicitly teach them and to provide support as teachers give students opportunities to practice using them in their writing.

Selecting Language Structures to Match the Language Forms

"So how do we figure out which language structures we should teach in a particular lesson?" Mrs. Littleford asked at the next study group meeting. Ms. Ramos explained that the first step is to decide what students will do with language and how they will use language during the lesson. Then teachers need to think about the intended learning outcomes of the lesson, and they need to have a clear idea in mind about their learning goals. Teachers' manuals often state objectives for each lesson. The verbs in those statements can serve as a guide for determining the focus of the language use to be addressed in the lesson.

Ms. Ramos then discussed the geometry lesson that she used to describe the brick and mortar concept. She asked the teachers to think about the following questions: Is the goal to have the students describe spatial relationships of the lines, curves, and angles in the geometric shapes? Will they be comparing and contrasting various geometric figures? Or, will they be expected to explain how to find the size of a particular angle? She reminded teachers that it is wise to incorporate no more than one or two language purposes in a single lesson. In content area lessons, reading, writing, speaking, or listening will usually not be the content objective. These language modalities are merely the means by which information is transmitted from one person to another. For example, in the goal statement: "Students will write a comparison of isosceles, equilateral, and right triangles," writing is not the communicative purpose for which students will use language. Comparing triangles is the purpose. Writing will be the means by which students communicate their ideas. The students, in other words, will be using writing to perform the communicative task of comparing triangles. Once they have determined what students will be using language to accomplish, teachers can prepare to explicitly teach the kinds of language structures that students will need to achieve that purpose.

One of the teachers brought in math journals as an example. Ms. Ramos found some entries in which the students compared and contrasted different geometrical shapes, defined various geometrical terms, and in still others, simply asked clarifying questions about geometric forms. Ms. Ramos explained that each of these communicative purposes is valid. The choice of which one to teach depends on the goals of the lesson. She then asked the teachers what kinds of language students would need if they wanted to compare and contrast. One teacher responded that they would need to use comparatives such as *greater than, less than,* or *equal to.* Ms. Ramos agreed and then asked more specifically what language structures students might need to be able to compare and contrast different kinds of triangles.

Mrs. Littleford commented that the students might say something like, "Equilateral, isosceles, and scalene triangles all have three sides, but equilateral triangles have three sides of equal length, isosceles triangles have only two equal sides, and scalene triangles have sides that have all different lengths." Ms. Ramos directed the teachers' attention to the language structures in this comparison statement. She illustrated that in addition to comparatives and superlatives, forms typically used in comparing and contrasting include adjectives, such as *equilateral, isosceles,* and *scalene,* conjunctions such as *and* and *but,* and adverbs such as *only.* While vocabulary words such as *equilateral, isosceles,* and *scalene* form the brick of the language structure, other words and phrases such as *long, short,* and *equal* (adjectives); *and* and *but* (conjunctions); *longer than, shorter than,* and *of equal length* (comparatives); and *longest* and *shortest* (superlatives) become the mortar words of a geometry lesson, along with brick words such as *angle, equilateral, isosceles,* and *scalene.*

Ms. Ramos gave a second example to help clarify the concepts. In a science lesson on thunderstorms, students might write a report in which they show *cause and effect* or in which they *sequence* the events in the weather cycle of thunderstorms. To teach the language structures associated with the purpose of communicating *cause and effect,* Ms. Ramos showed the teachers how to focus on verb forms, including past tense (The tree *fell* down when it *was struck* by lightning.), present tense (When lightning *strikes* trees, they *fall* down), or future tense (The tree *will fall* down if it *is struck* by lightning). If students will be *sequencing* a series of events related to a thunderstorm, they should focus on adverbs of time (*yesterday, today, first, next, then, finally, just, already, still*), relative clauses (clauses that begin with *who, which, whose, whom,* or *that,* such as *that fell on the house, who forecast the storm, which destroyed many crops*), and subordinate conjunctions (*as if, even though, since, now that, until, whenever,* etc.). Ms. Ramos was pleased to see that the teachers were beginning to recognize the kinds of language structures that they would want to front-load when teaching a lesson like this one. She reminded them that when choosing a language purpose and the language structures that will be taught and practiced in a lesson's writing session, they should state for the students the *reason* for their writing. A teacher might say, for example, "Today you will write about the damage that lightning caused during last Thursday's thunderstorm."

USING BRICK AND MORTAR IN THE WRITING PROCESS

The teacher study group was eager to try the ideas of brick and mortar, along with focusing on language purposes and structures, in teaching writing. They taught the writing process beginning in second grade and wanted to know how the brick and mortar ideas applied to instructional methods. Ms. Ramos began discussing the complexity of the writing process by quoting Flowers and Hayes (1980):

> The writer must exercise a number of skills and meet a number of demands—more or less all at once. As a dynamic process, writing is the act of dealing with an excessive number of simultaneous demands or constraints. Viewed this way, a writer in the act is a thinker on full-time cognitive overload. (p. 33)

Indeed, as is discussed in Chapter 1, a student learning to write must coordinate handwriting, spelling, planning, organization, working memory, metacognition, use of strategies, and more. Ms. Ramos reminded the teachers that because writing is such a complex process, they would need to provide appropriate supports at every step along the way for ELLs, who must attend to constructing meaning on paper while at the same time dealing with both lower- and higher-level demands of the English language. She described some of the difficulties that ELLs encounter during the writing process and what teachers can do to provide support.

Prewriting

Prewriting activities are important for all children, but they are critical to successful writing in ELLs. ELLs have gaps in their vocabulary and English language structures. Prewriting activities are essential for ELLs because they help students to learn the language of the topic and start thinking about how they might express their ideas. ELLs need explicit instruction in the academic "brick" vocabulary of the topic that they will write about, as well as in the use of the "mortar" words that show relationships among the ideas. The bulk of the writing process should be spent on this step.

Ms. Ramos and the teachers discussed how the prewriting step extends front-loading and gives students experience with the words and structures that they will use to express their thinking. Ms. Ramos explained that for students who have some English reading skills, preparing to write about a topic by reading about it gives them experience with vocabulary and language structures that they will use in their compositions. For example, a student preparing to write an essay on the Jamestown Colony might read to better understand the concepts behind words such as *charter, expedition, gentry, artisans, craftsmen, Algonquins,* and *colonization,* while becoming familiar with language structures such as the past tense and irregular past-tense verb forms. Ms. Ramos told the teachers that after teaching these structures to students, the students can more easily generate ideas for different paragraphs, while having the syntactical and organizational features of social studies text modeled for them. These scaffolds give ELLs increased exposure to and practice with the kind of language that they will use in their writing, which frees up cognitive resources to focus on communicating their ideas. Ms. Ramos commented that it helps students to better understand how to "write like the book."

For students who have some oral/aural proficiency but have not yet developed reading skills in English, or for young primary-level students, Ms. Ramos suggested that listening to the teacher read texts aloud or listening to audio tapes can be of benefit. Hands-on experiences and language front-loading also help to bring meaning to abstract vocabulary. She added that holding whole-class or small-group discussions about different topics is another way of helping students practice the kind of language that they will use when writing. She reminded the teachers to not overlook any first-language literacy strengths that students might possess, as first-language reading materials can also help to reduce the cognitive overload that ELLs face when preparing to write in English.

Mrs. Littleford and the other teachers were understanding better that good planning is critical to successful writing for ELLs. They had learned that it is at this stage of the writing process that students should spend the bulk of their time. They were also becoming aware of how careful planning can reduce the amount of time that students need to spend on editing and revising and how prewriting can also reduce writing anxiety and "writer's block" that may interfere with students' ability to express themselves with ease in English. Planning gives ELLs the chance to think about how and when they will use specific vocabulary words and how they will structure their sentences. Ms. Ramos reassured the teachers that when they make their students aware of why planning is important and when students should use planning strategies, when they expect their students to preplan their writing assignments, and when they model planning strategies and encourage students to use them, they create a classroom climate that supports careful planning (Graham & Harris, 2007). Ms. Ramos suggested that teachers can support students as they plan their writing by conducting brainstorming activities, having students make lists, and using graphic organizers.

Drafting

Prewriting helps ELLs to begin thinking about the vocabulary and language structures that they will use in their writing. They may, however, still have difficulty learning how to compose sentences that make sense to an English reader. Teachers can support their ELLs' writing efforts by weaving grammar instruction into the writing lesson through mini-lessons in specific grammatical features that pertain to the particular language purpose of the paper. Ms. Ramos recommended that the teachers in the ELL study group create mini-lessons to address grammatical issues. For example, if students are writing to describe something, the teacher can give mini-lessons in using adjectives to add detail. Teachers can support ELLs' drafting efforts through activities such as sentence combining and manipulating and practicing with sentence and paragraph frames. (See Chapter 5 for an example of a paragraph frame.)

Editing

ELLs are often not familiar enough with the English language to recognize immediately what "sounds right," so they aren't able to identify their writing errors. Many elementary- and intermediate-level teachers use peer editing as a means of providing students with feedback on their writing. Collaboration with peers can scaffold students' language abilities at this stage of the writing process. Ms. Ramos presented the benefits of peer editing for ELLs to the teachers in the study group. She emphasized that teachers should be explicit about teaching the editing process itself, encouraging students to point out errors relevant to grammar points taught in that day's lesson or by providing a checklist of potential errors to be corrected. Having examples of correct and incorrect spelling, language structures, and conventions on a checklist can help ELLs more fully participate in editing, allowing them to give valuable feedback to classmates while raising consciousness of their own errors at the same time. Ms. Ramos showed the teachers the editing checklist that she had developed (see Figure 2.1), and asked them to try it with their students. Mrs. Littleford commented that a checklist such as this one could help all students, not just ELLs, edit their written work.

Revising

Even if ELLs can identify their writing errors, they may not necessarily feel confident about revising their work independently. Ms. Ramos encouraged the teach-

FIGURE 2.1. Editing checklist with examples.		
Editing Checklist for Science Reports Grade level: 3–5 Assignment: Last Thursday's thunderstorm		
		Circle Yes or No
I used capital letters to start sentences and periods to end sentences most of the time.	Period: . Capital Letters: *The, If, Next*	Yes No
I put words in the right order, even if I made a few grammar mistakes.	The dark cloud The cloud was dark	Yes No
I described a sequence of events. I added some details.	First Next Then Finally	Yes No
My story has a main idea.	Last Thursday's thunderstorm	Yes No
I added a lot of details to my sentences.	Describe: • Colors • Odors • Shapes • Sights • Sounds • Your feelings	Yes No
I used vocabulary that makes sense for science, and I spelled my words correctly.	Word list: • Cloud • Electricity • Forecast • Lightning • Loud • Pour (pours, pouring, poured) • Rain (rains, raining, rained) • Strike (strikes, striking, struck) • Thunder • Weather	Yes No

ers in the study group to challenge their ELLs to use revising as an opportunity to practice using academic language. As students "fix" their vocabulary, spelling, grammar, and convention errors, find better ways to express their ideas, and "polish" their writing, teachers can provide scaffolds by reviewing language points that students have had difficulty with and by modeling clearer and more appropriate ways of saying what students want to say. Focused instruction helps students who continue to have difficulty with aspects of the English language to know not only what they are supposed to say, but how to say it (Kucer & Silva, 1999). Ms. Ramos added that ELLs should be encouraged to experiment with appropriately challenging language structures for their proficiency levels.

Publishing

By the time they reach the publishing stage of the writing process, ELLs should feel the satisfaction that they have done their best work and that they have learned more about the English language through the writing experience. However, they might not always feel that they have expressed their knowledge adequately. One way to extend the publishing of student work beyond just neat copying onto good paper is to have students illustrate their writing pieces. In the content areas, illustration can be a means through which ELLs convey an understanding that their limited writing skills do not yet allow them to express. There is research evidence that "pictorial representation can serve effectively not only as an adjunct to text, but as a direct instructional mode. Learner-generated drawings can contribute directly to the learning process, not just as an extension or filler activity. Students should be encouraged to use descriptive explanatory drawing to convey meaning" (Edens & Potter, 2001, p. 228). Ms Ramos told the teachers that illustrations serve the purpose of conveying meaning rather than merely decorating the paper; students can gain an additional opportunity to express understanding of content area material. Labeling their drawings and writing captions gives ELLs additional practice in writing key vocabulary words in a student-created context. She showed the teachers an example of an illustrated published writing piece similar to the example in Figure 2.2.

WHAT TO EXPECT FROM STUDENTS AT DIFFERENT PROFICIENCY LEVELS

The teachers in the school we introduce in this book teach at all grade levels and have several ELLs in their classrooms. They have students at different proficiency levels in their classes who perform differently on a spectrum from simple to complex language use.

Ms. Ramos is charged with improving the language and literacy development of all struggling readers and writers, including the ELLs. She explained that students proceed through levels of English language proficiency while at the same time moving through developmental stages as they advance grade levels.

FIGURE 2.2. Published second-grade student writing sample with illustration.

Moving

I moved in an airplane.
I went to the airport. We got in the airplane.
We got a toy of some family.
It took one day to get here.
We slept in a hotel.
Then we got to see our house for the first time.
Then we got to see our bedroom, but first our living room and our dining
        room.
That day I found out about the garage.
It took a long time for the container to get there. Finally the container
        came.
We took the things out of the container.
It took days for them to pick up the container.
I miss my best friend.
I miss all my friends, but here I get new friends.
My best friend's dog died. That was my favorite dog.
I got a letter from my best friend that said about the dog.
I can get friends, maybe 2 or 3 or 4 or more. I want enough or more. I
        wonder how many I can find?
But I get friends that are good.
In school it can be fun. So can it not.
And that is the end, so The End.

I moved in an airplane.

Many strategies can be used to scaffold students' academic English writing development at each language proficiency level. Since there is much overlap in proficiency levels, especially when a child is transitioning from one level to the next, these strategies can be used not only at the level indicated, but the one below and above it as well. For example, at the beginning level, teachers can label objects commonly used in the classroom, such as desks, pencils, and doors, and teach simple sentence structures explicitly through the use of sentence frames. They can post vocabulary items on a word wall so that students can see how they are written. For early intermediate-level students, teachers can give opportunities to label objects, using both common words such as furniture in a room and content area vocabulary such as parts of a flower. They can provide models for paragraph writing and use sentence frames to model and practice using sentence structures found in different content areas and academic vocabulary. At the intermediate level, teachers should explicitly teach the grammar points, including verb tenses that students must know to express their thinking in different content areas. They should give students opportunities to practice writing complex sentence structures with the support of sentence frames and teach academic vocabulary that includes synonyms, antonyms, and idiomatic expressions. They can also provide focused instruction on how to plan and organize writing. For early advanced-level ELLs, teachers should continue to explicitly teach content area vocabulary and review grammatical structures that tend to be problematic. They should model strategies such as outlining, so that students will be able to write essays with a strong thesis and supporting evidence. At the advanced level, ELLs benefit when teachers build on their prior knowledge of both language and content. Teachers should continue to expand students' academic vocabulary and model writing elements such as transitions and organizational strategies. They should create meaningful contexts for students to write and give students plenty of opportunities to practice and develop their writing skills.

Many states currently have guidelines to help teachers know what to expect from ELLs at different proficiency levels. These guidelines will help teachers to know at what level of English proficiency their students are performing and what they can look for as evidence that their students' writing is transitioning from one level to the next. At all proficiency levels, students should be expected to use capitalization, punctuation, and spelling that is appropriate to the child's level. Figure 2.3 lists guidelines to help teachers understand the proficiency stages. (You might want to check your State Department of Education website to find the specific standards for your state.)

The teachers in the ELL study group asked Ms. Ramos to help them understand what they should expect from students at different English-language proficiency levels and how to set expectations that are both challenging and appropriate for each student. Some of the teachers had looked at the English-language proficiency standards for speaking or reading, but only a few had seen the standards for writing. Ms. Ramos was happy to see the teachers' interest.

(text resumes on page 39)

FIGURE 2.3. English language development performance standards for writing.

Adapted from English language development standards from the following sources: Alaska Department of Education & Early Development. (2005). ELP: Alaska English Language Proficiency Standards. Retrieved November 7, 2009, from *www.eed.state.ak.us/tls/assessment/elp/ELPStandards/ELPBOOKFinalMarch2006.pdf*. California State Board of Education. (2009). English-Language Development Standards for California Public Schools: Kindergarten Through Grade Twelve. Retrieved November 7, 2009, from *www.cde.ca.gov/be/st/ss/documents/englangdevstnd.pdf*. Idaho State Board of Education. (2006). Idaho Content Standards: ELD Standards. Retrieved November 7, 2009, from *www.sde.idaho.gov/ContentStandards/lepstandards.asp*. Washington State Office of Superintendent of Public Instruction. (2003). English Language Development (ELD) Language Proficiency Levels. Retrieved November 7, 2009, from *www.k12.wa.us/MigrantBilingual/ELD.aspx*.

	Beginning	Emerging	Intermediate	Early fluent	Advanced
Grades K–2					
Handwriting and spelling	Copy or trace the letters of the alphabet. Follow a model to write student's own name. Write from left to right.	Follow a model to write upper and lower case letters. Copy words posted in classroom.	Independently write some upper and lower case letters. Begin to write using phonetic spelling to write high-frequency words. Copy phrases and simple sentences.	Write the upper and lowercase letters of the alphabet legibly. Use phonetic spelling to represent some sounds in one or two high-frequency words. Write phrases and simple sentences with some assistance.	Independently write all upper and lowercase letters of the alphabet legibly. Use phonetic spelling to represent all sounds in one or two high-frequency words. Independently write phrases and simple sentences.
Writing to express ideas			Identify sentences that have been written for different purposes.	Write for more than one purpose.	Write for several different purposes.
Planning and organizing writing around a topic	Participate in group writing process by using gestures and drawings in discussions.	Participate in group writing process by using simple words to express ideas. Write simple complete sentences with some assistance.	Participate in group writing process by using simple phrases and sentences to express ideas. Independently write simple complete sentences.	Participate in group writing process by contributing ideas to discussions. Independently write a simple complete paragraph on a single topic.	Fluently participate in group writing process by contributing ideas to discussions. Independently write sentences and paragraphs that demonstrate good organization of ideas.

(cont.)

FIGURE 2.3. *(cont.)*					
	Beginning	Emerging	Intermediate	Early fluent	Advanced
Drafting sentences and paragraphs	Copy familiar words.	Independently write familiar words and phrases.	Begin to use sentence and paragraph frames to write about main ideas and details. Write descriptive words and phrases.	Use sentence and paragraph frames to write about main ideas and details. Write simple descriptive sentences.	Independently write a paragraph on a single topic with one or two supporting details. Write a short, simple paragraph that describes something.
Revising and editing	Listen during group revising and editing.	Participate in group revising and editing.	Revise writing with teacher assistance.	Revise and edit writing with teacher assistance.	Revise and edit own writing using an editing checklist.
Vocabulary	Write two or three words related to a topic.	Write several words related to a topic.	Write some grade-level content words.	Write sentences using some grade-level vocabulary.	Write sentences using grade-level content vocabulary.
Grammar	Identify one or more features of English grammar.	Use some features of English grammar with frequent errors.	Use grade-level English grammar with frequent errors.	Use grade-level standard English grammar inconsistently.	Use grade-level standard English grammar most of the time.
Conventions	Capitalize the first letter of names.	Use some grade-level punctuation. Capitalize the first letter of names and beginnings of sentences some of the time.	Use grade-level punctuation inconsistently. Capitalize the first letter of proper names and beginnings of sentences with occasional lapses.	Use grade-level punctuation with occasional lapses Capitalize the first letter of proper names and beginnings of sentences most of the time.	Consistently use grade-level punctuation. Consistently capitalize the first letter of proper names and beginnings of sentences.
Grades 3–5					
	Beginning	Emerging	Intermediate	Early fluent	Advanced
Handwriting and spelling	Begin to use invented spelling. Write sight words and other familiar words.	Use phonetic knowledge to write unfamiliar words. Inconsistently spell high-frequency words correctly.	Use phonetic knowledge to write two or three multisyllable words. Write several high-frequency words correctly.	Use phonetic knowledge to write several multisyllable words. Write most high-frequency words correctly.	Use phonetic knowledge to write various multisyllable words. Consistently write high-frequency words correctly.

(cont.)

			FIGURE 2.3. *(cont.)*		
	Beginning	Emerging	Intermediate	Early fluent	Advanced
Write to express ideas	Identify more than one audience to write for.	Begin to write for different audiences.	Begin to write for different audiences and purposes.	Write for a variety of audiences and purposes.	Write for a wide variety of audiences and purposes.
Planning and organizing writing around a topic	Participate in group writing process by using simple words to express ideas. With assistance, write a list of words that are related to a single topic.	Participate in group writing process by using simple phrases and sentences to express ideas. Write a well-organized paragraph on a single topic.	Participate in group writing process by contributing ideas to discussions. Write two or more paragraphs that contain beginning, middle, and end.	Fluently participate in group writing process by contributing ideas to discussions. Independently write sentences and paragraphs that demonstrate good organization of ideas.	Fluently participate in group writing process by contributing ideas with supporting information to discussions. Independently write paragraphs that have logical organization and that contain a beginning, middle, and end.
Drafting sentences and paragraphs	Use graphic organizer to show main idea and details. With assistance, write a rough draft containing two or more sentences.	Begin to use sentence and paragraph frames to write about main ideas and details. Write simple rough draft with assistance.	Use sentence and paragraph frames to write about main ideas and details. Independently write rough draft. Use several different sentence types.	Write two paragraphs on a single topic, using topic sentence and supporting details. Use a variety of sentence types to add interest to paragraphs. Use some transitions in multiple paragraph essays and reports. Use narrative genre.	Write three or more paragraphs on a single topic with topic sentence and supporting details. Use a wide variety of sentence types to add interest to paragraphs. Effectively use transitions in multiple paragraph essays and reports. Use narrative and expository genres.
Revising and editing		Revise rough draft with teacher assistance.	Revise rough draft using a checklist.	Revise and edit with minimal assistance.	Revise and edit independently.

(cont.)

FIGURE 2.3. *(cont.)*					
	Beginning	Emerging	Intermediate	Early fluent	Advanced
Vocabulary	Write several words related to one content area.	Write a variety of academic content words.	Use some grade-level academic vocabulary in sentences.	Use grade-level academic vocabulary across content areas most of the time. Choose words that contribute to interest of paragraphs.	Use grade-level academic vocabulary across content areas. Choose from a wide range of words that contribute to interest of paragraphs.
Grammar	Write simple sentences with Standard English word order.	Use subject/verb agreement and Standard English word order inconsistently.	Demonstrate increasing control over subject/verb agreement and Standard English word order, conjunctions, pronouns, and other grammatical forms.	Use grade-level Standard English grammar, including subject/verb agreement, word order, conjunctions, pronouns, and other grammatical forms, with occasional lapses.	Consistently use grade-level Standard English grammar, including subject/verb agreement, word order, conjunctions, pronouns, and other grammatical forms.
Conventions	Capitalize proper nouns.	Use punctuation and capitalization inconsistently.	Correctly use ending punctuation, and capitalization with occasional lapses.	Demonstrate increasing control over punctuation, including use of commas in a series, and capitalization.	Demonstrate grade-level control over punctuation, including use of commas in a series, and capitalization.
Grades 6–8					
	Beginning	Emerging	Intermediate	Early fluent	Advanced
Handwriting and spelling	Begin to use invented spelling. Write sight words and other familiar words.	Use phonetic knowledge to spell a few multisyllable words. Use correct spelling inconsistently in high-frequency words.	Demonstrate increasing control over correct spelling. Write most high-frequency words.	Demonstrate grade-level control over correct spelling most of the time.	Write all high-frequency words. Consistently demonstrate grade-level control over correct spelling.

(cont.)

	Beginning	Emerging	Intermediate	Early fluent	Advanced
			FIGURE 2.3. *(cont.)*		
Write to express ideas	Begin to write for one or more purposes.	Begin to write for a variety of audiences and purposes.	With some assistance, produce writing for a number of different purposes.	Independently produce writing for a number of different purposes.	Independently produce writing for a wide variety of purposes.
Planning and organizing writing around a topic	Participate in group writing process by using simple phrases and sentences to express ideas. Use a paragraph frame to show main ideas and details.	Participate in group writing process by contributing ideas to discussions. Write simple paragraph that contains a main idea and supporting details.	Participate in group writing process by contributing ideas and supporting information to discussions. Use topic sentence and supporting details to maintain focus of paragraph.	Participate in group writing process by contributing ideas and supporting information to discussions. Write essays of at least two or three paragraphs containing a beginning, middle, and end.	Fluently participate in group writing process by contributing relevant ideas and supporting information to discussions. Write multiparagraph essays with logical organization, containing a beginning, middle, and end.
Drafting sentences and paragraphs	Write simple sentences. Begin to write using sentence and paragraph frames and other models. Write several sentences on a single topic.	Begin to use basic conjunctions to combine sentences. Write simple sentences and paragraphs with some assistance. Write simple rough draft.	Use basic transitions and sentence combinations. Write simple sentences and paragraphs independently. Independently write rough draft containing two or more paragraphs. Use narrative genre.	Use a variety of sentence types. Use topic sentence and details to develop a topic. Independently write rough draft containing multiple paragraphs. Use narrative and expository genres.	Use a wide variety of sentence types. Use topic sentence and relevant details to develop a topic. Independently write longer rough drafts. Use narrative, expository, and persuasive genres.
Revising and editing	Revise rough draft with teacher assistance.	Revise and edit rough draft with teacher assistance.	Revise and edit independently using an editing checklist.	Revise and edit rough draft with minimal assistance.	Revise and edit rough draft with minimal assistance.
Vocabulary	Write simple sentences with assistance, using content vocabulary words.	Write sentences using content vocabulary words.	Use some academic vocabulary in some content areas.	Use academic vocabulary across content areas.	Use complex academic vocabulary across content areas.

(cont.)

	Beginning	Emerging	Intermediate	Early fluent	Advanced
FIGURE 2.3. (cont.)					
Grammar	Use punctuation and capitalization inconsistently.	Correctly use ending punctuation and capitalization with occasional lapses.	Demonstrate increasing control over grammatical forms such as conjunctions, pronouns, and subject/verb agreement.	Correctly use grammatical forms such as parts of speech, quotation marks, and clauses.	Use Standard English grammar, including parts of speech, quotation marks, irregular verbs, plurals, and subordinate clauses, with few lapses.
Conventions	Begin to use correct capitalization.	Use correct ending punctuation, contractions, and capitalization with modeling.	Use ending and in-sentence punctuation and capitalization with increasing consistency.	Use grade-level ending and in-sentence punctuations, commas, and capitalization with occasional errors.	Consistently use grade-level ending and in-sentence punctuations, commas, and capitalization.

When the ELL study group met the next time, Ms. Ramos showed the teachers that the English-language development standards are divided into five different proficiency levels. The standards are further divided by group level. In addition, there are several different writing strands that are addressed by the standards.

Beginning Level

Ms. Ramos started by discussing the beginning level of language proficiency standards for writing. She told the teachers that in the primary grades, beginning-level ELLs can be expected to copy the alphabet and copy words that are on the chalkboard or posted on a word wall. They can also write a few words or phrases about a story that the teacher has read aloud or about an experience that a character in a story has had.

In grades 3–5, beginning-level ELLs can be expected to write the alphabet without needing to copy it. They can write the names of common objects, such as *door* and *chair*, especially if they have seen the objects labeled in the classroom, and they can write simple sentences in English with help from the teacher or a classmate. When given a model, they will be able to follow the model to write a short narrative. Beginning-level ELL students can participate in small-group writing in the classroom, and can produce short stories or narratives that include a few standard grammatical forms.

At the sixth- through eighth-grade level, assuming that the student has had some previous education in his or her home country, students can be expected to write simple compositions using a few standard grammatical forms. They will be able to compose simple paragraphs that include a main idea and a few details. They will also be able to fill out simple business forms with information such as their addresses.

Ms. Ramos told the study group that by labeling objects commonly used in the classroom, teaching simple sentence structures through the use of sentence frames, and posting vocabulary on a word wall teachers can support their beginning-level ELLs in their English writing development.

2 Early Intermediate Level

Ms. Ramos continued the discussion about proficiency levels by talking about the early intermediate level. She told the teachers that in the primary grades, early intermediate-level ELLs will be able to write simple sentences about characters or events from a familiar story that has been read aloud to them. They can use words that are posted on the word wall or written on the board, and that are regularly used in the classroom to compose simple sentences. Early intermediate-level ELLs in the intermediate grades can write short narrative stories that contain a few elements of character and setting. They will also be able to write simple sentences in response to familiar literature, showing their understanding of the text, and using drawings, lists, or charts to further express their thinking.

At the early intermediate level, third, fourth, and fifth graders can write simple sentences about topics in content areas such as math, science, and social studies. They can also follow a model to write a friendly letter. Although their writing will be understood when it is read, students may not consistently use standard grammatical forms. At the sixth- through eighth-grade levels, early intermediate-level ELLs can write simple responses to literature, include main ideas and some details in short paragraphs, and write words and simple sentences related to content areas.

Giving students opportunities to label objects, using both common words and content area vocabulary, providing models for paragraph writing, and completing sentence frames that use sentence structures found in different content areas and academic vocabulary, are some of the ways that Ms. Ramos recommended to the teachers for helping early intermediate-level ELLs develop academic language skills.

3 Intermediate Level

The teachers continued to listen as Ms. Ramos explained the standards for the intermediate level. Young intermediate-level ELLs in the primary grades are able to write short narrative stories that use some elements of character and setting. Their independent writing may contain inconsistencies in standard grammatical forms, but the reader will be able to understand it. By using a model, they will be able to work through the writing process and produce a written piece of at least three lines. In content areas such as math, science, or social studies, they are able to write simple sentences that express their thinking about content concepts. At this level, children can write short friendly letters.

Intermediate-level ELLs in third through fifth grade will be able to write about a sequence of events using some level of detail. Their independent writing will develop an idea and will be understood by the reader, even if they have not consistently used standard grammatical forms. At this level, students will begin to write in a variety of genres, including both narrative and expository writing as well as poetry. Their content area writing becomes more complex, and they use a wider variety of academic vocabulary and more complex sentence structures. Students have a larger repertoire of verbs and can use them in more tenses in their writing at this level. Their vocabulary is richer than it was at earlier stages, and they can use synonyms, antonyms, and some idiomatic expressions. They will also be able to independently write a letter using sentences that contain details.

By sixth grade, intermediate-level ELLs can be expected to write brief expository compositions that include a thesis and some supporting details. They can also demonstrate their understanding of literary selections by writing responses that give details and use appropriate transitions. They can write short fictional biographies using complex sentences and details, write outlines and use other note-taking strategies, write brief essays on topics that they have researched, including using appropriate citations, and write business letters. Ms. Ramos showed the teachers a sample of an intermediate-level composition written by a sixth-grade student as an illustration (see Figure 2.4). The author of the intermediate-level writing sample includes some researched information and uses standard grammatical forms, conventions, conjunctions, and sequencing words, but uses little variety in sentence structures and does not edit effectively for spelling.

Because writing at the intermediate level is becoming more sophisticated, teachers can provide support by explicitly teaching the grammar points, including verb tenses that students must know to communicate their thinking in different content areas. Giving students opportunities to practice complex sentence structures with the support of sentence frames is helpful, as is instruction in academic

---

FIGURE 2.4. Sixth-grade intermediate-level writing sample.

Oregon Trail

In 1803 Lewis and Clarck reached the Pacific Ocean. They had also found Oregon. They thought they had found the Oregon trail, but they were wrong. Their Oregon trail was not good for wagon. Finaly someone did find the Oregon trail, and many people went to Oregon but only about half of them made it. In 1959 Oregon became part of the U.S.A. In 1970 the Oregon Trail was no use any more cause they already had a railroad going to Oregon. Today the railroad is no use cause we have airplanes flying to Oregon.

vocabulary that includes synonyms, antonyms, and idiomatic expressions. Teaching that focuses on how students can plan and organize their writing is helpful to all students at this level and especially helps ELLs attend to these aspects of the writing process.

Early Advanced Level

The early advanced level, commented Ms. Ramos, is often the highest proficiency level at which students receive specialized instruction in English language development. Many school districts do not provide services beyond this level. In the primary grades, early advanced-level ELLs can write short narrative stories that include elements of setting, characters, and events. They can use the writing process to produce writing pieces that maintain a consistent focus. Their use of standard grammatical forms is fairly consistent, and they can write independently. Their content area writing is becoming more sophisticated and complex, using more variety of grammatical forms and a broader range of vocabulary. Ms. Ramos displayed a sample of a second-grade student's writing at this stage similar to the one found in Figure 2.5. In this writing sample, the author uses standard grammatical forms and sentence structure in the imperative. The sample has elements of character, events, and setting, and the theme is well developed. The paragraph has some inconsistencies with regard to capitalization and punctuation, and some words are spelled incorrectly.

Early advanced-level ELLs in third through fifth grade are able to write detailed summaries of stories, multiple paragraph narratives, and content area essays that are well organized. They can independently produce simple responses to literature and persuasive letters with relevant supporting evidence. In the content areas, their sentence structures are complex, standard grammatical features are used consistently, and their use of academic vocabulary is sophisticated.

Early advanced-level ELLs who are in the middle school grades will be able to write in a coherent, focused manner in a variety of genres, using language variations that are appropriate for specific content areas. They can demonstrate careful reading in their responses to literature by appropriately citing parts of a text. Their

---

FIGURE 2.5. Second-grade early advanced-level writing sample.

Wake up

Wake up and open your eyes. Do not slow down. Get ready for your party. You are going out to eat. You're already seven. And big! But who cares. And have a good time. But do you want to have gifts? And you're a big girl.

fictional writing is detailed at this level. They can use strategies such as outlining and note taking to write clearly structured and organized drafts that contain a thesis with strong supporting evidence.

Ms. Ramos recommended that the teachers support the writing development of ELLs at the early advanced level by continuing to explicitly teach content area vocabulary and by reviewing grammatical structures that tend to be problematic. They can also scaffold essay organization by modeling strategies such as outlining, so that students will be able to write essays with a strong thesis and supporting evidence.

Advanced Level

Ms. Ramos emphasized that advanced-level ELLs still need support in academic writing, whether they receive specialized language support services or not. She explained that advanced-level ELLs in the primary grades can write short narratives that describe setting, characters, objects, and events and expository pieces that use vocabulary and genres that are relevant to content areas. They are able to use correct grammatical forms in independent writing and use the writing process to produce clear, coherent pieces that have a consistent focus.

In the intermediate grades, advanced-level ELLs are able to write short compositions in the genres that are appropriate to various content area topics. Their writing will include standard grammatical forms, and they will be able to navigate independently through the writing process. Ms. Ramos showed the teachers a writing example of a fifth-grade advanced-level ELL (see Figure 2.6). The teachers could see that the theme was well developed in this multiparagraph writing sample, which contains elements of both expository and persuasive writing. The topic had been researched and details were included. Ms. Ramos pointed out that the writer consistently used standard grammatical forms with only minor errors and included a variety of sentence structures.

Middle school students at the advanced English proficiency level use various discourse elements including purpose, speaker, audience, and form. They can write in narrative, expository, persuasive, and descriptive genres, and use rhetorical devices such as analogies, quotations, facts, and statistics that support the thesis of their report. Their narrative writing includes elements such as coherent plot development, characterization, setting, dialogue, and suspense. They are also able to write career-related pieces, such as memoranda and business letters.

Ms. Ramos encouraged the teachers to give students at this stage the support they need by continuing to expand their vocabulary, by modeling the use of more complex verb tenses, and by focusing instruction on persistent grammatical problems.

After listening to descriptions of the different proficiency levels, Mrs. Littleford commented that writing in a foreign language, without an adequate vocabulary or knowledge of the structure of the language, must be in some ways like trying to draw a picture without good artistic skills. The aspiring artist can visu-

FIGURE 2.6. Fifth-grade advanced-level writing sample.

Trading Card Games

Trading card games are fun, easy to play. The basic principle of trading cards is this: I have cards, you have cards, and we will play against each other using the cards. Each Game is unique, making games better.

Some parents disagree. Why waste money on cards, ask the parents. I ponder about it, and in the end I came up 3 answers: Trading Card Games are fun, cool, and attractive. Of course those aren't reasons (well, to parents anyway), but having a good time to a kid is like earning a million dollars, and kids don't often, or rarely get $1,000,000.

I kept searching until one day I came across a book called The Ultimate Guide To Trading Card Game by Michael G. Ryan. It had a number of good reasons, and a good explanation of five trading card games (From now on I'm just going to call trading card game TCG).

History of TCG

TCG was created by a man named Richard Garfield, who start the game Magic: The Gathering. Since then, other games came out: Pokemon in 1998 (2000 in U.S), Yu-Gi-Oh in 2002, Chaotic in early 2008, Bakugan in late 2008. Even now, new cards are still coming out.

Well, Trading cards do have a long history (16 years). If your kid like Bakugan or something, don't discourage them, encourage them! If you let them join tourniment, they might make new friends. (might) !

alize exactly what the picture is supposed to look like but is unable to transfer the mental image to the paper in a satisfactory way. Ms. Ramos, pleased with this metaphor, continued by saying that ELLs with cognitive skills that have been developed through the home language may have excellent ideas, but can be frustrated by their inability to express themselves adequately in English. Ms. Ramos mentioned that for advanced-level ELLs to develop writing fluency, they should be encouraged, when necessary, to use circumlocution, the process of finding alternative words to describe a concept for which they do not know the word. This lessens the need for dictionary use, which can interrupt the flow of a student's thoughts during the writing process. If students can convey their thinking during content-area writing, even without specific vocabulary words, teachers can know that their ELL students are learning content-area concepts.

Finally, Ms. Ramos commented that teachers can support advanced-level ELLs by building on their prior knowledge of both language and content, continuing to expand the students' academic vocabulary, and by modeling writing elements such as transitions and organizational strategies. Teachers, she cautioned, can also create meaningful contexts for students to write and can give them plenty of opportunities to practice and develop their writing skills. Teachers will need to create a balance between emphasis on language and emphasis on content.

SUMMARY

As Ms. Ramos explained to Mrs. Littleford and the other teachers in the ELL study group, teachers can make the writing process a rich language learning experience for ELLs by providing explicit instruction and appropriate scaffolding. There are many ways that teachers can support ELLs during the writing process. Identifying the "brick" and "mortar" words that are relevant to a given lesson helps teachers know which vocabulary and syntactical features of the English language to teach explicitly. "Front-loading" key vocabulary items before shifting focus on lesson content helps ELLs access the content material more successfully. For ELLs, a significant portion of writing time should be spent on prewriting activities such as reading, brainstorming, and discussing, as well as on careful planning of the writing piece. Explicitly teaching relevant grammar and sentence structures to ELLs before they write their first draft helps them to focus on practicing specific language structures. When editing, teachers and peers should focus on identifying errors in the specific vocabulary, spelling, and grammar features being taught. Having an error checklist with examples allows ELLs to participate more fully in the peer-editing process. Teachers can explicitly review aspects of language that students are having difficulty with during the revising phase of the writing process. As students publish their writing, labeling and captioning illustrations can help ELLs to better express themselves and practice key vocabulary. Many states have developed proficiency descriptions of ELLs' language and literacy development. A variety of proficiency levels can be found in most ELL classrooms.

WEB RESOURCES

By Request
www.nwrel.org/request/2003may/

Articles on language acquisition theory, ELL policy, and strategies for teaching ELLs.

E. L. Achieve
www.elachieve.org/index.php/research--articles?47cefd1ed643d7f5e3485507f579c12a=50e74692fa cc2582e8961ae7a91f7bbc

Articles of interest to teachers of ELLs, including Dutro and Moran's landmark article.

English Language Development Standards for California Public Schools
www.cde.ca.gov/be/st/ss/documents/englangdevstnd.pdf

Lists ELD standards for reading, writing, speaking, and listening at each proficiency level in grades K–12.

Language & Literacy
www.jeffzwiers.com

Resources and articles of interest to teachers of ELLs.

Project G.L.A.D.
www.projectglad.com

Vision, components, features, and strategies of the GLAD model.

SIOP: Making Content Comprehensible for ELLs
www.everythingesl.net/inservices/using_siop_model_08621.php.php

An overview of the SIOP model, with links to other SIOP-related resources.

CHAPTER 3

Facilitating Writing Fluency

Rana, a newcomer from India who was in fourth grade, learned how to communicate with her classmates and teacher quickly, but she wrote hesitantly. She was able to learn English words and phrases with no trouble and was pleased that she could communicate with her classmates. When it came to writing what she was thinking, however, Rana froze. Rana had learned the Indian alphabet in school before she arrived in the United States and was surprised that the letters that formed the English alphabet were very different. Ms. Wilson, Rana's teacher, worked with her and other newcomers to learn the English alphabet and simple sight words. With Ms. Wilson's expert teaching, Rana was able to learn how to write letters and short words in a few weeks. She also began learning simple rules of conventions, such as capitalizing the first letter in a word. Rana practiced writing sentences and, although she made many mistakes, she knew she was improving. Within a few months, Rana felt comfortable writing short sentences, but she still couldn't express all of her feelings and ideas in English. Ms. Wilson knew that she needed to help Rana and her other students develop writing fluency as she taught them the rules that govern English, so she contacted Ms. Ramos, the literacy coach, for ideas.

Students like Rana can have a difficult time incorporating their ability to learn conversational English into writing. According to Herrera, Perez, and Escamilla (2010), "The skills that allow a student to understand and/or speak English do not automatically transfer to writing" (p. 193). This is because writing is an output activity and thus is more complex than either listening or speaking. Many teachers are familiar with the notion that comprehensible input is necessary for language learning (Krashen, 1985). Ms. Wilson knew that speaking in class so that the ELLs could understand her was an example of comprehensible input. According to Anthony (2008), the output of ELLs is as important as language input. Output is defined as the product of learning, such as when students answer a question or take a test (Swain, 2005; VanPatten, 2003). When ELLs are producing language in output activities, they are accessing their knowledge of words, syntax (word order), and morphology (word forms). They are also "testing" how words go together through trial and error. Just participating in output activities, such as speaking and writing, help ELLs practice ways to use English in different contexts. Anthony suggests that output activities, such as writing, need to be practiced so that they become automatic.

The ability to write automatically is commonly called writing fluency. This chapter explains the reasons why teachers need to focus on writing fluency, the challenges ELLs face when learning to write, and instructional strategies for facilitating writing fluency.

WHAT IS WRITING FLUENCY?

Writing fluency is the ability to produce texts without drawing heavily on working memory (McCutchen, 2006). Since Rana was a new learner of English, she had to remember how to form the letters, how words are spelled, and how words form sentences. Since Rana could be classified as a beginning-level ELL writer who was transitioning into an early intermediate-level ELL writer (see Chapter 2 for stages of writing development), she needed to spend much of her cognitive capacity accomplishing basic writing skills. Her ability to form ideas worked much faster than her ability to write them down. Julio was another of Ms. Wilson's students. He had been in American schools for 3 years and was an intermediate-level writer. Julio was able to compose English sentences without much difficulty and was able to write down his thoughts quickly. According to McCutchen (2006), writers like Julio who are able to compose sentences quickly can use a higher percentage of their cognitive capacity to achieve higher-order tasks, such as organizing thoughts and choosing words.

When ELLs write, they are experimenting with English and trying out ways to express themselves. It's much like learning any new skill. Think about a skill you have learned or that you watched someone else learn. For example, think about learning to play the violin. Imagine for a moment taking the violin in your arms and lifting the bow to the strings. Then imagine a teacher explaining the fingerings for the notes, how to read music, and how to move the bow across the strings. After being taught each one of the skills, would you be ready for a performance? You need to practice and practice. The same principle holds true for writing. Students, especially ELLs, need to practice writing in order to build the kind of writing fluency that good writers need (Watts-Taffe & Truscott, 2000).

Facilitating Writing Fluency

Writing fluency can be developed by participating in informal writing activities. Informal writing activities can take the form of writing in journals, responding to reading, or writing to learn. In each case, ELLs express what they are thinking without focusing too much on the conventions of language. With informal writing, it is the work of the mind that is more important than language conventions. Students need to know that for informal writing, it's the thought that counts, but more formal writing requires attention to details such as conventions.

There are two main reasons why informal writing activities are important for all writers, and especially for ELLs. Effective writing depends on being able to use low-level writing skills, such as letter production and the use of function words, automatically (Lesaux, Koda, Siegal, & Shanahan, 2006). When that is the case, writers are able to devote more cognitive capacity to expressing ideas and feelings. This is especially important for ELLs who are learning both the vocabulary and the grammar of a new language. In addition, informal writing can help ELLs learn. "Writing is not simply a way for students to demonstrate what they know. It is a way to help them understand what they know. At its best, writing is learning" (National Commission on Writing, 2003, p. 13).

ELLs need time to write. "Writing maturity develops through practice and trial and error. We must first challenge our writing to improve it. Safe writing allows no room for growth" (Sjolie, 2006, p. 39). Ms. Wilson learned that she needed to provide many opportunities for Rana and the other students to write in a nonthreatening environment. Before Ms. Wilson could get all of her students writing, however, she knew that she needed to address their knowledge of the English alphabet.

ALPHABETIC FEATURES

Students won't be able to write fluently if they're not used to the English alphabet. Ms. Wilson had 10 ELLs, four of whom spoke Spanish and were familiar with most of the letters in the English alphabet. Six of the students were not. Olga and Leo spoke Russian and knew the Cyrillic alphabet; Xiaoqin was from China and used Chinese ideograms; Kaliq was from Syria and used the Arabic alphabet; and Rana and Bansari spoke Hindi and used the Indian alphabet. Ms. Wilson decided that she needed to learn about the language systems of the world to determine how best to teach these fourth graders the English alphabet. She contacted Ms Ramos who gave her some basic information about the world's writing systems.

The World's Writing Systems

The writing systems of the world are divided into two kinds: those that represent consonants and vowels (alphabets) and those that represent syllables (syllabaries). A few writing systems do both (Parker & Riley, 2010). Most of the 400 languages spoken in the United States are based on alphabets (Shin & Bruno, 2003) and are based on the five main language families: Latin or Roman, Cyrillic, Indian, Arabic, and Chinese (Bukiet, 1997). Each of these writing systems is briefly described as follows.

Latin

The Latin alphabet, also called the Roman alphabet, was first used to write Latin and is the most widely used writing system in the world today. The Latin alphabet is the basis for English and most of the languages of Europe. The languages based on the

Latin writing system, especially English and Spanish, were spread around the world during the age of colonialism. Basic modern Latin alphabets have changed over the centuries but they all use at least 26 letters. Some of the modern languages that use the Latin alphabet are Africaans, Basque, Catalan, Czech, Danish, Dutch, English, Estonian, Filipino, Finnish, French, German, Hungarian, Kurdish, Malay, Modern Latin, Norwegian, Romanian Slovak, Spanish, Swedish, and Zulu (Bukiet, 1997).

Cyrillic

Cyrillic writing is the most recent of the scripts. It resembles Greek and is used by many people in Eastern Europe and the former Soviet Union. The languages that use Cyrillic do not necessarily use all of the 31 letters of the Cyrillic alphabet. Some of the languages that use Cyrillic are Belarusian, Bulgarian, Macedonian, Russian, Serbian, and Ukrainian. It is also used by the following non-Slavic languages: Kazakh, Kyrgyz, Tajik, and Uzbek, of the former Soviet Union, and Mongolia. Cyrillic has become the third official alphabet of the European Union (*www. omniglot.com/*, June 5, 2009).

Indian

The Indian alphabet is based on Phoenician and appeared in India before 500 B.C.E. In the Indian alphabet, each of the letters represents a consonant, vowels are indicated with diacritical markings, letters are grouped according to the way they are pronounced, and many letters have more than one form. Some of the modern languages that use the Indian script are Assamese, Bengali, Gujarati, Hindi, Kannada, Kashmiri, Konkani, Maithili, Malayalam, Marathi, Nepali, Oriya, Punjabi, Sindhi, Tamil, Telugu, and Urdu. Hindi is spoken by approximately 40% of the people of India (Gupta, 2009).

Arabic

Arabic is used primarily by the countries of the Middle East and Northern Africa. In addition to Modern Standard Arabic, which is the language of literacy, other spoken dialects exist across the region such as Egyptian Arabic, Gulf Arabic, Iraqi Arabic, Levantine Arabic, and Maghrebi Arabic. These dialects are generally mutually intelligible with the exception of Maghrebi Arabic, which is spoken in Northern Africa. The Arabic script is written from right to left. Only the consonants and the three long vowels are represented by the Arabic alphabet. Short vowels are orthographically represented with diatrics; that is, marks that are placed over or under the letters (S. Al-Widyan, e-mail communication, January 31, 2009).

Chinese

The Chinese writing system is the only nonalphabetic language in use today and is the world's oldest writing system. Chinese is based on ideograms that represent ideas or words. Each character represents one syllable each of which has a meaning. Chinese script spread to Korea with Buddhism in the seventh century and from there to Japan. It is currently used by one-fifth of the world's population and can be found in Chinese, Japanese, Korean, and Vietnamese. Although the Chinese dictionary has more than 47,000 characters, educators note that it takes the knowledge of only 4,000 characters to be literate in Chinese, 2,000 of which a child learns by age 10 (Bukiet, 1997; Parker & Riley, 2010).

Directionality of Writing Systems

Not only do different writing systems contain different alphabets, writing systems can also be written in different directions. Most of the modern languages are similar to English and are read from left to right horizontally. Some languages, however, are written from right to left horizontally; some are written left to right vertically; some are written right to left vertically; and still others can be written in more than one direction. Although scholars do not know with certainty why the languages were written in different directions, it is supposed that the different directions are based on the writing surfaces writers originally used and the writing implements they used. Figure 3.1 is a chart with various languages and the direction in which they are written.

Teaching the English Alphabet

Ms. Wilson realized that she needed to teach some of her students about the Latin alphabet and even the directionality of reading and writing. She and Ms. Ramos decided to expand their repertoire of ideas by talking with a kindergarten teacher. Ms. Wilson learned that teachers of young children have some good ideas that can be incorporated into all grade levels for students who need to learn the basics of English. Two of those ideas, teaching concepts about print and using alphabet books, are described next.

Concepts about Print

The knowledge about directionality of language is typically learned when children are very young (Teale & Sulzby, 1989). Children who are exposed to books in English learn that reading moves from left to right horizontally and that pages are turned from right to left. Even looking at environmental print, such as signs and billboards, provides children with information about how the language works. Clay (1985) termed this knowledge "print concepts."

ELLs who have learned print concepts that are different from English can be taught through shared reading and writing. Ms. Wilson decided to pair her ELLs with native speakers to learn these concepts. She gave each pair a book and told the English speakers to read the book while moving their fingers under the line of print and turning the pages slowly. After repeating this process a few times, Ms. Wilson then asked the English speakers to help the ELLs move their fingers

FIGURE 3.1. Directionality and languages.	
Left to right Horizontal	Armenian, Batak, Bengali, Blackfoot, Burmese, Cherokee, Cree, Cyrillic, Dehong Dai/Tai Le, Ethiopic, Fraser, Georgian, Greek, Gujarati, Gurmukhi (Punjabi), Hmong, Inuktitut, Irish Uncial, Javanese, Kpelle, Lanna, Lao, Latin alphabet languages, Limbu, Malayalam, Manpuri, Modern Mayan languages, Modi, Naxi, Ojibwe, Oriya, Ranjana, Redjang, Santali, Sinhala, Soali, Sorang Sompeng, Sourashtra, Syloti Nagri, Tagalog, Tai Dam, Tai Lue, Tamil, Telugu, Thai, Tibetan, Yi
Right to left Horizontal	Arabic*, Aramaic, Chinese, Hebrew, Mende, N'Ko, Tifinagh *In Arabic numerals are written from left to right.
Left to right Vertical	Manchu, Mongolian
Right to left Vertical	Chinese, Japanese, Korean
Variable	Chinese can be written from right to left in vertical columns, left to right in horizontal lines, or occasionally right to left in horizontal lines. In Taiwan it is often written in vertical columns, while in China it is usually written horizontally from left to right. In newspapers and magazines with vertical text, some of the headlines and titles are written horizontally right to left across the top of the main text. Japanese can be written from right to left in vertical columns or left to right in horizontal lines.

Data from Bukiet, S. (1997). *Scripts of the world.* Lathrup Village, MI, and Cincinnati, OH: Multi-Cultural Books & Videos and AIMs International Books. Gipe, J. P. (2010). *Multiple paths to literacy: Assessment and differentiated instruction for diverse learners K–12.* Boston: Allyn & Bacon. Omniglot: Writing systems and languages of the world. *www.omniglot.com.* Parker, F., & Riley, K. (2010). *Linguistics for non-linguists: A primer with exercises* (5th ed). Boston: Allyn & Bacon.

under the print and turn the pages. The student pairs repeated this activity over several days until the ELLs learned the direction they were supposed to read in English.

Alphabet Books

Alphabet books are not just for young children; they can be just as appropriate for older students. Alphabet books have letters arranged in sequential order from *A* through *Z*. There are many alphabet books that range over a multitude of topics. Some alphabet books are whimsical, such as *Jazz ABZ* (Marsalis, 2005), and others are serious, such as *A to Z China* (Fontes & Fontes, 2003). Some alphabet books also contain poems, such as *B is for Beaver: An Oregon Alphabet* (Smith & Smith, 2003), and some have informational paragraphs for each letter. Reading alphabet books helps students become familiar with the names, sounds, letters, and order of the alphabet. They are also excellent for teaching phonemic awareness and alliteration.

Reading alphabet books to ELLs or having them read the books paired with native speakers facilitates the learning of the alphabet. While reading, the teacher should point out any special features and eventually encourage the ELLs to recite the alphabet along with them. Teachers can also have students write alphabet books at all ages and can differentiate the assignment by having students write words, phrases, sentences, or paragraphs (Evers, Lang, & Smith, 2009). Teachers can also write alphabet books for their students, as exemplified in Figure 3.2.

FIGURE 3.2. *B Is for Bilingual,* edited by Anna Tachouet and McCale Ashenbrenner.

A is for alphabet, reading and writing in both.
B is for bilingual, being bicultural, bi-literate and living in the best of both worlds.
C is for communication, connecting to other people.
D is for dedication, devoting yourself to a multicultural world.
E is for enthusiasm, emitting energy and empathy.
F is for food, eating your way into countries and cultures.
G is for games, using play to gain global perspectives.
H is for hope, helping students understand the possibilities.
I is for immersion, using ingenuity to stay afloat.
J is for joyous, when joining the bilingual community.
K Is for knowledge, discovering grammar, vocabulary, culture and more.
L is for love of learning, always longing for new challenges.
M is for music, helping to memorize through melodies.
N is for necessity, the increasing demand for languages in a global society.
O is for optimism, having an open mind and positive attitude for what's new.
P is for people and places, sharing your personality and perspective.
Q is for quality, quickly and concisely saying what you mean.
R is for relevance, remaining engaging and pertinent.
S is for speech, showcasing your language learning skills.
T is for travel, oh the places you'll go when you have two languages in tow.
U is for unique, understanding your own perspective.
V is for visuals, seeing a language come alive.
W is for wanderlust, always searching to broaden horizons.
X is for being excellent at crossing cultures.
Y is for yes, a positive attitude has you always yearning to learn more.
Z is for zeal, now you're ready to share your enthusiasm and knowledge.

Language Differences with the English Alphabet

After teaching alphabet books for several days, Ms. Wilson noticed that some of her students were still having difficulties with certain letters. According to Olshtain (2001), teachers should help students whose own alphabet is similar to English, like Spanish, by focusing only on the differences between the alphabets. So Ms. Wilson decided to spend some extra time teaching her Spanish-speaking students English sounds that are not found in Spanish, such as /v/ in *vote*, /th/ in *then*, /z/ in *zoo*, /zh/ in *measure*, and /j/ in *jump* and also blends with an /s/ such as *wasp*, *last*, *desk*, and *star* (see Johns & Lenski, 2010, for additional language differences). For students who know a completely different alphabet, Olshtain suggests that teachers spend extra time working on the recognition of the English consonants and vowels, again focusing on sounds that are new to students.

English Consonants

English is not a completely phonetic language, but it does have a group of rules that govern it (Chomsky & Halle, 1968). ELLs tend to look for a one-to-one letter–sound correspondence and this works well with the 21 English consonants. A few English consonants have more than one sound: The letter *c* can have the sound /k/ when followed by the letters *a, o, u, l,* or *r,* but it has the sound /s/ when followed by the vowels *e* or *i.* The letter *c* has a different sound when followed by the letter *h,* such as *chocolate* or *choir,* or the letter *k,* such as *chicken.* The consonants *g* and *h* also have a few more rules than do the other consonants.

English Vowels

The English vowel sounds are more complicated, but they do have some rules that can be widely applied. There are five vowels in English (*a, e, i, o,* and *u*) that result in at least 11 different sounds. Olshtain (2001) suggests that teaching the vowel sounds by focusing on the types of letter environments works best. For example, the letter combination consonant–vowel–consonant (CVC) most often results in the short vowel sound, as in the words *cat, dog,* and *bag.* Long vowels are typically found in the combinations consonant–vowel (CV) and consonant–vowel–consonant–silent *e* (CVCe) as illustrated by the words *he, see,* and *game.* As teachers use the letter combinations to teach vowel sounds, they should also be aware that the terms *long* and *short vowel sounds* might be confusing to some ELLs. Some students might think that the terms *long* and *short* are used to express the length the sound is spoken as it does in some languages rather than how the vowel sounds.

ACTIVITIES FOR BEGINNING AND EARLY INTERMEDIATE ENGLISH PROFICIENCY WRITERS

Ms. Wilson taught fourth grade but sometimes she felt as if she were teaching first grade. She considered five of her students as beginning-level ELL writers even though it was February. (See Chapter 2 for a description of writing stages.) Four of her ELLs and one other student still needed practice writing simple words. Ms. Wilson knew that beginning-level ELL writers should be encouraged to write words and sentences. Fourth-grade beginners should be able, at the very least, to copy words and the alphabet, according to the writing standards found in Chapter 2. She also agreed with the British author Cowley (2002) that she should have all of her ELLs teach the class how to write a few words in their own language, so she had each one share five words from his or her language. To encourage the beginning-level ELL writers, Ms. Wilson was able to adapt activities from her primary teaching colleagues and Ms. Ramos to help them learn to write simple words. Four of the activities she used were signing in, writing the room, sharing the pen, and teaching sight words.

Signing In

Researchers have found that having students sign their names when they enter the classroom promotes literacy development (Richgels, 1995). Name writing empowers beginning-level ELL writers and provides an entry point through which they gain insights into written language (Clay, 1975). As students learn to write their names, they practice writing English letters and begin to notice the sounds associated with the letters. Once students are able to write their names, they can begin writing other words next to their names on the sign-in list. Ms. Wilson also placed a column on the sign-in list for things like favorite foods, colors, girls' names, boys' names, and so on. Students practiced writing their names and one other word every day. After several weeks had passed, Ms. Wilson began to encourage students to write lists. She asked all of her students, for example, to write as many words as possible that begin with the letter *b* or all of the things they could think of that were white. Ms. Wilson began using this as a prewriting activity. As students became more competent at writing lists of words, she was able to have them write sentences.

Writing the Room

Ms. Wilson had already labeled all of the features of her classroom and had as much environmental print as possible for students to read. She also had logos from household articles posted on her bulletin board (Prior & Gerard, 2004). In addition, Ms. Wilson had a sentence wall to help her students learn how academic words are used in sentences (Carrier & Tatum, 2006). Students were given time each day to "write the room." They were given paper and markers and were asked to write any words or sentences that they saw around the room. Students were also allowed to add words or sentences to their pages. This activity helped many of the students become more comfortable writing English words and sentences.

Sharing the Pen

Literacy instruction for ELLs tends to focus on drill and practice of decontextualized skills rather than on authentic writing (Manyak, 2008). While attending to discrete skills has its place in writing instruction, activities in which students write sentences or paragraphs that express their ideas can support students' literacy development. One activity that Ms. Wilson used to promote authentic text is called Sharing the Pen.

Students and teachers "share the pen" as they create text with interactive writing (Pinnell & McCarrier, 1994). This activity begins with teachers and students thinking of a shared experience or familiar story to write about. Then the teacher composes the first sentence that describes the events and writes it on the chalkboard. Students copy the sentence on their paper. The teacher then asks the students to think of the next sentence. After the students agree on the sentence, the teacher asks them to write it down. If students have trouble with any of the words, he or she can assist them. The teacher scaffolds the students' writing by helping them spell or write any of the words they don't know, allowing them to focus on the ideas as well as on the mechanics of writing. The teacher and students continue to "share the pen" until they have finished the description.

Teaching Sight Words

Knowledge of sight words is critical for fluent reading and writing. When students know sight words, they are able to read, write, and say the words automatically. There are 13 basic sight words in English that account for nearly 25% of the words that occur in texts (Fry, Fountoukidis, & Polk, 2000). They are *a, and, for, he, in, is, it, of, that, the, to, was,* and *you.* Basic sight words are a necessary, but insufficient, basis for fluent reading and writing. The Revised Dolch List comprises approximately 50% of the words children encounter in reading (Johns, 1981). The most common sight words are listed in Figure 3.3.

FIGURE 3.3. Common sight words.

a	his	they
about	I	this
all	if	to
am	in	was
and	is	we
are	it	were
as	of	what
at	on	when
be	or	would
but	out	you
by	said	
can	so	
for	some	
from	that	
had	the	
have	their	
he	there	

Sight words are best taught through explicit instruction because the words themselves are abstract. Nor are most sight words easy to decode. Basic sight words, however, are common in speech so showing students words and phrases that are used in common speech patterns helps them remember sight words. Another way to teach sight words is to label classroom objects by using sight words with nouns, such as *the* lion, *a* pencil, or line up *by* the door. Students can then copy these sight words as they "write the room."

INFORMAL WRITING STRATEGIES

As the year progressed and as Ms. Wilson's ELLs spent time writing, all of them became competent using the English alphabet and writing sight words. Even Rana was able to write simple sentences fluently. Some of the ELLs, like Rana, had learned how to compose writing in their native language, so once they learned how to use English, their writing skills grew rapidly. Other students in Ms. Wilson's class were intermediate writers and were quickly learning how to write. Ms. Wilson found that using storytelling, translated stories, and journal writing helped all of her students become more fluent writers.

Storytelling

Many of the students in Ms. Wilson's class came from backgrounds that value oral language so she decided to use storytelling as the basis for encouraging students to write. Cultures that have primarily oral traditions, such as Hawaiian, Hmong, Latin American, and many African cultures, use storytelling and songs as entertainment, passing on traditional values, and sharing history (see Thao, 2006). Stories are used in these cultures to instill cultural knowledge, share personal experiences, inspire, entertain, and examine or share individual and cultural identities (Johnstone, 2001; Ochs & Capps, 2001). Stories are also used to share a community's beliefs, values, and attitudes (Heath, 1983). According to Bruner (1996), people "swim in a sea of stories" that are used to construct a model of a version of themselves in the community they inhabit.

According to Perry (2008), storytelling is an important cultural practice for many marginalized communities in the United States, and using storytelling in the classroom can influence students' literacy practices. Ms. Wilson knew that stories from different cultures can have different structures, but that stories are typically defined as a sequence of events that tells an actual or fictional experience (Labov, 1972). She decided to capitalize on the stories that her students knew from their home culture as a "border-crossing" activity. (Border-crossing is Zhang's [2007] term for importing practices from different contexts.) Ms. Wilson knew that all of her students, not only those from cultures with oral traditions, have stories to share. Some stories students know or create are mixed with popular culture, such as music, movies, and television (Dyson, 2003), but all of her students tell stories.

Ms. Wilson decided to use storytelling as a springboard for building writing fluency. To begin, she asked students to think about stories they knew or could create. Some students needed help, so she used an activity adapted from Lenski and Johns (2004) called "Let Me Tell You a Story" (see Figure 3.4). In this activity, students read a list of ideas to spark their memories about stories they knew and placed a check mark next to some of the items on the list. Then Ms. Wilson divided her class into pairs and had each member of the pair tell a story. After all of the students had shared their stories, Ms. Wilson asked them to write the stories on paper without worrying too much about the conventions of language. She emphasized that writing fluently meant getting the words down on paper and that they would correct spelling and usage errors at another time.

Translating Stories to English

As ELLs learn English, they are frequently responsible for interpreting communications and translating documents from their home language to English (Martinez, Orellana, Pacheco, & Carbone, 2008). Ms. Wilson knew that most of her ELLs translated for their parents and grandparents as they learned English. Some of their translations focused around school communications, and so Ms. Wilson decided to connect students' home lives with her writing program. She asked her ELLs to list the kinds of interpreting and translating they already do. The list included translating notes from the school, telephone conversations, doctor's visits, and translating mail. Ms. Wilson then encouraged her ELLs to also ask their family members to tell them stories from their childhood or from their home country. She knew that translating stories into English would help students value their home culture (Dworin, 2006). At school, Ms. Wilson was able to help students find the English words they needed to complete their stories. Ms. Wilson asked the students to translate as much of the stories as they could and write them down in their journals. An example of a story told by a Russian grandmother and translated into English can be found in Figure 3.5.

Journal Writing

Ms. Wilson had given students journal topics for a number of years but she was never sure what her purposes were. She instinctively knew that having students write in journals could make them more comfortable with writing. And she was right. Journal writing helps students develop fluency (Newman, 1983). Journals are typically notebooks where students can write whatever they want. They are often used as places for students to write down what they think, see, feel, or have experienced. When students write in journals, they are formulating ideas and practicing expressing themselves in English. They are learning how to string together ideas into sentences and paragraphs to make their thoughts comprehensible.

Writing in journals, however, is not only a way to express thoughts; it can also be a process of discovery. Journal writing can be a spontaneous, unplanned means of understanding oneself (Giorgis, 2002). When writing in journals, students can

FIGURE 3.4. "Let Me Tell You a Story."

Please ask me to tell you a story about the ideas I've checked.

____ my family	____ my favorite food
____ a fun party	____ work I do
____ a TV show	____ a time I helped someone
____ when I was little	____ a video game
____ things I like	____ my neighbors
____ my family	____ my town
____ my pet	____ places I've lived

FIGURE 3.5. Translated Russian folk tale.

Once a man planted a turnip. The turnip grew to be the biggest turnip anyone had seen. The man decided to pull the turnip and make soup for his family. He started to pull the turnip, but he couldn't get it out of the ground. He pulled and pulled and pulled. Finally, he called his wife to help him.

The wife took hold of the man and they pulled together, but couldn't pull out the turnip. So they called their daughter. The daughter took hold of the wife who took hold of the man. They pulled and pulled, but they couldn't pull out the turnip.

The daughter called the dog. The dog took hold of the daughter who took hold of the wife who took hold of the man. They pulled and pulled, but they couldn't pull out the turnip.

The dog called over the cat. The cat took hold of the dog who took hold of the daughter who took hold of the wife who took hold of the man. They pulled and pulled, but they couldn't pull out the turnip.

So the cat called the mouse. The mouse took hold of the cat who took hold of the dog who took hold of the daughter who took hold of the wife who took hold of the man. They pulled and pulled and they finally pulled out the turnip!

(When the story is told in Russian, the words form a tongue twister.)

---

relive experiences from a different vantage point and let their imagination redefine reality; they can explore new worlds, and become more cognizant of their own beliefs. When writing in journals, students can learn what they truly think and who they really are (Piper, 2006). Artists, scientists, engineers, and dancers write in journals to record events and to reflect on their reactions. Anderson and Anderson (2003) expressed a common feeling about journal writing: "Sometimes I don't know what I think until I see what I write" (p. 94).

Just asking students to write in journals may not result in much writing. That's why Ms. Wilson usually provided her students with one or more journal prompts. She also gave students the option of writing about whatever they wanted. One year Ms. Wilson tried giving journal prompts almost every day. She found that the students grew tired of the activity so she now gives journal-writing prompts twice a week. Figure 3.6 contains a short list of journal-writing prompts that Ms. Wilson has found useful. Ms. Wilson often wrote questions back to her ELLs to clarify words or ideas that they were struggling to come up with. In this way, she could model vocabulary and sentence structures without correcting students' writing.

Journal-Writing Issues

There are a number of issues to consider when giving students journal-writing assignments. First, journals need not be graded or even read. The audience for journals should be the students, so it is not necessary for teachers to read students' journal entries. Ms. Wilson reads two to three students' journals every day on a rotating basis so that in 2 week's time she has read one entry from each student. When she collects the students' journals, she asks them to tag the page they want her to read. Because students know that their teacher will read their journal occasionally, they know that they should not write about personal issues that they don't want read. Teachers in many states are mandatory reporters, which means that if they suspect any type of abuse, they must report it to social services. Sometimes students write things in journals that they really want to keep private, and at times students exaggerate during journal writing. Teachers should let students know that journal entries are part of schoolwork and are not strictly private.

Another issue Ms. Wilson had to face was whether to allow students to write in their home language or whether she should encourage students to write only in English. Since the goal of the writing assignment was to encourage fluency in writing English, Ms. Wilson told students that they should attempt to write in English, but that they could use their home language if they couldn't think of the English word for something and they didn't want to interrupt their writing to ask someone. Switching languages in this way is called "code-switching" and is commonly accepted in certain types of student writing (Wheeler & Swords, 2006).

FIGURE 3.6. Journal-writing topics.

About my family . . .
What I did last night . . .
Places I've seen . . .
Favorite TV programs . . .
Weekend chores . . .
My dreams . . .
What surprises me . . .
Things that scare me . . .
What I learned . . .
My family . . .
Places I want to see . . .
What I wish . . .
Valuable possessions . . .
People I admire . . .
How I spend my time . . .
My biggest problem . . .
Things I wonder about . . .
What bothers me . . .
When I grow up . . .

Some teachers prefer to have students write using both languages so that they can write more fluently. If students have the opportunity to learn literacy in their home language, it will help them develop a repertoire of strategies for writing in English.

RESPONDING TO READING AS AN INFORMAL WRITING ACTIVITY

Ms. Wilson read her class a picture book or a chapter in a novel every day. She knew that students needed to hear stories in English to learn how language works. She also decided to have students write in response to reading so that they could reinforce their knowledge of the story and practice writing. After each day's reading, she would ask the class to name a dozen or so vocabulary words from the story that they wanted her to spell out for them. These words she listed on the board.

When students write in response to stories, they begin to listen in new ways. They are listening to retell the story or they are listening for something specific. When students respond to reading, they are bringing their background knowledge and experience to the reading event (see Rosenblatt, 1978). According to Echevarria and Graves (2003), ELLs are more successful and have a better attitude toward learning when they can use their background knowledge to respond to reading. This personal response may not indicate a complete understanding of the story but it could show that the student was trying to make meaning of the story.

Ms. Wilson was able to develop a number of activities that gave her ELLs opportunities to write as well as to respond to reading. Some of these activities were two-column response charts, response cards, and e-mail dialogue journals or blogs.

Two-Column Response Charts

Two-column response charts (Ollmann, 1991/1992) are designed for students to think more deeply about specific things that authors write. Authors include many facts, ideas, and emotions that different students respond to in different ways. For example, in the book *If You're Not from the Prairie* (Bouchard, 1995) the author writes about different aspects of living on the prairie, such as the wind, the flat landscape, and the snow. When students hear this book, they can write something they hear in the left side of the chart. On the right side, they write a response, usually what they think or how they feel about the statement. The comments students make can lead to a lively discussion about the story that can, in turn, lead to more writing.

Ms. Wilson would sometimes pair her lower-proficiency-level ELLs with native English speakers. The ELL would dictate a response to the native speaker, who would write it down. The ELL would then copy what the native speaker had written.

Response Cards

When ELLs read grade-level text independently, they may miss important parts of the story and have minimal comprehension as a result. When students have to write responses after reading, they stop and reflect, thus increasing their understanding of the story (Berger, 1996). Students could also be encouraged to write responses to the self-selected reading. Figure 3.7 includes some ideas that Ms. Wilson used to encourage students to write responses to stories they heard or read. Taking notes on their reading can serve the dual purpose of practicing writing while keeping track of the flow of ideas in reading passages. Ms. Wilson supported her ELLs by giving them paragraph frames to help them write their responses to the stories.

E-mail and Blogs

E-mail is a familiar tool for almost every student today and can be a good method for students to respond to stories. When students write an e-mail, they typically do not pay close attention to the conventions of writing; instead, they concentrate on getting a message to the reader. This type of writing illustrates what teachers want students to do when writing informally. Students should concentrate on writing as much as they can, making the text readable, but not being overly concerned about writing in Standard English. (That can come later and with other types of writing assignments, and the spell-check feature can help students with spelling.) Students can write e-mails about a story they heard or read, either to a friend or to a teacher. Many teachers also have the capacity for developing blogs. For some reason, some students will eagerly write a blog about a book when they typically don't like to write. Encouraging students to write e-mails or blog in response to reading can motivate even the most reluctant writer.

Asking ELLs to write using e-mail, blogs, or word-processing programs assumes that they have some level of keyboarding skills. Once ELLs acquire these skills, e-mailing and blogging can be an effective way for them to develop writing fluency.

WRITING TO LEARN WITH LEARNING JOURNALS

Ms. Wilson was pleased that all of her students, including her ELLs, were writing in journals and responding to reading. She wondered, however, whether there were other ways students could practice writing so that they learned science, social studies, and other academic subjects. Ms. Wilson talked with another teacher who told her about learning journals. Learning journals are places for students to record what they have learned. They provide the double benefit of helping students practice writing in English using academic language and in solidifying their knowledge of academic subjects.

Asking students to record what they have learned helps them understand what they know (Fulwiler, 1987). This is particularly important for ELLs who need

FIGURE 3.7. Response cards.

Questions about Authors

How do you picture the author?

What would you ask the author if you could?

Why do you think the author wrote this book?

Questions about the Plot

What happened in the story?

What was the problem in the story?

What part was most exciting?

Questions about the Characters

How would you describe the main characters?

Would you choose one of the characters as a friend?

How are the characters like or unlike one of your friends?

How do the characters change in the story?

Questions about the Setting

Where did the story take place?

When did the story take place?

Questions about the Theme

What was the point of the story?

Questions about the Style

How did you feel while you were reading this book?

Did you like the first sentence in the book?

Did the author use words that were interesting?

a great deal of practice with academic language (Hadaway, Vardell, & Young, 2002). For this reason having students write in order to learn is a powerful learning tool, both in content area learning and for writing instruction. Students learn content material through the mental processes they experience as they write (Elbow, 1981; Farnan & Dahl, 2003).

Ms. Wilson remembered what she had learned in the ELL study group with Ms. Ramos and the other teachers. She knew that she would need to support her ELLs' content area writing by teaching them to write and properly use academic vocabulary, or brick words, and the other word patterns that characterize the various content areas, or mortar words. To do this, Ms. Wilson kept a word wall with key content vocabulary words on display in the classroom, arranging the words by subject area. She also made use of sentence and paragraph frames, providing ELLs at different proficiency levels with just enough scaffolding so that they could successfully write about their lessons.

Learning Journal Prompts

Ms. Wilson found that she needed to supply students with a variety of learning journal prompts to get them to write about academic subjects. Through trial and error, she was able to develop a list that included easy and difficult questions (see Figure 3.8). She most often allowed students to make choices about which prompt to use, but at times she found that she needed to target particular questions for some students. For example, Abdisa, an immigrant from Ethiopia, tended to answer the first question whenever given the choice. Ms. Wilson, therefore, decided to push Abdisa to connect what he was learning in social studies class to the present day. Once Abdisa tried a new question, he felt confident enough to try to think in other ways about the subject he was learning (see Figure 3.9). Generating ideas for writing is the hardest part for almost all writers. Having students explore a topic

---

FIGURE 3.8. Learning journal prompts.

What did you learn from today's lesson?

How do you feel about the subject you are learning?

How did this lesson relate to your life?

Select an idea from the lesson and explain it.

Write a letter to a historical figure discussing an event.

Write a letter to a contemporary figure discussing a historical event.

Compare what you learned in this lesson to a previous lesson.

Explain how you would teach this lesson to a friend.

What else do you know about this topic?

How does this lesson connect to other things you've learned?

FIGURE 3.9. Writing sample from a sixth-grade Ethiopian immigrant student.

Dear President Roosevelt,

I'm a photographer who traveled the country documenting the effects of the Great depression. In this time lot people life looks miserable. They doesn't have any job and shelter. This people needs food. shelter. clothing and job. Mr. President this people have victims of the Depression. I saw lot people hurt by losing house and they didn't get enough food. I felt fear and so sad. I smelled dirty and I heard when childrens cried to get food. Mr. President you should do to help hurting Americans, you should create the job. You should make rules to help this poor people. I hope you'd change everthing. The time has com. Thank you for everything you do.

sincerely Abdisa Godana

---

through reading and discussion before writing will help them to have ideas about what to write. Taking notes while they read helps students to remember what they have read and gives them additional writing practice.

BENEFITS OF INFORMAL WRITING ACTIVITIES

Ms. Wilson was pleased with her students' progress when she gave them informal writing assignments such as writing in journals, responding to reading, and writing in learning journals. Her students were becoming more confident, fluent writers. She was especially pleased with Rana's progress. By the end of the year, Rana was able to compose her own sentences and short paragraphs. However, Ms. Wilson was concerned that students were not learning how to write Standard English by using these informal writing assignments.

Informal writing can be beneficial on its own, and it can also help students in other areas of writing. Chapters 4 and 5 describe narrative and expository writing, respectively, and explain how to teach the writing process. Much of the informal writing done by Ms. Wilson's students ended up being rough drafts for other types of writing. Ms. Wilson also used some of the informal writing that she read to inform her instruction about English grammar and usage.

Circles of Writing

Students' informal writings can be used as prewriting for other more formal pieces of writing (see Chapters 4 and 5). Hughey and Slack (2001) suggest that students develop Circles of Writing to help them use their informal writing pieces as the springboard for stories and expository pieces (see Figure 3.10). Ms. Wilson

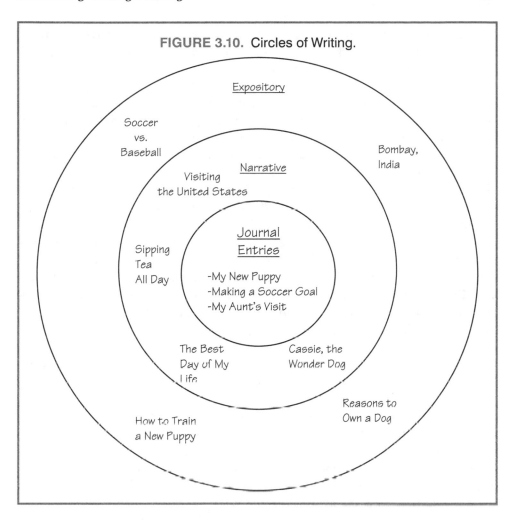

FIGURE 3.10. Circles of Writing.

used this strategy to help Rana develop as a writer. She wrote the names of some of her personal and learning journal pieces in the center of the circle. Then she helped Rana identify some of the stories that were of most interest to her to use as drafts for narratives. In the outermost circle, Rana identified some topics from her journals that could be the basis of expository pieces. Using the Circles of Writing, Ms. Wilson was able to help students see that their informal writing pieces were "thought pieces" that could be used in other writing situations.

Distinguishing between Talk and Writing

Informal writing is similar to speech in that it doesn't focus on the conventions of language as much as producing written output. This kind of writing helps students explore their thoughts and ideas, make tentative responses to literature, and investigate their learning. When students write using informal writing activities, they use words and language to discover the meaning of their experiences and of their learning (Murray, 1982). It's almost like writing down thoughts and speech without paying too much attention to editing.

Ms. Wilson knew that she needed to scaffold students' ability to distinguish between conversation and writing so they wouldn't be confused when they were assigned formal writing activities. When students write informally, they often write what they hear in conversation. For example, many of Ms. Wilson's ELLs wrote *kinda* rather than *kind of* and *wanna* rather than *want to*. Ms. Wilson used the information she got from looking at students' informal writing for on-the-spot teaching. She told students that when English speakers talk, they shift their pronunciation of function words. In English, function words are not given the same emphasis as content words (Allington, 2009) so that when people talk their words sound as if they are running together. For example, when Ms. Wilson's students heard the words *want to* from fluent English speakers, it sounds like *wanna*. Ms. Wilson used this and other examples to show students how to write these common English phrases to scaffold students' English learning so that as students developed writing fluency they also continued to develop their competence in their knowledge about the English language.

SUMMARY

ELLs come from a variety of language groups, some of whom may not be familiar with the English writing system. These ELLs need to learn the English alphabet and the directionality of English. All ELLs, from beginning to advanced English proficiency writers, need practice writing connected text. Teachers can provide ELLs with writing practice by helping students build writing fluency.

Writing fluency is the ability to write without spending cognitive effort on sight words or on conventions. Students who write fluently focus primarily on communicating their thoughts or feelings. Teachers can facilitate writing fluency through a variety of activities including writing in journals, responding to writing, and writing to learn.

WEB RESOURCES

Alphabets of the World
www.word2word.com/alphabet.html

Excellent resource for information about the world's alphabets.

EFL/ESL Lessons and Lesson Plans from the Internet TESOL Journal
iteslj.org/Lessons

A variety of ideas for all of the language arts.

Language Variations
www.mla.org/census_main

A map of language variations in the United States.

Omniglot: Writing Systems and Languages of the World
www.omniglot.com

Information about all of the world's languages, past and present.

Sentence Fluency Lessons
www.teacher2teacherhelp.com/six-trait-writing/sentence-fluency-activities-and-minilessons

Lessons that teach students how to build sentences.

Spanish Cognates
www.latinamericalinks.com/spanish_cognates.htm

A list of Spanish cognates organized alphabetically.

Story Corp
www.storycorps.net

Stories told from different generations across the country.

Write Source Writing Topics
www.thewritesource.com/writing_topics

A variety of journal-writing topics.

CHAPTER 4

Teaching Narrative Writing

wish I could do this.

Mr. Jones reads picture books to his second graders every day. Of the 23 students in his classroom, 10 are ELLs, five of whom are newcomers from Latin America. Mr. Jones is aware that his ELLs came from cultures with strong oral traditions so he also gives them opportunities to share stories that they heard at home. After hearing stories from each of his ELLs, Mr. Jones talked with Ms. Ramos, the literacy coach, exclaiming, "The stories of the students from Latin America are so different from those of my other students. I couldn't follow their plots at all!" Ms. Ramos explained that stories from cultures other than the United States can have different plot structures and, consequently, some ELLs may be unfamiliar with the way Americans tell or write stories.

text-text connections

When native English speakers read a story or watch a television program, most of them have intuitive knowledge about what will happen next. The reason they have this knowledge about a story's organization is because they have many experiences with texts. Texts are written in organizational patterns, called genres, that have been developed over several centuries. Writers have refined genres over time in ways that are culturally accepted so that genres have developed differently by culture. As a result, discourse styles that are specific to European-based cultures, which are the predominant genre types in American stories, may differ from those of the language-minority students (see Donovan & Smolkin, 2006; Lesaux et al., 2006).

So we're the odd ones?

Research on the discourse patterns of different groups reveals that people who speak English share a dramatically different way of expressing stories and academic texts than do other language groups. Narrative texts in the United States follow a sequence of events that moves the plot to a conclusion. Hererra et al. (2010) state, "The English discourse pattern is very linear, and academic writing in English typically has a distinct introduction, body, and conclusion" (p. 197). Many ELLs follow a different discourse pattern that is less linear than English. Although the directionality of English is easy for teachers to understand, Kaplan (2005) found that ELLs tend to view their own discourse pattern as linear, even when it does not seem so to English ears. ELLs who are unfamiliar with English stories need to be explicitly taught the discourse patterns of English. In this chapter, we discuss how to teach ELLs narrative structures, how to help students focus on content, and how the writing process can be facilitated in mainstream classes with diverse learners and in ELL classrooms.

NARRATIVE TEXT STRUCTURE

In English-speaking North America, texts tend to be divided into two categories: narrative and informational (Donovan, 2001). Narrative texts are stories with a plot that directs a sequence of events toward a goal. Students who have been socialized in English-speaking families and have heard stories told or read to them, or who have watched American television, will most likely have a good understanding of narrative text structure. Stein and Glenn (1979) found that even young children could identify the plot, setting, and characters of stories even when they had not had instruction on these story elements. Research indicates that when students read fictional texts, they can use their knowledge about the story structure to store, retrieve, and summarize information (Meyer, Brandt, & Bluth, 1980). These abilities with the structure of a language, along with the understanding of the setting, role of participants, and register, are among the skills necessary to be competent in a language (Hadaway et al., 2002).

Influence of Translated Books

Not every ELL will be unfamiliar with the American plot structure so it's important that teachers do not generalize. Mr. Jones found this when he began examining the plot structure of the stories his ELLs told. José's stories were told in a sequence that had a clear beginning, middle, and end. As Mr. Jones learned more about José, he found out that José's older sister had attended a school in Guatemala that had a library of books donated from the Nassau Reading Council of New York. Although all of these books were in Spanish, they were translated from popular picture books written in the United States. Therefore, José already was familiar with the plot structure of American stories.

Many picture books that are popular in the United States have been translated into other languages, especially Spanish. These translated books are used in some schools in Latin America. When that is the case, students are being exposed to the American story structure rather than the one that is more typically used in their culture. Moreover, students who watch American television are also exposed to the same kind of story structure that is taught in schools.

TEACHING ELLs TO WRITE NARRATIVES

Mr. Jones realized that he needed to teach the organizational structures of texts to all of his students and to be particularly explicit with the ELLs. As Mr. Jones began to develop a writing program, he once again conferred with the literacy coach. Ms. Ramos reminded Mr. Jones that organizational structure is just one component of writing. Thoughts and ideas are the content of writing, and the content depends on the writer's reasons for writing, the topic of the piece, and the audience for whom the piece is written. The process that writers use has been documented and refined by a variety of educators, most notably Donald Graves (1983). Mr. Jones developed a writing program that balanced teaching narrative organization with selecting topics and audiences for writing.

Teaching Narrative Organization

Students become aware of text patterns primarily through reading and listening. Writing, however, is another matter. Writers generally need to be taught the genres of texts. Inexperienced writers sometimes think that writing is simply talk written down (Wray & Lewis, 1997). It's not. Formal writing follows accepted organizational rules so that readers can comprehend content while following the train of thought presented in the texts.

2nd Graders·

Students need to learn the patterns of the texts that they are expected to write. Students who have had many experiences hearing stories will learn the pattern of narrative easily and apply the organizational features of narrative when writing (Lancia, 1997). They will understand that the story takes place in a particular setting with main characters who are involved in a plot and that the story will most likely have a theme. Teachers can teach narrative elements by reading aloud to students and through explicit teaching of plot structure with activities such as the plot relationship chart and plot diagrams. (See Figure 4.1 for a list of the elements of narrative texts.)

FIGURE 4.1. Elements of narrative texts.	
Term	**Definition**
Point of view	The perspective from which the story is told (e.g., first person, third person).
Setting	The time the story is set and the location.
Characters	Main and minor characters who are the subjects of the plot.
Plot	The sequence of events that tell the story.
Climax	The point of greatest tension and the turning point of the action.
Conflict	The struggle between two or more forces: person versus person, person versus self, person versus nature, person versus society.
Resolution	The point in the story where the conflict has been settled or worked out.

Reading Aloud

Mr. Jones was right in reading to his students every day. ELLs learn vocabulary and sentence structure from hearing stories. They also learn how stories are organized. According to Donovan and Smolkin (2006), students can learn about genre features from listening to stories, and they suggest that teachers reread particular books so that students can hear and then identify the story elements. This is particularly true for ELLs (Hickman & Pollard-Durodola, 2009).

Mr. Jones asked Ms. Ramos to demonstrate how to scaffold his students' knowledge of text structure. Ms. Ramos came to class with *Willy the Wimp*, a book by one of the students' favorite authors, Anthony Browne (1984), which is about how a gorilla, Willy, who was very timid, tries to change his nature through self-help activities. Ms. Ramos read the book through the first time, stopping only once to ask students to make predictions. Many of the ELLs in the class simply repeated the predictions of other students, but Ms. Ramos knew that peer modeling was an important part of learning for ELLs. Knowing that students understood the main plot, Ms. Ramos read the story a second time, requesting that students look for the beginning, middle, and end of the story. Ms. Ramos made sure to teach the sequencing words *beginning, middle,* and *end* for the ELLs. After the second reading, she had students draw pictures retelling the plot. Each student drew three pictures; one for the beginning, one for the middle, and one for the end of the story. Later in the week, Ms. Ramos returned to the class and read the story a third time. This time she talked about the sequence of events in the story and had students list what happened in the order they occurred. She wrote the list of events on sentence strips and had students order and reorder them. Ms. Ramos made one more trip to the class to reread the story the next week. During that reading, she had students pay attention to how the main character, Willy, met a challenge and changed through the story. Ms. Ramos taught a mini-lesson about ways characters are developed in narrative and how conflict is generally resolved.

Plot Relationship Chart

Beginning writers and younger ELLs can learn how to understand plot structure by using the Plot Relationship Chart (Schmidt & Buckley, 1991). Mr. Jones tried this strategy with his students. He first asked who the character, or the "Somebody," was in the story *Willy the Wimp*. The students responded, "Willy." Then Mr. Jones asked what Willy wanted. The students discussed this for awhile and finally came to the conclusion that he wanted respect. Mr. Jones suggested that identifying what the character wanted helped students understand the main point of the story. Mr. Jones then asked students what was preventing Willy from getting respect and explained that this is the conflict of the story. The students were able to quickly find an answer: that the Suburban Gorillas thought Willy was a wimp. Mr. Jones smiled and continued, asking how the story ended. He explained that American stories are typically resolved by the obstacle being overcome. The students told

[handwritten margin note: ✓ revisiting familiar books to look for story elements. ↓ more than 2×.]

Somebody	Wanted	But	So
Willy	To be respected	Other gorillas thought he was a wimp.	He changed his appearance.

FIGURE 4.2. Plot Relationship Chart for *Willy the Wimp*.

Mr. Jones that Willy did many things to gain the respect of his girlfriend, including getting strong. Mr. Jones helped the students formulate what happened and wrote it in a Plot Relationship Chart (see Figure 4.2). He then reinforced narrative organization by having students develop their own chart about another book.

Plot Diagrams

Older students and intermediate to advanced English proficiency writers (see Chapter 2 for a classification of writers) can learn a more sophisticated method of identifying narrative structures. The organization of narrative depends on a sequence of events. The narrator or the main character encounters a problem or a conflict that he or she needs to resolve (see Figure 4.3). The events of the plot typically move through a period of introduction, rising action, climax, falling action, and resolution. Older students and advanced writers can be taught how the plot moves through reading and analyzing some picture books, chapter books, and short stories. ELLs will need to be taught these words before they are expected to use them.

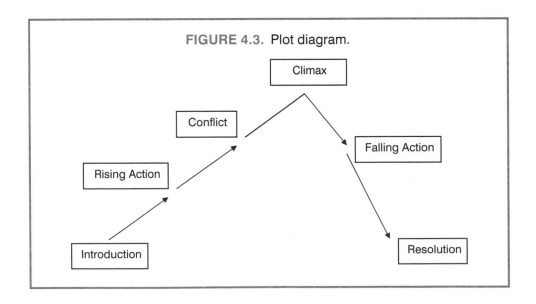

FIGURE 4.3. Plot diagram.

Teaching Transition Words

English has specific transition words that are used in narrative texts. Transition words signal what is coming next. Following Dutro and Moran's (2003) architectural metaphor, these are mortar words that help to show relationships among key (brick) words in the text. Students may not be familiar with transition words because they are not used quite as often in speaking as in writing. Speakers use other ways of alerting their listeners about what is coming next in their story. Teachers, therefore, need to explicitly teach students the words that hold sentences together. In the Systematic English Language Development paradigm (Dutro & Moran, 2003), transition words are also part of the mortar, the general-utility words needed to build sentences. Transition words show the relationships among words, phrases, sentences, or paragraphs with regard to time or location.

There are a variety of transition words that are used in narrative writing to make the transition between one thought and the next (see Figure 4.4). Other phrases such as *once upon a time, long ago,* and *in a faraway place* are used to signal stories and tales. Mr. Jones found that he needed to teach transition words explicitly in a number of ways before students felt comfortable using them. He used sentence combining to teach students how to use connective words when writing sentences, and he used paragraph frames to teach them how to connect sentences.

Sentence Combining

The research on sentence combining indicates that this activity can help writers develop longer, more complex sentences (Hillocks & Mavrogenes, 1986). Mr. Jones

FIGURE 4.4. Narrative transition words.

Beginning Writers		
First	The next day/week	Immediately
Second	Since	Finally
Third	Now	Afterward
Then	Today	Eventually
After	Yesterday	During
Later	Next	In the future
		Meanwhile

Transition Chains

first . . . second . . . third . . .
generally . . . furthermore . . . finally
in the first place . . . also . . . lastly
in the first place . . . pursuing this further . . . finally
to be sure . . . additionally . . . lastly
in the first place . . . just in the same way . . . finally
basically . . . similarly . . . as well

had students brainstorm a list of kernel sentences, such as "I played," with a list of adjectives, adverbs, prepositional phrases, and other kernel sentences. He then had students create a variety of combinations and discussed the transition words that connected the words and phrases. For example, Maya connected the two phrases, "I played my video game all day" and "I didn't get to level 10" with the connecting term *but*. Mr. Jones discussed how this word connects two short sentences. Like the mortar that holds two bricks together, the word *but* holds the ideas, "I played my video game all day" and "I didn't get to level 10" together, turning two simple sentences into one complex sentence. It also shows the relationship that Maya intended between her two ideas. Think about how the meaning would change if she had used the transition word *because* or *therefore*.

Paragraph Frames Using Transition Chains

Mr. Jones knew that his students needed practice using transitions between sentences as well as within sentences so he developed a number of paragraph frames (see Figure 4.5). He had beginning English proficiency writers use these types of paragraphs until they were able to use transition words without support. Some ELLs needed the frames most of the year while others learned how to connect sentences after just one or two tries. The paragraph frames helped many of Mr. Jones's students learn how sentences are connected using transition words.

TYPES OF NARRATIVES STUDENTS CAN WRITE

Narrative writing has a specific structure, as discussed earlier in this section. Not all narratives, however, are the same. Narrative writing that is typically taught in schools can be divided into two main genres: personal experience stories and fictional narratives. Students should learn each of these kinds of narratives and know how they are similar and different.

Personal Experience Stories

"My dog had puppies," Raquel exclaimed as she skipped into Mr. Jones's class one morning. Students regularly come to class with stories about their lives. They tell stories about themselves to their teachers, their friends, and even to strangers. Students' lives are filled with stories that they are more than willing to share. One task of the teacher is to help students discover the stories of their lives and to write about them (Furr, 2003). These stories can illustrate how the students are making sense of their lives by the way in which the writers position themselves in relation to their family, their friends, and their community (Wortham, 2001).

Personal experience stories are written true accounts of anecdotes from writers' lives. They typically emphasize one event or incident. When students write personal narratives, they bring their private lives into the classroom, which leads to a stronger sense of community (Buss & Karnowski, 2000). Many teachers don't

FIGURE 4.5. Paragraph frame.

My friend, _____, and I went to

_____. First,

we _____

_____.

Then _____

_____.

After that we _____

_____.

We had a _____ time.

have time to listen to all of the stories their students have to tell, so they find college students or senior citizens to elicit stories from students (see Armon & Ortega, 2008).

Personal experience stories are different from autobiographies and memoirs that may also be taught in schools. Autobiographies are a chronology of a writer's life, and memoirs relate a part of a writer's life. Personal experience stories narrow the writer's experience further by relating a single incident, event, idea, or theme. Since authors of personal experience stories write about themselves, the stories are written in the first person using the personal pronoun *I*. Personal experience stories typically have a beginning that introduces the experiences and the author's reactions to them, a middle that describes the events in a sequence, and an ending that summarizes the events and expresses the writer's feelings. ELLs and other students will need instruction in this story structure. An example of a student's personal experience story can be found in Figure 4.6.

Mr. Jones read Raquel's personal experience story and recognized several problems with the story that are common to novice writers. First, Raquel did not focus on one event. Mr. Jones talked with Raquel about the story and suggested that she write a story about her new puppy, Ruby. He also asked Raquel to explore how she felt about her puppy in general and specifically when the dog ate her dad's plants. Mr. Jones knew that personal experience stories are pretty dull if they don't include the writer's feelings, reactions, and learning. The purpose of personal experience stories is to share the writer's feelings about an event or experience. According to Maryanne Wolf (2007) who writes about the science of the *reading brain,* one of the jobs of the reading brain is to connect feelings to the words on the page. Writers help readers make those connections by expressing their feelings in personal experience stories.

Mr. Jones wanted his ELLs to express their emotions in their personal experience stories, but he found that they most often used the words *sad, happy,* and *mad.* Many students, not only ELLs, have difficulty putting their feelings into words. To help students add depth to their stories, Mr. Jones decided to develop a list of words that expresses emotions (see Figure 4.7).

FIGURE 4.6. Student example of a personal experience story.

My name is Raquel I am in 5th grade. My Teachers name is Mrs. Bray.

I like art and reading. I have amom name Sara and my Dad name is Ezequel. I have to sister my older sister name is Synthia and my younger sister name is Johanna.

I have a pupy name Ruby. Ruby Loves eating my dad plants in the summer. I have 11 best friend one name Luara, Ashley, Zeinab, Roide, Kiley, My Mom, My Dad, My tow sister. And My puppy. When I grow up I want to go to College and graduate and becam a vet or disaine cloths.

FIGURE 4.7. List of emotions for personal experience stories.

Add Emojis?

Angry	Foolish	Scared
Awful	Friendly	Shy
Bashful	Furious	Silly
Bold	Glad	Sorry
Brave	Gloomy	Stressed
Cheerful	Good	Strong
Clumsy	Great	Superb
Confident	Happy	Terrific
Courageous	Important	Thoughtless
Daring	Joyful	Thrilled
Delighted	Lonely	Tough
Depressed	Pleased	Uneasy
Downhearted	Proud	Weak
Dreadful	Relaxed	Wise
Excellent	Rough	Wonderful
Fantastic	Sad	Zealous

Fictional Narratives

Fictional narratives have a unique structure that is similar to personal experience stories. The difference is that fictional stories are not true. Stories can have a single character or many characters. These characters have qualities that are revealed through their thoughts, actions, appearances, and speech. The characters are people or personified animals that are the focus of the story.

The characters of fictional stories are involved in a series of events that make up the plot. The plot is the action that takes place in the story, usually beginning with a problem to be resolved and ending with a resolution. The problem may be as simple as deciding which kind of dog to buy or as complex as surviving an avalanche. The characters and the plot take place in a setting. The setting of a fictional story is the time and place of the story. Through the character, plot, and setting, the author of a fictional story frequently introduces a thought or idea that is called a theme. Themes can range from simple to complex. Finally, all stories are written from a point of view. Most fictional stories are written in the third person with the author relating the story using the characters' names and the pronouns *he, she, they,* and so on. Some fictional stories are written in the first person. These stores are written as if the author is telling the story. Students can create fictional stories using the plot outline described earlier in this chapter, or they can begin by describing a character. An example of a portion of a student's fictional story is found in Figure 4.8.

Mr. Jones had his students brainstorm a number of possible characters, settings, and themes for fictional stories. He wrote the students' ideas on a word list so that his ELLs and other students who needed extra support could see them. Mr. Jones realized that some of his ELLs might not be familiar with English pronouns, so he presented a mini-lesson on how to use pronouns in story writing.

FIGURE 4.8. Excerpt from a student's fictional story.

It is said that long ago the Quileute tribe settled on the Island. The Quileutes are decendants from wolves. They lived peaceful until they noticed someone was hunting on their land. These creatures were not like the white faces; they had icy-pale skin and each one of them perfect, beautiful, and gracful. They moved at the speed of light and drank blood.

The Quileutes decided to talk to the creatures that called themselves the Cullens. The Cullens claimed they were different and that they didn't drink humans blood, so the Quileutes made a deal with them, and made their very own border line dividing them both, but if any vampire were to cross on the Quileutes side they would be killed. Now we all live in peace.

GENERATING TOPICS FOR NARRATIVES

"I don't know what to write about," Maria complained when Mr. Jones asked her to write a story. This statement, echoed by many students, expresses an important concern for teachers. Content is the essence of writing. Every other part of writing, the organization, the mechanics, and the style, takes a distant second place compared with content. Helping students generate topics for writing, therefore, is a key issue for teachers.

There are three areas from which students can choose topics for writing: personal experiences, imagination, and outside knowledge. Some writing educators suggest that when writing narratives, students should write primarily from their personal experiences (Graves, 1994). Students also should write about topics outside their experiences and from their imaginations according to Stotsky (1995). Having students write from their imaginations is important, which is why fictional narratives should be taught as well as personal experience stories. Just where creative ideas originate is somewhat of a mystery (Sharples, 1996). Many students are able to take their background experiences and knowledge and organize them in unique ways. Although imaginative ideas might be based on prior knowledge, having students use their imaginations to generate writing topics motivates some students to write. ELLs, like all students, have vivid imaginations. By providing the extra support that ELLs need, teachers can help them put their ideas into writing.

A day in the life of a...

In *The Power of Story* (2007), Jim Loehr posits that people tell stories about five major subjects: work, family, health, happiness, and friendship. Mr. Jones believed that his students were able to use these five subjects to generate ideas for writing. He listed them on a bulletin board (substituting *school* for *work*) and had students brainstorm possible writing topics about each one. Mr. Jones also used interest charts (Lenski & Johns, 2004), topic trees (Rog, 2007), and "I Am From" poems (Lyon, 1999) to help students think of writing topics. He paired his ELLs with native English-speaking classmates who could help them with these activities.

make 2 column or Top Down

Interest Charts

One way to get students to think about topics about which to write is to help them identify their own interests. Mr. Jones used an Interest Chart for the students who had difficulty thinking about topics. Tom was one of those students. He just couldn't think of anything to write so Mr. Jones asked him about the things he liked. Tom replied that he liked ice cream, soccer, and pizza. Mr. Jones probed this topic a bit more by asking Tom whether there was anything else he liked. Tom thought for a while and then replied that he also liked snakes and cougars. Mr. Jones listed these things on Tom's Interest Chart. He encouraged Tom to look at books in the classroom library about snakes and cougars so that he could find vocabulary words to describe them. Tom decided to write about the time he saw a cougar when he was hiking with his father. Mr. Jones helped Tom fill out the other sections of the Interest Chart throughout the year (see Figure 4.9).

FIGURE 4.9. Example of a second grader's Interest Chart.		
Things I Like Ice cream, soccer, pizza, Snakes, cougars	**Things I Don't Like** Homework, spinach, ballet	**Hobbies** Bug collection
Books I've Read Magic School Bus	**Sports I Like** Soccer, baseball, kickball	**TV and Games** "Simpsons"
Things My Family Does Tells stories, plays games, watches TV, sings	**Good Things about Me** Responsible, honest	**Things about Me That Aren't So Good** Get angry sometimes, forget things

Topic Trees

Mr. Jones encouraged his students to develop topic trees as they thought about ideas for personal experience stories. Topic trees begin with a general idea and then get more specific. For example, Mr. Jones asked Anna to think about a topic to write about. She said she could write about the time she was visiting her family in Mexico. Mr. Jones asked Anna to write about it at the bottom of her paper and to think about the family members who she saw on her trip. Anna said she spent most of her time with her cousins and her grandparents. Anna wrote those words in the next lines above the bottom. Then Mr. Jones asked Anna to think of the kinds of things she did with both her cousins and her grandparents and to write them above the terms. Anna did and then had four topics from which to choose (see Figure 4.10).

Good way to zoom in.

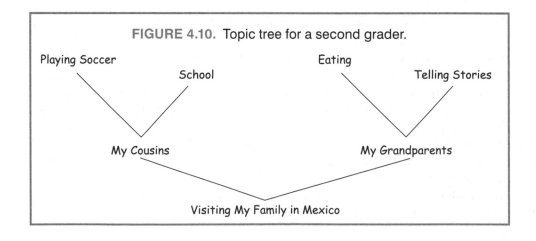

FIGURE 4.10. Topic tree for a second grader.

Playing Soccer   School   Eating   Telling Stories

My Cousins   My Grandparents

Visiting My Family in Mexico

I Am From . . .

George Ella Lyon published a format for "I Am From . . . " poems in her book for teachers titled *Where I'm From, Where Poems Come From* in 1999. Since that time, teachers around the country have had students create their own "I Am From . . . " poems. Mr. Jones talked with his newcomers to find out about their lives before coming to America. As he learned about each student, he was able to coauthor "I Am From . . . " poems with them (see Figures 4.11 and 4.12).

WRITING FOR AN AUDIENCE

"If you want to give the best possible gift to a writer, give an audience" (Elbow, 1981, p. 122). Writing is primarily a social act. The main purpose of writing is for the product to be read by another person. Britton, Burgess, Martin, McLeod, and Rosen (1975) identified four main audiences for students' writings: themselves, the teacher, a known audience, and an unknown audience. These researchers read 2,000 pieces of writing and found that more than 95% of them were written for the teacher. The teacher, of course, can be an authentic audience, but more often the teacher is an evaluator. In Britton's study more than half of all of the writing written for the teacher was read as an evaluator rather than as an authentic audience.

Students understand that when a teacher reads their writing in the role of an evaluator, the teacher is not a real audience. Ray (2001) wrote, "For publishing to make any sense at all in our writing workshops, students need to feel the pull of readers waiting for them" (p. 257). In school, the purposes for writing often do not go beyond completing an assigned task with the teacher as the audience (Bright, 1995). When students consistently write for the teacher as the audience, they have difficulty developing a sense of audience awareness. Audience awareness becomes apparent when writers think about their audience while writing (Rubin, 1998).

Thinking about the audience for a piece of writing shapes the process and the product of writing. Xiaquin, an ELL in Mr. Jones's class, wanted to write a story to let her classmates know about her grandmother's experiences during the Chinese Cultural Revolution. She wanted her friends to understand why her grandmother was so suspicious of the government. The audience Xiaquin selected would ultimately shape her writing. She knew she had to write her grandmother's story in simple terms, and she also had to include some Chinese history to contextualize the story. If Xiaquin had selected a different audience for her story, she would need to change some of the content she included in her piece.

As writers visualize their audiences, they decide what to include, what to omit, and whether to write informally or formally. It is the awareness of audiences that influences many writing decisions (Dahl & Farnan, 1998). Some students have difficulty visualizing their audiences. Fisher, Frey, and Lapp (2009) suggest that teachers give ELLs photographs of potential writing audiences. As students look at the photographs, they should think about how to write for that particular audience. Photographs should include pictures of the teacher, other students, teachers in the school, and public audiences.

Writing for your classmates. ↓ alternative audiences.

FIGURE 4.11. Form for creating "I Am From . . ." poems.

I am from _____

and from _____ .

(two things in your house)

I am from _____ and _____

(plants or nature around your house)

_____ .

(one nature memory)

I'm from _____ (two foods)

from _____ and _____ .

(parents' last names)

I'm from _____ .

(two sayings)

I'm from _____ .

I'm from _____ and _____ .

(two foods with unique smells)

From _____

_____ .

(physical description of family members)

Under my bed is _____

_____ .

I am from those moments—

I am _____ (race/culture).

I am _____ (your name).

FIGURE 4.12. Example of a student's "I Am From . . ." poem.

I am from a cinder block house with a dirt floor
and from an oven heated with wood.
I am from chickens pecking in the soil around my feet.
I am from flowers wilting in the heat and grass matted into dust,
From volcanoes ringing the lake that was down the road from my village.
I'm from beans and tortillas
From Perez and Vivres.
I'm from "May God Go with You" and "Who Knows."
I'm from "Take care of your sisters" and "Listen to your teacher."
I'm from blanched corn and aromatic coffee.
From flashing teeth and backs stooped from heavy loads, from cinder-strewn
hair and rainbow-colored clothes.
On the dirt floor underneath my bed are my soccer ball, my notebook, and my
only pair of shoes.
I am from those moments—
I am Guatemalan.
I am José Alejandro Francisco Perez Vivres.

Public Audiences

Submitting writing on the Internet challenges writers' ability to visualize their audiences. Black (2005) suggests that students use the fanfiction site to submit stories. Fanfiction is a site that publishes writers' responses in the following categories: anime/manga, books, cartoons, movies, plays, comics, TV shows, and games. There are a variety of other websites that publish students' writing.

Additional audiences for student writing can be found in Figure 4.13.

CHOOSING WORDS TO TELL THE STORY

The human voice underlies each piece of writing (Graves, 2003). Voice lets readers know that a piece of writing is the product of one person rather than another. Yagoda (2004) likens voice and style to a person's fingerprint or the sound of a friend's voice on the phone. Voice in writing is distinctive; it reveals the writer.

According to Spandel (2009), word choice enhances a writer's voice because voice comes from how a writer chooses and arranges words. Many ELLs don't realize that their writing should be a formal version of their own voice. ELLs' writing can reflect their tendency to grow in conversational vocabulary more quickly than academic vocabulary, and they need to be reminded to write more formally (Fisher et al., 2009). Teachers can ameliorate this problem by teaching students word connotations and synonyms to expand their word choices.

FIGURE 4.13. Audiences for student writing.

1. Students in your class
2. Students in other classes in your school
3. Pen pals from other countries
4. Administrators or staff in the school
5. School board members
6. Relatives
7. Local newspaper
8. City officials
9. State or federal representatives
10. Government officials
11. Local organizations
12. Travel bureaus
13. Chamber of commerce
14. Public or school libraries
15. Waiting rooms in dentists' or doctors' offices
16. Radio stations
17. Book authors
18. President
19. Blogs
20. Social networks

Voice intersects with writing style. Some experts believe that voice reveals the writer's personality while style encompasses the tools writers use to express themselves in different contexts (Yagoda, 2004). "It is frequently the case that writers entertain, move and inspire us less by what they say than by how they say it. *What* they say is information and ideas and (in the case of fiction) story and characters. *How* they say it is style" (Yagoda, 2004, p. xi). Style is hard to define, and some teachers believe that each writer's style is a function of his or her personality and unchangeable. According to Yagoda, however, there are also aspects of style that can be taught, especially those that consist of word choice and sentence arrangement.

Different writing styles are valued in different countries. For example, one of the most common writing styles in the United States is short, direct sentences (see Strunk & White, 2000). Writers from other parts of the world, especially Latin American countries, value longer, more complex sentences. ELL teachers, therefore, need to be cognizant of ways to help ELLs express themselves in their own voices while conforming in some sense to the style used in academic settings in the United States.

Don't drown out the cultural voice.

Mr. Jones wanted each of his students to write with his or her own voice and to develop a style that fit both his or her personality and the writing assignment. To do this, he tried to read a different children's book every day showing students how each writer used a different way of expressing him- or herself. He also encouraged students to conduct author studies and look at ways the writing in an author's books is similar. He then had students draw a picture of the way they visualized the different authors after reading the books and discuss why they visualized the author that way.

List?

SCAFFOLDING STUDENTS' WRITING

When Mr. Jones began his teaching career more than 15 years previously, he had no ELLs in his classroom. For 5 years, however, an increasing number of immigrants had moved to the area and enrolled in school. As stated earlier in this chapter, Mr. Jones now has 10 ELLs. Mr. Jones was proud of his ability to keep up with the field of education through reading and professional development, and he was conscientious about incorporating what he understood about best practice in his classroom. The problem he faced, however, was whether the practices he was using for native English speakers would be the same as those for ELLs. For example, Mr. Jones had incorporated the writing workshop approach in his classroom (see Calkins, 1994), and he wondered whether he would be able to scaffold his ELLs' writing in this informal setting. So, once again, Mr. Jones called on Ms. Ramos for assistance.

Ms. Ramos explained that ELLs need authentic writing experiences similar to those of native English speakers and that the practice of waiting until ELLs know the language before having them write stories hinders their potential development (Hadaway & Young, 2002). Research indicates that ELLs can write in English long before they have complete command of the oral and written systems of their new language (Peyton, 1990), and the composing process of ELLs is similar to that of native English speakers (Peregoy & Boyle, 2008; Persky, Daane, & Jin, 2003). Writing can, in fact, help students develop their reading, speaking, and listening skills. Ms. Ramos believed, however, that many ELLs needed more scaffolding than native English speakers.

At the time when writing workshop approaches were becoming increasingly popular, Lisa Delpit (1988) introduced a counterargument about the use of writing workshop for students who speak a dialect other than Standard English. She suggested that students who did not grow up hearing Standard English were at a disadvantage when teachers used instructional practices that deemphasized explicit instruction. Delpit suggested that dialect speakers, especially African American populations, need to be taught the structure of Standard English language explicitly (see Chapter 6 for a discussion about teaching grammar). Ms. Ramos told Mr. Jones that the same holds true for ELLs. Providing them experiences to progress through the writing process in authentic situations was important, but Mr. Jones also needed to provide explicit scaffolding about English writing.

Ms. Ramos illustrated her point with an example adapted from Allington's (2009) work. According to Allington, the usual sequence in speaking is noun–verb (e.g., "Mr. Jones told me that I need to bring in a picture of myself for the bulletin board"). In writing, the word order is often reversed (e.g., "Bring in a picture of yourself," said Mr. Jones). These distinctions in English need to be taught to ELLs who are learning to write narratives because they have fewer experiences with the English language than do native speakers.

Using the Writing Process

Writing narratives for an audience usually needs several days (or more) to complete. Donald Graves (1983) studied good writers and found that they typically move through a process that includes prewriting, drafting, revising, editing, and sharing. The stages in the writing process are not always discrete; writers can edit as they revise, for example. And the stages in the writing process can be of different lengths. It is outside the scope of this book to explain how to incorporate writing workshops into the classroom, but there are many excellent books available on this subject. Earlier in this chapter we discussed generating topics, which is one of the most important components of prewriting and writing for audiences. Students need to also revise and edit their writing.

Revision

Britton (1996) stated, "Good writing is largely a matter of rewriting" (p. 323). Rewriting turns a string of sentences into an engaging story. Revising takes place throughout the writing process. During writing, writers often put down words that do not completely capture their thoughts and ideas. Instead, these initial drafts reflect the surface thoughts of the writer. As students revise ideas, they might stop and rewrite a phrase, sharpen an image, or check the spelling of a word. Students need to learn how to stop and think while writing and to make changes that capture their thoughts.

Revision takes time, thought, and work, and is resisted by many students. Since revision takes a great deal of time, Graves (2003) suggests that not every piece of writing be taken through the revision cycle. Even beginning writers, however, can learn how to revise their writing. For example, teachers can write sentences on the board and make changes to them to show students how to revise. Mr. Jones supported his ELLs through brainstorming activities that focused on how to add detail to a story and detail words that students could use.

Editing

Writers rarely compose totally correct text. That's why writers edit their work throughout the writing process. We address ways students can help each other edit their writing in Chapter 5, and we discuss grammar and usage in Chapter 6.

Writing Conferences

Teachers have used writing conferences to scaffold students' writing for several decades. Writing conferences are conversations between the teacher and students individually or in small groups about their writing (Graves, 1983). Beach and Friedrich (2006) underscore the need for teachers of ELLs to spend time talking with students about their writing. Writing can be a window into ELLs' language development. According to Slaughter (2009), teachers can use heterogeneous groups for conferences, or they can group students by the skills they need to learn. Mr. Jones used both types of conferences. He used heterogeneous conferences when he wanted the students to support each other's learning. He used skill conferences when he wanted to focus on a specific aspect of narrative writing. When Mr. Jones conferenced with his students, he learned where they were in the process of learning to tell stories in a way that is accepted in English, and he was able to use that knowledge to scaffold their learning.

SUMMARY

The structure of narrative writing used in the United States tends to be more linear than the kinds of stories that many ELLs know. Teachers of ELLs, therefore, need to explicitly teach the elements of narrative texts. Typically, personal experience stories and fictional stories are taught in school. Students need to learn how to incorporate emotions into personal experience stories and how to develop characters and plot in fiction. Teachers can use a variety of activities to support ELLs as they learn how to write narratives. Teachers can also teach the writing process while they focus on a specific genre. The writing process includes generating topics, drafting, revising, editing, and thinking of audiences. Teachers can scaffold ELLs' writing development through writing workshops and other teaching structures.

WEB RESOURCES

Fanfiction
www.fanfiction.net

Site in which writers submit reactions and additions to books, comics, TV shows, and movies.

Kim's Korner for Teaching Tips
www.kimskorner4teachertalk.com/readingliterature/literary_elements_devices/plot.htm

Lessons on teaching plot structure.

Online Writing Lab
owl.english.purdue.edu/handouts/esl/eslaudience.html

Tips for ESL writers on writing for an American audience.

Reading and Writing Online
www.ncte.org/library/NCTEFiles/Resources/Journals/CC/0182-nov08/CC0182Audiences.pdf

Discusses how to use online venues to widen the audience pool for students.

Story Skeletons
shutta.com/storyskeletons.pdf

Ideas for teaching plot structure through picture books.

Topics for writing
www.youthonline.ca/penpals/bltopics.shtml

A list of ideas for writing topics.

CHAPTER 5

Academic Writing Genres

Description, Exposition, and Persuasion

Mr. Kerry was assigned to teach fifth grade after spending 8 years as a fourth-grade teacher. He was reluctant to begin the new grade level because he knew his students would be given the state writing test. Mr. Kerry had 11 ELLs in his class. All of the ELLs had attended school in the United States for at least 3 years and had excellent conversational English. Mr. Kerry knew, however, that most fifth-grade students have difficulty writing descriptive, expository, and persuasive essays and that ELLs have special problems organizing writing that is non-narrative. Mr. Kerry decided to talk with Ms. Ramos, the literacy coach, to learn more about ways to help his ELLs experience success on the state writing test and become competent in academic writings genres.

In the United States, there are four agreed-upon rhetorical modes of writing: narrative, descriptive, expository, and persuasive. Narrative writing is by far the easiest mode of writing to teach, as was discussed in Chapter 4. Descriptive, expository, and persuasive writing are typically more difficult because students have fewer experiences with them. Therefore, students need explicit instruction in the ways texts are organized and they need practice with all of the writing modes, which are termed *genres* in schools (Kern, Andre, Schilke, Barton, & McGuire, 2003).

According to Resnick and Hampton (2009), students learn to write in fairly predictable ways. Beginning writers need many experiences learning that the written word is communication and, as they experiment with language, they also need to learn how sentences and texts are organized. Most students, and ELLs in particular, also need explicit instruction in how academic sentences are structured and how longer texts are organized (Herrera et al., 2010). Neglecting to teach academic genres can deny students access to higher-level schooling. Teachers need to spend time demonstrating academic writing and, at the same time, they need to teach students that genres are not rigid structures but are organizational frameworks (Resnick & Hampton, 2009). In this chapter, we focus on the academic genres of writing. First, we discuss the types of writing that are most frequently taught in schools, and then we present teaching activities that facilitate good academic writing.

DESCRIPTIONS OF WRITING GENRES

Mr. Kerry, the fifth-grade teacher introduced at the beginning of this chapter, needed to know more about the academic writing genres. Mr. Kerry brought Ms. Ramos several different books that he had in his classroom, such as the *Magic School Bus* series, that he thought were examples of expository text. He was aware that informational books had not been emphasized enough in schools (see Duke, 2000), and he was trying to increase students' exposure to these kinds of texts through read-alouds.

Ms. Ramos explained that the informational texts that Mr. Kerry had been reading to his classroom were beneficial, but they were not the same kind of text structure that students needed to learn to write. She explained that informational texts are frequently confused with expository texts. Informational texts can be narrative, expository, or a combination of the two (Kletzien & Dreher, 2004). For example, narrative–informational texts are in story format, such as the ones that Mr. Kerry often read. Those texts are great to read but do not have the organizational structure of the kinds of writing genres students need to learn in order to produce academic writing.

Academic writing is culture specific. According to Herrera et al. (2010), the discourse pattern of academic English is much more linear than Semitic, Asian, Romance, Russian, and Navajo languages. Therefore, the discourse patterns taught in school are likely different from the ways texts are organized in the ELL's country of origin (Lesaux et al., 2006). We discussed this idea in Chapter 4 where we illustrated how narratives in the United States could be different from those of other countries. The differences between narratives and the academic genres discussed in this chapter are even more distinctive. Most students, even newcomers, have many experiences with the ways stories are told in the United States. Students watch stories on television, they hear stories on the playground, and they listen to their teachers read stories aloud. The language from the other genres is heard much less often and is far removed from daily experiences (Fang, 2008).

The organizational patterns of English academic texts are unfamiliar to most ELLs and the transitions and function words are also new—even for those students who are proficient in conversational English (Carrier, 2005). For example, consider the following sentence: "One of the negative by-products of river dams is the decline of the salmon population because the salmon cannot jump over the dams." The preceding sentence has a cause–effect structure and uses the connectors: "One of the" and "because." ELLs who are able to read the words in this sentence may still be unfamiliar with these connecting words and may therefore have difficulty understanding the meaning of the sentence. In the same way, ELLs may have difficulty composing academic sentences because they are unfamiliar with the sentence structure, and they also may not have the knowledge of transition words.

The non-narrative genres are descriptive, expository, and persuasive. Although authentic writing is often a combination of these genres, Ms. Ramos suggested that Mr. Kerry teach each genre individually so that students could learn to distinguish between them and become competent in each one (see Fleischer & Andrew-Vaughan, 2009). The following are detailed descriptions of the academic writing genres.

Descriptive Writing

Descriptive writing presents an object, a place, or a person in a way that creates a vivid impression in the reader's mind. The reader gains a rich, comprehensive, and detailed picture of what is being described. The writing also clearly conveys a mood, attitude, and/or perspective about the subject so that the reader feels part of the writer's experience. The organizational pattern that is typically used is to begin with a main idea, to add details, and to conclude with a summary statement. Writers often use their five senses as they consider their descriptions and use the literary devices of similes and metaphors to make their meanings more vivid.

The transition words that are typically used in descriptive writing include *above, across, along, appears, as in, behind, below, beside, between, down, for example, for instance, in addition, in back of, in front of, in particular, looks like, near, onto, outside, over, specifically, such as, to be* and *under*. A graphic organizer for descriptive writing and a sample piece can be found in Figures 5.1 (page 94) and 5.2 (page 95), respectively.

Expository Writing

Expository writing provides information, gives directions, explains a situation or event, details a process, clarifies, or defines. There has been an increasing interest in teaching expository writing in schools because so much of the print we read in life is one kind of expository writing, such as reading directions, manuals, textbooks, and memos. Letters can also be expository when they describe or explain a situation or event.

Before students can write expository texts, they need to have knowledge about a specific subject. Expository writing is predicated on knowledge that is organized and shared. For example, Mr. Kerry was teaching an American history unit that focused on the causes of the Civil War. He wanted students to write about some of the causes and their effects. Before he could ask students to write this piece, he needed to make sure students knew enough information to be able to have the content about which to write.

Expository writing informs or amplifies the reader's understanding through a carefully crafted presentation of key points, explanations, and supportive detail. The main point is usually clearly stated or implied. It is developed and supported by facts, the facts are presented in an orderly way, and the writing is directed toward a specific audience (Buss & Karnowski, 2000).

There are a variety of organizational patterns that are typically considered to be expository writing. Among the most common patterns are simple explanation, steps in a process, comparison–contrast, cause–effect, and problem–solution. Each

FIGURE 5.1. Graphic organizer for descriptive writing.

What you are describing . . .

How it looks, feels, sounds, smells, and/or tastes . . .

Conclusion

FIGURE 5.2. Sample descriptive writing.

The houses in Belgium are mostly small. They are made out of Bricks. most of the houses are stacked in a row. in Belgium, the people make Belgium Waffles and Belgium pancakes. a lot. people can buy French Fries at the french frie store. Belgium chocolate is super good! once my daddy took me for a ride on a bike. I sat on a little seat on his bike. his bike had two little seats and one big seat. Sometimes we would ride on the train. It would scare me to death when the trains went Through The tunnel Where we were waiting. They made such a loud noise! Sinter klaas comes to my house evry year on December 6th. That's his brthday. if I'm good all year, he gives me candy. Sometimes the children put carrots in their shoes for his horse. If you're not good all year, he will give you rocks or sticks.

---

of these types of expository writing has a slightly different organizational pattern (Englert, Okolo, & Mariage, 2009).

Explanation–Definition

This type of writing will be familiar to some students. Many trade books and textbooks have sections that are organized by simple explanation. That means the writing begins with a main idea, details are given to support the main idea, and examples are given to illustrate the details. Although the main idea of a paragraph can be anywhere in the paragraph, or not even directly stated, most explanation writing that students will read or hear begins with a main idea. Explanation–definition writing is one of the easiest types of expository writing to teach students.

There are many different transition words to teach students. Transitions words for opening a paragraph initially or for general use could include *admittedly, assuredly, certainly, for example, generally speaking, granted, in general, in this situation, no doubt, nobody denies, obviously, of course, to be sure, undoubtedly,* and *unquestionably.* Transition words or the internal sentences of a paragraph or essay include *finally, first, lastly, next,* and *then.* For the end of the paragraph, transitions words include *after all, all in all, all things, finally, in brief, in conclusion, in short, in summary, in the final analysis, in the long run, on balance, on the whole, to sum up,* and *to summarize.* A graphic organizer and an example of explanation–definition writing can be found in Figures 5.3 (page 96) and 5.4 (page 97), respectively.

Sequence or Steps in a Process

This text presents information in order of time, sequence, or as a process. Teachers frequently have students give step-by-step directions, such as directions to make

FIGURE 5.3. Graphic organizer for explanation–definition writing.

Topic

Detail #1

Examples

_____

_____

_____

_____

Detail #2

Examples

_____

_____

_____

_____

Detail #3

Examples

_____

_____

_____

_____

Conclusion

FIGURE 5.4. Explanation–definition writing sample.

I would give a special mug to my mom because she likes them and uses them and lets me use them and because she is my mom and because she's nice and because she loves me and I love her and because I dont get to see her as much and because she helps me and because she makes me laugh.

---

a sandwich or directions to walk home. The important part of steps in a process is to give clear, concise directions that are sequential. Mr. Kerry asked his students to write a process paper on how to tie their running shoes. He then placed a run- *how to modify?* ning shoe with laces in front of every student and asked them to exchange papers and to try to follow the written directions. After this demonstration, Mr. Kerry emphasized how important it is to give precise directions. Transition words for sequence or steps-in-a-process papers include *additionally, after, afterward, another, as soon as, before, during, finally, first, following, immediately, initially, last, later, meanwhile, next, not long after, now, preceding, a second, soon, then, third, today, tomorrow, until, when, yesterday,* and *first, second, third, last, next,* and *then.* A graphic organizer and an example of a process paper can be found in Figures 5.5 (page 98) and 5.6 (page 99), respectively.

 *often on ACCESS*

Comparison–Contrast

A comparison–contrast paper describes the similarities and differences between two or more things, places, events, ideas, and so on. We compare and contrast things all of the time. We compare and contrast baseball teams, prices in stores, and even teachers in school. Because our society compares and contrasts things often, students may be familiar with the thinking process that is needed for comparison–contrast writing. Transition words typically used in comparison–contrast writing include *alike, also, although, as opposed to, as well as, both, but, by contrast, compared with, different from, either or, even though, however, in common, in comparison, instead of, like, on the other hand, otherwise, similar to, similarly, still, unlike, whereas,* and *yet.*

A graphic organizer and an example of comparison–contrast can be found in Figures 5.7 (page 100) and 5.8 (page 101), respectively.

Cause–Effect

Cause–effect writing is a bit more complex than other types of expository writing. In this type of writing, a cause is stated with its effect. Throughout students' lives, they have learned that there are consequences for actions. In cause–effect writing students can learn the thinking and writing processes behind actions and consequences. Transition words for cause–effect writing include *accordingly, as a*

FIGURE 5.5. Graphic organizer for steps-in-a-process writing.

Name of process

Steps in the process

1. _____

2. _____

3. _____

4. _____

5. _____

6. _____

Conclusion

FIGURE 5.6. Steps-in-a-process writing sample.

I know how to tie my shoes and I can tell you how to do it to. First you have to put the shoe on the foot and then you get the two ends of the laces. You have to twist the laces and make too bows. Then you twist the bows together and pull them tight. If your laces come apart you have to tie them more tight.

---

result of, because, begins with, consequently, due to, for this reason, if . . . then, in order to, is caused by, leads to, may be due to, so that, steps involved, thereby, therefore, and *thus*. A graphic organizer and an example of cause–effect writing can be found in Figures 5.9 (page 102) and 5.10 (page 103), respectively.

Problem–Solution

A problem–solution text identifies an issue and how the issue is solved. Students are also used to this type of thinking. Mr. Kerry capitalized on his students' background knowledge by posing several school problems on the board, such as "the amount of graffiti on the school sidewalks," "the quality of food in the school cafeteria," and "the rules about cell phones and iPod use." Transitions typically used in problem–solution texts include *because, consequently, despite, dilemma is, if . . . then, problem is, puzzle is solved, question–answer, resolved, result, so that,* and *thus*. A graphic organizer and an example of problem–solution writing can be found in Figures 5.11 (page 104) and 5.12 (page 105), respectively.

*CR–
→ personal
interest
+
debate*

Persuasive Writing

Persuasive writing attempts to convince the reader to agree with a particular point of view and/or to persuade the reader to take specific action. The topic is debatable because there are clearly reasons for more than one point of view and the piece is focused to a manageable scope. Persuasive writing differs from expository writing in that it does more than explain; it also <u>takes a stand</u> and endeavors to <u>persuade the reader to take that same stand</u>. When a specific audience has been identified, the nature of the arguments and the style of presentation are designed to appeal to that audience.

The art of persuasion and creating effective arguments is not a natural human ability but must be learned (Fulkerson, 1996). Mr. Kerry illustrated how persuasion could be used when one of his students asked if the class could get a salamander for a pet. When Mr. Kerry asked for reasons why they should get a salamander, the student replied, "Because." Mr. Kerry explained that to persuade him, the students needed to make a claim, offer reasons for that claim, provide examples or details that illustrate the reasoning, and provide reasons and opinions for counterclaims.

FIGURE 5.7. Graphic organizer for comparison–contrast writing.

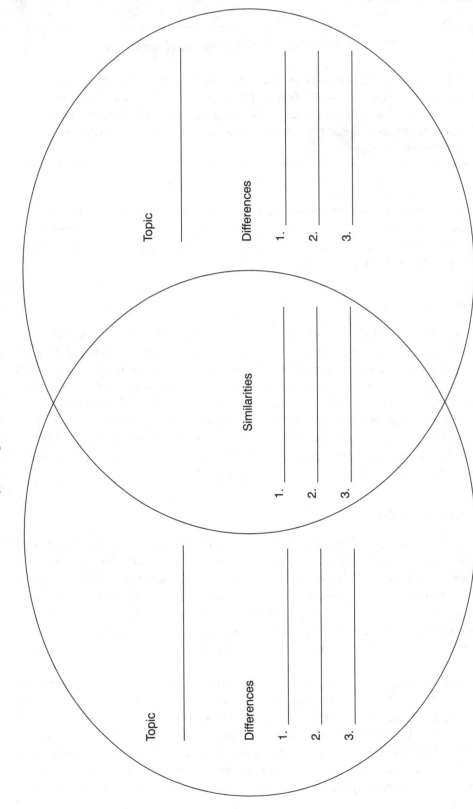

Topic _____

Differences

1. _____

2. _____

3. _____

Similarities

1. _____

2. _____

3. _____

Topic _____

Differences

1. _____

2. _____

3. _____

FIGURE 5.8. Comparison–contrast writing sample.

Sum peple like dogs and some like cats. I like dogs better. Dogs are friendly and lik your face and wag its tail and cats do not do that so much. cats scrach and bite and can run away from you house. Dogs like to live in the house but my mom makes us keep ours in the yard. Dogs are more fun and play ball and like to run and cats climb trees. Dogs are cuter and I love dogs.

Students are more likely to understand how to write using the persuasive writing genre if they have had the opportunity to use persuasive writing to make an actual difference. Mr. Kerry decided to give his students the opportunity to convince him to purchase a salamander. He had his students develop a series of statements about the topic and provided them with a graphic organizer and a list of transition words. Students were eventually able to develop a group paper that convinced him. The transition words he taught included *also, because, but, certainly, conversely, for that reason, however, in my opinion, in the same way, in this situation, nevertheless, on the other hand, specifically, though, unquestionably,* and *yet.* A graphic organizer and an example of persuasive writing can be found in Figures 5.13 (page 106) and 5.14 (page 107), respectively.

ACADEMIC WRITING INSTRUCTION

Once Mr. Kerry understood the different types of writing, he was able to adapt the classroom routines and activities he was already using in his classroom to teach academic writing genres. In past years, Mr. Kerry had allowed students to use whatever genre fit their writing topic. Most of his students, however, had not been instructed in academic genres so most of them wrote narratives. In addition to teaching academic genres, Mr. Kerry decided to encourage students to practice these genres during writing workshop and to assign the genre in other class assignments. Some of the classroom assignments that Mr. Kerry used follow.

Genre Examples and Mentor Texts

Ms. Ramos explained that showing ELLs the organizational structure of each text and demonstrating how to use transition words is critical. According to Filmore (2005), mere exposure to language may not necessarily translate into the understanding of academic writing.

The first thing Mr. Kerry did to teach academic writing genres was to find writing samples as mentor texts. He searched through the samples of writing that students had done in the past, asked Ms. Ramos and other teachers for examples they had, and looked on the Internet for writing samples completed by students.

FIGURE 5.9. Graphic organizer for cause–effect writing.

Topic

Causes		Solutions
	→	
	→	
	→	
	→	
	→	
	→	

Conclusion

FIGURE 5.10. Cause–Effect writing sample.

When you make a mistake in school you might get a detention. If you do something bad like disrupt the class or walk in late and the teacher puts you name on the board then you can get a detention and stay after school. Sometimes if you fight the teacher will send you to the principal and she will call your mom. The you are in BIG trouble because mom will be mad and maybe tell dad and you might get grounded. It's better to act good in school.

Mr. Kerry taught students one writing genre at a time by showing them the mentor text, explaining the way the text was organized, and highlighting the transition words. He then gave the students a graphic organizer to use and brainstormed ideas as a class that fit in the categories. This strategy worked for the majority of his students. A few of the newcomers who were still beginning-level English proficiency writers (see Chapter 2 for classifications of writers) needed more scaffolding with strategies such as sentence and paragraph frames.

Sentence and Paragraph Frames

Most ELLs need explicit instruction in the language used in academic writing and need to see how language, such as transition words, is used in authentic texts (Ehlers-Zavala, 2008). One way to do this is through teaching sentence and paragraph frames (Montelongo & Hernandez, 2007). A sentence frame for teaching transitions, for example, provides an outline of a sentence using the transition words. Students fill in the blanks with content words and read the sentences aloud to hear how academic sentences sound. As students become more mature writers, they can write the entire sentences by themselves. Sentence frames can be used to teach other aspects of academic language as well.

Mr. Kerry decided to introduce writing frames for all of his fifth graders, including the native English speakers. He was teaching a unit on weather and erosion and developed the following sentence frames. In the first frame, Mr. Kerry discussed how academic sentences often describe something. The words *is* and *that* are words that connect the ideas together. The second sentence frame illustrates a cause–effect sentence using the transition word *because*.

[handwritten margin note: Cards w/ vocab. + transition relationships (CE, CC, etc.)]

- Ground *(water)* _____ is *(precipitation)* _____
  that soaks into the *(ground)* _____ .
- Destroying natural *(habitats)* _____ eventually affects
  (people) _____ because of food
  (chains) _____ and habitats that are
  (destroyed) _____ .

FIGURE 5.11. Graphic organizer for problem–solution writing.

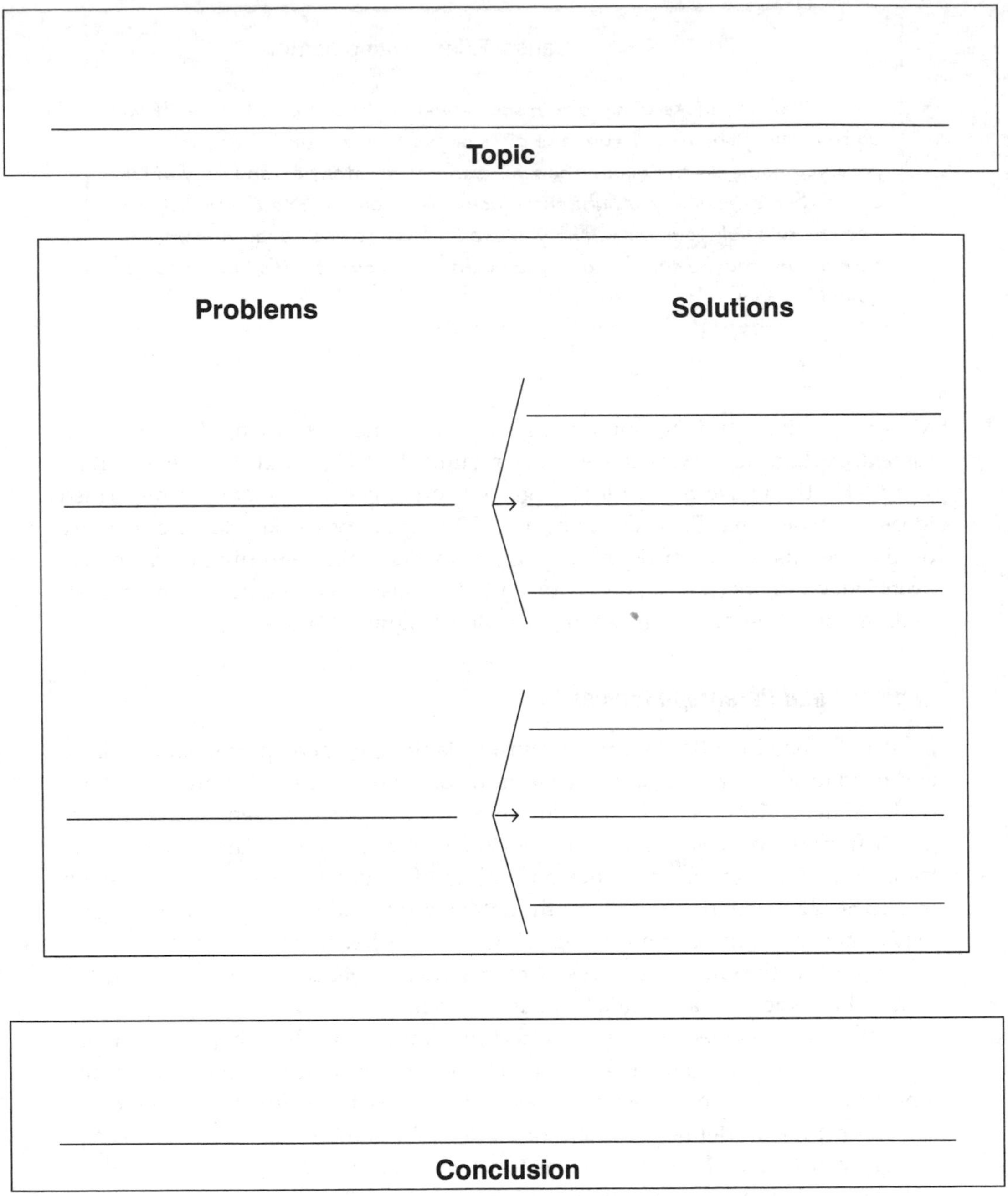
Topic
Problems
Solutions
Conclusion

From *Writing Instruction and Assessment for English Language Learners K–8* by Susan Lenski and Frances Verbruggen. Copyright 2010 by The Guilford Press. Permission to photocopy this figure is granted to purchasers of this book for personal use only (see copyright page for details).

FIGURE 5.12. Problem–solution writing sample.

We have a problem and that is people don't recycle. When we dont' recycle we have to much trash and the trash will take over the world and we will live in a bad place but we can recycle at school and at home and at everyplace we go except my grandmother says we dont have to recycle but we realy do. We can recycle by putting our papers in the paper bin and we can compost our food that we do not eat at lunch and we can put our soda cans in the bin to so that we don't' have so much trash and the world is better.

Mr. Kerry found that all of his students were able to use the sentence frames to learn how to write about the science content he was teaching and to become familiar with academic sentences. After a few weeks, he decided to try paragraph frames for the intermediate-level English proficiency writers. Cunningham and Cunningham (2010) recommend the use of paragraph frames with ELLs to help them learn text organization. They suggest that paragraph frames should be prepared so that ELLs can become more familiar with academic discourse patterns as well as the content being taught. Paragraph frames are used just like sentence frames. The teacher prepares an outline of a paragraph, and students fill in the content words. After completion, it is important that students read or hear the entire paragraph out loud, focusing on how the transition words are used in the paragraph. An example of a paragraph frame about the American Revolutionary War can be found in Figure 5.15 (page 107).

for tests?

Dialogue Journals

"An excellent way to familiarize ELLs with syntactical patterns is to engage in written conversation with students or to use dialogue journals" (Gunning, 2010, p. 481). As ELLs write and read dialogue journals, they can develop an "ear" for what sounds right in English, especially if their teacher is intentional in the responses. Consider the following example from Mr. Kerry's class:

Juan	On Saturday my brothers and me play soccer. We play in the field. It was fun.
Mr. Kerry	Soccer is one of the fastest growing sports in our town because so many people like to play it. I'm so glad you are having fun playing soccer at the field. Do you play on the field next to the school?
Juan	Yes, on the field next to the school. I was the goalie and stop my brother from making two goals.
Mr. Kerry	You must be a good player if you stopped your brother twice. Do you play soccer at recess? If you do, I'd like to watch you play next week.

FIGURE 5.13. Graphic organizer for persuasive writing.

Topic

Reason #1

Examples

_____

_____

_____

_____

Reason #2

Examples

_____

_____

_____

_____

Reason #3

Examples

_____

_____

_____

_____

Conclusion

FIGURE 5.14. Persuasive writing sample.

Should people lost their jobs if it helps the environment? No. I say that before they close down something, they should make sure the people have a job. That way, it's fair for both people and the environment. If someone isn't looking for a job and the factory finds out, they should give that person a warning. If that doesn't work, they should close the place anyway. Another solution is having the government pay the people that give up their job for the environment.

In this example, Mr. Kerry scaffolded Juan's knowledge of English syntax by replying in complex sentences that introduced new vocabulary and used prepositions and verb tenses that Juan was in the process of learning. Ms. Ramos had told Mr. Kerry that it is better if he would respond thoughtfully rather than with a quick "I'm glad," or "That's great." Mr. Kerry tried to respond to each student in his class once a week. He collected five dialogue journals each day and responded to them while the class was doing independent reading.

Daily News Strategy

Many teachers, including Mr. Kerry, use a daily news strategy as a classroom routine to begin their day. Ms. Ramos suggested to Mr. Kerry that he use this activity to show students how to use the main idea–detail pattern that is used in academic writing similar to the way Manyak (2008) described it. When students entered the classroom, Mr. Kerry had one student talk about something he or she had done over the past few days. Some of the stories that students volunteered were narratives. Mr. Kerry wrote the news stories using a narrative structure, scaffolding the student by asking pointed questions, and making changes that would make the story conform to the narrative organization (see Figure 5.16). Mr. Kerry then used

---

FIGURE 5.15. Paragraph frame about the American Revolutionary War.

The American *(Revolutionary)* _____ War, also known as the American War of *(Independence)* _____ , began as a war between *(Great Britain)* _____ and *(13)* _____ former British *(colonies)* _____ . In 1775, revolutionaries gained control of *(colonial governments)*, set up the Second Continental *(Congress)* _____ , and formed an *(army)* _____ . These actions resulted in Great Britain declaring the revolutionaries to be *(traitors)* _____ . The Americans responded by formally declaring their *(independence)* _____ as a new *(nation)* _____ .

FIGURE 5.16. Daily news stories.

Narrative Story

Last weekend my brother and I played soccer all afternoon. We went to the field by the school and found some of our friends already playing. We waited on the sidelines until Robbie saw us and invited us to play. We were on different teams, and I played goalie for a while. I also kicked a ball that went into the net and made a goal. I laughed all the way home because I made a goal.

Expository Text

Soccer is a game that is growing in popularity in the United States. Soccer, known more commonly as football, has been played all over Europe and South America for generations. If you go to one of these countries you see soccer on television at almost any time of day. Children play soccer in the fields and in the street. This trend is picking up in the United States as well with the U.S. soccer team becoming competitive in the World Cup tournament.

---

something from the news story that could be written using one of the academic writing genres. After that he demonstrated how to write a short paragraph using this mode. At times the students told news stories that were not narrative. Mr. Kerry wrote the stories while explaining how he composed the main idea sentence, details, and concluding sentence.

Using Student Translations

Many of Mr. Kerry's ELLs were more fluent in English than their parents and translated letters and documents for their families. According to Martinez, Orellana, Pacheco, and Carbone (2008), the translations that ELLs do at home can be used in schools to help them learn academic writing. Mr. Kerry talked to the ELLs about the translations that they did for their families and emphasized that translations are important and valuable. He then asked the ELLs to keep track of the translations they did and invited them to bring the materials to class. Mr. Kerry gave students time occasionally to discuss their challenges when translating. For example, some of his Spanish-speaking students did not know the Spanish words for ideas they were learning at school. When appropriate he showed some of the original English documents to the entire class. He showed students how the documents were organized; he highlighted the transition words, and he identified the genres that were present in the text. These strategies helped his ELLs understand the relevance of learning academic genres in school.

WRITING WORKSHOP

The topic for academic writing is often assigned by the teacher. McGinnis (2007) interviewed ELLs and learned that the students found their writing assignments to be "boring" and that they wanted their assignments to be more authentic and more creative.

According to Díaz-Rico and Weed (2010), using a process approach, such as in writing workshops, is especially important for ELLs because they are developing oral language while they are learning how to write. Using writing workshops involves a great deal of oral communication, a variety of interactions, planning, and revising/editing. ELL teachers can use the flexibility of writing workshops to teach the writing genres that are described in Chapter 4 and in this chapter. In a study of one ELL teacher, Ranker (2009) found that the teacher was able to successfully teach genre while offering the resources and tools that students needed to develop academic writing.

We discuss ideas for planning and prewriting in the chapter on narrative writing (Chapter 4). Those ideas apply to academic writing as well. In this chapter, we next describe some ideas for helping ELLs revise and edit their writing. Again, these strategies could also be adapted for narrative texts.

Revising Writing

Revision is re-visioning or rethinking a piece of writing. As writers compose a first draft, they often do not completely capture their thoughts and ideas. Instead, these initial drafts reflect the surface thoughts of the writer. After writing an initial draft, writers often reread their original sentences and change them to make the words express their intentions more clearly. As Donald Murray (1991) wrote, "I believe that if I attend to the draft, read it carefully, and listen to what it says, the draft will tell me what a reader needs" (p. 85).

According to Graves (1994), not all papers that students write should be revised. Students should write so much that they do not have time to take every piece of writing to the sharing stage. If students are writing every day, much of their writing need not be revised. However, when students are writing for an audience, even if it is their classmates, they need to make their writing as close to Standard English and as clear as possible. That's when they need to revise their writing.

Revising writing does not always take place at a certain time during the writing process. Even though many writers revise after drafting a piece, the writing process is recursive, and revision can take place at any time. When students begin a piece of writing, they need to keep their audience in mind, even if that audience is only the teacher. Students need to be cognizant of their audience as they revise. They revise their pieces on many levels, examining their logic, ideas, sentences, grammar, words, and sequence. Revision is necessary to produce high-quality writing. They might stop to rewrite a phrase, sharpen an image, or check the spelling of a word. Students can learn how to stop and think while writing, even reading the piece aloud, to make sure they have written using English syntax. According to Fearn and Farnan (2001), when students revise, they learn the recursive nature of the writing process.

Teaching ELLs How to Revise

Sometimes students have the misconception that revising is simply recopying their paper in neater handwriting or in typing. Most ELLs in kindergarten through eighth grade are novice writers who do not know all of the rules that govern the English language. Therefore, ELLs need to spend time polishing their writings to make sure they are as correct as possible. To produce writing that is correct, ELLs may need their teacher's assistance.

Even writers in kindergarten need to learn about revision. Ms. Ramos worked with teachers at all levels. She suggested that kindergarten and first-grade teachers write a sentence on the board, such as "I bought a puppy." The teacher can then show students how to revise by adding words to the sentence, such as "I bought a new puppy from the shelter last weekend." Young ELLs learn that writing can be changed.

Teachers of students in second grade and higher can teach students that they can make changes to their drafts to make their writing better. They can ask students to reread their first drafts and think about what they were trying to express. Then teachers can either have the writer or another student offer suggestions for changes. Some teachers may want students to get in small groups to read each other's writings. Students often do not know what to say about pieces of writing. Figure 5.17 gives some examples of questions to ask their writing partners.

FIGURE 5.17. Sample questions to ask writing partners.

- How do you like your writing so far?
- Why did you choose this topic?
- Which is your favorite part? Why?
- Are you finished? If you want to write more, what do you plan to write?
- Could you tell me more about . . . ?
- What did you mean by . . . ?
- Did you say what you wanted to say?
- Who is your audience?
- What is your purpose for writing this piece?
- Does the piece end the way you want it to end?
- Have you checked the spelling?

Editing

Editing is polishing a piece of writing into its final form by correcting surface features, or mechanics. Correct mechanics, such as spelling, usage, punctuation, capitalization, paragraphing, sentence structure, and handwriting/typing, can make a difference. According to Graves (1983), "Poor spelling in the midst of a good piece of writing is like attending a lovely banquet but with the leavings of grime and grease from the previous meal still left on the table" (p. 18).

Written words need to express as clearly as possible what the author means. When a writer gives a piece of writing to a reader, the writer loses control of the meaning of the text. It is then the responsibility of the reader to construct meaning, and if the writer hasn't been specific, the reader could misinterpret the author's point.

Most students tend to be poor editors, and ELLs have additional obstacles to editing. One of the reasons students aren't very good at cleaning up a piece of writing is that they have had very few chances in their lives to edit writing. Editing is a skill that is typically learned in schools.

Mr. Kerry wanted his students to edit their own writing that they would be sharing with an audience. He partnered the ELLs who had the most difficulty writing English with students who were proficient writers. He gave the students an editing checklist that they used in their groups (see Figure 5.18, page 112). Students used the editing checklist to make final changes to their writings before they gave them to their audiences (see Chapter 7 for additional assessment ideas).

SUMMARY

Academic writing in North America includes descriptive, expository, and persuasive discourse patterns. These patterns are organized differently by culture. ELLs need to learn the patterns of academic writing and the transition words that are commonly used. Teachers can teach academic writing patterns through graphic organizers and mentor texts. Additional activities that are useful are sentence and paragraph frames, dialogue journals, daily news, and using translations. Academic writing can be taught through teacher-generated assignments and through writing workshops. Revision and editing are especially important in academic writing.

WEB RESOURCES

Breaking News English
www.breakingnewsenglish.com/index.html

EFL/ESL lesson plans and podcasts for studying current events and news. Great for learning academic writing.

FIGURE 5.18. Editing checklist.

1. I read the writing to myself and it makes sense. ☐

2. I read the piece to a writing partner and used some of the suggestions. ☐

3. The purpose of my writing is clear. ☐

4. My writing style fits my audience. ☐

5. The writing is focused and clear. ☐

6. I have enough details to make my writing interesting. ☐

7. I have included interesting words. ☐

8. I have an interesting first sentence. ☐

9. The title for this writing fits the content. ☐

10. The ending has punch. I am satisfied with this piece of writing. ☐

11. I checked the piece for spelling errors. ☐

12. The capitalization is correct. The punctuation is correct. ☐

13. The subjects and verbs agree. ☐

14. The paragraphs are indented. ☐

15. The words are used correctly. ☐

16. The writing is legible. ☐

ESL Teaching/Learning Resources
academics.smcvt.edu/cbauer-ramazani/Links/esl_writing.htm

Resources for academic writing, including graphic organizers.

Everything ESL
www.everythingesl.net/about

Lesson plans, resources, and teaching tips.

Fostering Academic Success for English Language Learners
www.wested.org/policy/pubs/fostering

Provides information to answer questions about ways to foster better educational practice for ELLs.

Marie Nuzzi's ESL Page
www.eslconnect.com/links/html

Links to more than 200 ESL sites.

Web English Teacher
www.webenglishteacher.com/expwriting.html

Strategies and examples for teaching expository writing.

CHAPTER 6

How Language Works

Grammar and Usage

Amir proudly handed his teacher, Ms. Brennan, a short description of his family written in English. It was the first time he felt as if he had produced a good piece of English writing. He knew that he was an accomplished writer in Arabic, but composing in English was far more difficult. As Ms. Brennan read his work, Amir scanned her face for clues. Was it good enough? Ms. Brennan gave Amir a small smile and gently said, "Do you remember how to write sentences? Just listen to how the sentences sound. Does this sound right?" Amir read his paper out loud and replied, "I can't hear any problems. Don't you like my paper?"

Ms. Brennan discussed Amir's response with Ms. Ramos, the literacy coach. Ms. Ramos explained that it would take some time for Amir and other ELLs to "hear" how to apply Standard English in their writing. Ms. Ramos explained that learning a second language involves more than replacing a native language with the new language. ELLs typically construct an interlanguage (Selinker, 1972) in the process.

Teachers like Ms. Brennan often expect ELLs to respond to writing instruction in the same way that native speakers do. Native speakers and permanent residents often acquire English by "ear" from exposure to the language in oral contexts. Unlike native speakers, however, ELLs do not have years of listening to English and internalizing its grammatical structures so they need different kinds of grammar instruction than their English-speaking classmates (Frodesen, 2001). Understanding the grammatical nuances of a language is critical to writing that is understood and accepted by its readers.

The purpose of writing is to express ideas for an audience. The degree to which readers are able to construct meaning from a piece of writing, however, depends on the way the piece is written. Clear writing that conforms to standard usage is easier to read than writing that is unclear, dull, and full of errors. As Donald Graves (2003) reminds us, writing requires precision that spoken language doesn't require because writing doesn't offer the second chance that spoken words do. Writing with precision requires a number of specific accomplishments: knowing the structure of a genre, using words and idiomatic expressions to convey the intended meaning, applying the rules of grammar, and using the correct level of formality (Brisk & Harrington, 2000). This chapter provides research, teaching suggestions, and illustrations to help teachers teach grammar and usage to ELLs in ways that will help them become better writers.

DEVELOPMENT OF GRAMMATICAL KNOWLEDGE

We have known for decades that children learn their first language in stages (Parker & Riley, 2010). In 1975, Chomsky published a theory of universal grammar (UG) that illustrated how children learn languages. He suggested that UG is a set of principles, conditions, and rules that are elements of all languages. UG helped us understand that children are able to learn their own grammatical systems quite easily because the rules of language are innate. Native speakers are able to generalize the language systems they have heard since they were babies.

Most native speakers are able to "hear" the differences between syntactically different sentences. For example, Ms. Brennan spent time listening to some native speakers read their descriptions about their families. Jacob wrote, "My brother runs cross country at the high school he came in fourth place at the meet the team came in first place." When Ms. Brennan asked Jacob to read his work, he was able to hear where to put periods in his run-on sentence. He wasn't able to explain why he put in periods; he just knew how the sentences should sound.

Although native speakers are often able to hear how to correct their writing, they often do not have the terminology or explicit knowledge of grammar rules to explain their corrections. Many students do not see the need to learn the terminology for something they know intuitively. When students learn a foreign language with unfamiliar grammatical structures, however, grammar is usually taught explicitly and students say that for the first time they understand grammar. Ms. Ramos gave Ms. Brennan an example to illustrate this point. When native English speakers learn German, they have to put objects in a place different from where the objects would be found in an English sentence. Instead of saying, "It makes no difference to me," in German the speaker would say the English equivalent of "It makes me no difference." This placement of objects in German is different from English, and a German learner would have to learn what kind of word constitutes an object and how to use it in the German grammatical structure. For some reason, it seems easier to understand about objects when learning a new language; probably because the learners cannot use internalized grammatical knowledge. Explicit teaching of grammar raises ELLs' awareness of English grammatical structures, which is a first step in internalizing the grammatical system of the English language.

The Importance of Teaching Standard English

There is another reason why teachers need to teach grammar to ELLs. Learning grammar is inextricably linked with power (Ehrenworth & Vinton, 2005). Writers who are able to express themselves in Standard English are able to make choices that students who lack facility in language do not have. Delpit (1988) suggests that grammar is a gatekeeper for students who do not know how to use Standard English. When writers do not use Standard English, they are frequently subject to "linguistic prejudice" (Zuidema, 2005) by readers who make assumptions about the writer. When teachers ignore the use of power inherent in language by ignoring grammar instruction, they work against their students' ability to move into places of power (Dean, 2008).

Standard English is the dialect that is used in academic writing. It is a "collection of the socially preferred dialects from various parts of the Unites States and other English-speaking countries" (Wolfram, Adger, & Christian, 1999, p. 17). ELLs often quickly acquire the features of English that enable them to interact with their peers. The dialect of English that students learn from their peers differs among the regions of the country and social groups in those regions (Mac-Neil, Cran, & McCrum, 2004). The dialect that students use may not be a written language, but all dialects have grammar, follow rules, and are a variety of English (Dean, 2008). Learning Standard English for academic writing is a different skill set. It can take as many as 10 years for ELLs to be able to read and write academic language as well as their native English counterparts (Graves & Rueda, 2009). Yet effective precise academic writing is a prerequisite for success in high school and beyond.

Language Differences

When learning Standard English, ELLs sometimes generalize their native language grammatical rules in their writing. This language transfer is helpful in some situations but an obstacle to learning in others (Gass & Selinker, 2001). For example, a Spanish speaker might say, "I want that you help me," which follows a typical Spanish sentence structure, instead of "I want you to help me." Grammatical errors such as this one immediately identify the writer as a non-native speaker, and can be distracting to the reader, or worse, can invoke the linguistic prejudice described earlier (a list of transfer errors for different languages can be found in Figure 6.1).

Each language has its own grammatical system, and other languages diverge from English in critical ways. According to Haussamen (2003) English is potentially different from other languages in a number of key ways. In other languages:

- The nouns might take gender.
- Articles are used differently, or there are no articles at all.
- Plurals may be formed by adding words or syllables to the sentence or by giving context clues in the sentence.
- The word order may not follow the familiar subject–verb–object pattern.
- Pronouns may not have to agree in gender or number with its antecedent.
- There could be fewer prepositions or the preposition may precede its object.

FIGURE 6.1. Sample transfer errors.		
Based on Johns, J. L., & Lenski, S. D. (2010). *Improving reading: Interventions, strategies, and resources* (5th ed.). Dubuque, IA: Kendal/Hunt. Parker, F., & Riley, K. (2010). *Linguistics for non-linguists: A primer with exercises* (5th ed). Boston: Allyn & Bacon. Raimes, A. ESL Center: Language Transfer Tip Sheet. Retrieved June 5, 2009, from *college.cengage.com/english/raimes/keys_writers/3e/instructors/esl/transfer. html*.		

Language Features	Language	Sample Transfer Error in English
Double negatives are routinely used	Spanish	He don't know nothing.
Definite articles omitted	Chinese, Japanese, Farsi, Russian, Swahili, Urdu	He is farmer. Father bought car.
Personal pronouns restate subject	Arabic, Spanish	My uncle he lives in California.
No -*ing*	Arabic, Chinese, Farsi, French, Greek, Portuguese, Spanish, Vietnamese,	I enjoy to play tennis. She study now.
Be is omitted	Arabic, Chinese, Creole, Haitian, Russian	He always busy. She working now.
No tense inflections	Chinese, Thai, Vietnamese	He have a good time yesterday. When I was little, I always walk to school.
Verb tense	Arabic, Chinese, Creole, Farsi, French, Haitian	I study here for a year. I need help yesterday.
No distinction between subject and object forms of pronouns	Chinese, Korean, Spanish, Thai,	I gave the paper to he.
Verb precedes subject.	classical Arabic, Hebrew, Russian, Spanish, Tagalog	Good grades received every student in the class.
Verb last	Bengali, German (in dependent clause), Hindi, Japanese, Korean, Turkish	. . . (when) the teacher the books collected.
That clause rather than infinitive	Arabic, Creole, French, Haitian, Hindi, Russian, Spanish	I want that he stay. I want that you try harder.
Subject can be omitted (especially pronoun)	Chinese, Japanese, Spanish, Thai	Is raining.
No equivalent of *there is/there are*	Japanese, Korean, Portuguese, Russian, Spanish, Thai	This book says four reasons to exercise. In the garden has many flowers.
No plural form after a number	Chinese, Farsi, Korean	Five new book.

Immigrant Students with Prior Grammatical Instruction

Some ELLs have already studied English before they arrived in the United States. Some students learned English in their home country; others learned English in refugee camps; still others learned English from relatives or friends. The students in your class may have had a variety of experiences learning English, some heavy on grammar and some heavy on conversation and vocabulary. According to Frodesen (2001), immigrant students who have learned English in their home country generally received considerable explicit grammar instruction and are often able to recite grammar terms and rules. These students, however, often have difficulty applying grammatical rules in writing. Leki (1992) found that even after 10 or more years of studying English in classrooms abroad, ELLs may still have trouble writing effectively in English, even though they are able to explain the most complex grammar rules. Other students come from schools in different regions of the United States. According to Leki (1992), many ELLs who have had writing instruction have spent more time on grammar drills than actually communicating through the written word.

Because ELLs differ so much in their experiences learning English grammar, it is important that teachers learn as much as they can about their ELLs' grammatical experiences. Ms. Brennan, for example, had seven ELLs in her fifth-grade classroom. Amir, who moved to the United States from Jordan, had been in Ms. Brennan's school for 3 years and was fluent in conversational English. Amir had had some English instruction in Jordan both in his school and from an English-speaking father. One student was from Somalia but had lived in refugee camps for 2 years, where he learned basic conversational English. Two of the ELLs were newcomers from Mexico who spoke no English. Two of the students were cousins who emigrated from the Philippines; and one student was newly arrived from China. Each of these last three students had studied English in their home country.

When teachers like Ms. Brennan have a variety of ELLs, it can help to design a more effective writing program if they learn something about the students' background. The teacher will most likely give a battery of assessments to learn about the ELLs. For ELLs who know English, one of the assessments teachers could give them is a short survey about their grammatical background. Finding out about a student's background in grammar can save valuable time as teachers consider the best way to engage ELLs in writing. For example, in Ms. Brennan's class, Bayani and Dalisay had extensive instruction in English grammar in their Filipino school so Ms. Brennan gave them a survey about their grammatical knowledge (see Figure 6.2 for Dalisay's survey). They did not have much experience in applying the skills, but they knew the names of the parts of speech. Therefore, Bayani and Dalisay did not need to be taught as much grammar explicitly as the other ELLs, but they needed instead to spend more time with authentic writing activities so they could apply grammatical concepts. None of Ms. Brennan's other ELLs had any knowledge of English grammar. They all needed explicit instruction in grammatical terms and rules.

FIGURE 6. 2. Learning about students' grammar backgrounds: Grammar survey for a fifth grader.

Name *Dalisay*

1. In what country did you learn English?
   Phiippines

2. Did you learn English in a school or in another type of class?
   I learned English at school, and I spent time talking English with my cousins because we were going to move here.

3. What kinds of things did you learn?
   - How to understand spoken English?
     Yes, we learned how to understand English when the teacher talked to us.
   - How to speak English?
     We did not practice speaking English in school but we talked English at home.
   - How to read English?
     No, we did not read English.
   - How to write English?
     No.
   - English grammar?
     Yes, we did grammar worksheets every day. I was the best in the class. I love doing grammar worksheets.

4. How did you learn English?
   - Through conversations?
     A little bit.
   - Through reading?
     No.
   - Through worksheets?
     Yes, many worksheets.

5. How well do you know these grammar terms?

Terms	Know it well	Seen or heard it	Never heard it
Noun	X		
Verb	X		
Preposition		X	
Adjective	X		
Adverb		X	
Capital letter	X		
Period	X		
Comma			X

HOW TO TEACH GRAMMAR

The trend in teaching grammar has changed over the past two decades. When many experienced teachers attended school, grammar was taught through drill, practice, and workbooks. Newer teachers may have experienced little grammar instruction. Weaver (2007) points out the range of teacher knowledge about grammar in today's schools: "Many experienced teachers need to unlearn the tactic of drilling parts of speech, many mid-career teachers usually incorporate only small doses of language instruction because of their uncertainties about syntax, and many young teachers know precious little about grammar" (p. xiii).

Recent reviews of research indicate that grammar should be taught both explicitly and through writing (Hillocks & Smith, 2003; Smith, Cheville, & Hillocks, 2006). Teaching grammar explicitly does not necessarily mean teaching it in isolation. Explicit teaching helps to take the guesswork out of learning so that students can give more attention to other aspects of the learning task. Smith and Wilhelm (2006) suggest that teachers spend time teaching about common writing programs, especially those that don't interfere with understanding. Instruction in grammar and usage, however, needs to be balanced with other interventions and instructional ideas presented in this book. Instruction should also give students plenty of opportunities to practice applying grammatical structures in their writing.

In order for ELLs to learn how to write academic English, teachers should consider spending time teaching the following grammatical terms or principles; some of which are described further:

1. Parts of speech
2. Subject and predicate
3. Usage, such as subject–verb agreement
4. Fragments and run-on sentences
5. Punctuation
6. Sentence order (subject, verb, object)
7. Pronoun use
8. Homophones
9. Contractions
10. Spelling
11. Verbs, consistency of tense
12. Descriptive words (adjectives, adverbs, phrases)

Teaching the Parts of Speech

ELLs may need to learn the parts of speech in the same way teachers introduce other new vocabulary terms. Although grammatical terms are abstract and hard for most students to understand, they provide a name for the concepts that are needed in order to discuss writing. For example, if a student hands in a piece of writing in which the subject and the verb do not agree, it is easier to help the student understand how to express the ideas in English if you are able to say, "This noun is singular and needs a singular verb." Noguchi (1991) writes that "some words are necessary to talk about language, and the traditional terms are more universal" (p. 17). Teaching the names of parts of speech is not important on its own; it is only important as you apply parts of speech to writing.

The eight parts of speech that are typically taught are

- Noun
- Verb
- Adjective
- Adverb
- Preposition
- Conjunction
- Pronoun
- Interjection

For younger students or students new to English, teachers might begin with more general terms and transition to common grammatical terms during the year. For example, Rog (2007) suggests that teachers use the terms "name parts" and "doing part" of sentences. She continues

> Telling young children that a sentence is a "complete thought" can be very confusing to them. Many "complete thoughts" are not complete sentences. However, teaching students that a sentence is a special group of words that has a *who* or *what* and an *is* or *does* gives them a framework for understanding what a sentence is. (p. 43)

As students learn about language, teachers should then transition to the more standard terminology.

Instructional Strategies for All Writers

Some instructional strategies for teaching grammar that Ms. Brennan found useful are teaching the vocabulary of parts of speech through a four-square vocabulary concept map, using children's books, practicing parts of speech through writing cinquains, applying parts of speech in short authentic writing such as menu writing, writing sentence frames, and having students identify parts of speech in their own writing through games such as Parts-of-Speech Bingo.

Four-Square Vocabulary Concept Map

The names of the parts of speech should be taught just like other abstract vocabulary terms. Abstract terms are more difficult to explain because they cannot be defined easily. As students learn English, however, they can learn the basic parts of speech. One way to teach new words is through a Four-Square Vocabulary Concept Map.

The Four-Square Vocabulary Concept Map provides students with four quadrants that help them understand new vocabulary terms (see Figure 6.3). Typically, students begin with the vocabulary word in the upper left-hand quadrant. In the example, the word *noun* is used. The teacher works with students to create a definition that they write in the bottom left-hand quadrant. For example, a noun is a person, place, or thing. Older or more advanced-level ELLs can go beyond that simple definition and produce an expanded definition such as the one in the example. In the upper right-hand quadrant, teachers should have students write a sentence with the part of speech underlined. In some situations, teachers can also have students write examples of words that are nouns, but because parts of speech are dependent on how they are used in sentences (*input* is typically a noun but is now also used as a verb), simple words could cause confusion. In the bottom right-hand quadrant students should write a sentence in which the words that are not examples of nouns are underlined. Older or more advanced-level ELLs can also write the reason these words are not nouns.

Using Children's Books

Parts of speech can be illustrated by reading children's books that use the different terms in context. Ms. Brennan read one of these books each week to show how the parts of speech in English are used. Some of the books she found most helpful include

- Cleary, B. P. (2000). *Hairy, scary, ordinary: What is an adjective?* Minneapolis, MN: Carolrhoda Books.
- Cleary, B. P. (2002). *A mink, a fink, a skating rink: What is a noun?* Minneapolis, MN: Carolrhoda Books.
- Cleary, B. P. (2002). *To root to toot to parachute: What is a verb?* Minneapolis, MN: Carolrhoda Books.
- Cleary, B. P. (2003). *Under, over, by the clover: What is a preposition?* Minneapolis, MN: Carolrhoda Books.
- Cleary, B. P. (2005). *Nearly, dearly, insincerely: What is an adverb?* Minneapolis, MN: Carolrhoda Books.
- Cleary, B. P. (2006). *A lime, a mime, a pool of slime: More about nouns.* Minneapolis, MN: Carolrhoda Books.

FIGURE 6.3. Four-Square Vocabulary activity.

Word to learn Noun	*Examples* *Nadia* found three *frogs* in the *pond.*
Definition A noun is a person, place, or thing. It is only capitalized if it names something. Sentences can have more than one noun.	*Nonexamples and reason* Nadia *found* three frogs in the pond. *Found* is used as the action in the sentence so it can't be a noun.

- Cleary, B. P. (2006). *I and you and don't forget who: What is a pronoun?* Minneapolis, MN: Carolrhoda Books.
- Cleary, B. P. (2006). *Slide and slurp, scratch and burp: More about verbs* Minneapolis, MN: Carolrhoda Books.
- Cleary, B. P. (2008). *Lazily, crazily, just a bit nasally: More about adverbs.* Minneapolis, MN: Carolrhoda Books.

Writing Cinquains

Some poetic forms, such as cinquains, are formed from specific parts of speech. A cinquain is an unrhymed poem consisting of five lines that are arranged in a special way. Cinquains are written by selecting nouns, adjectives, and action verbs in the five lines (see Figure 6.4). After students know the meaning of the terms *nouns*, *verbs*, and *adjectives*, Ms. Brennan reinforced the terms by having her students create cinquains. First, Ms. Brennan showed students a cinquain and explained how each line follows the cinquain pattern. She had to make sure her students knew how each part of the word is used in the poem so she had students who had a solid understanding of parts of speech work with students who did not understand. Then Ms. Brennan had the students brainstorm a list of nouns that they could use to write their own cinquains. After the students wrote their cinquains, Ms. Brennan emphasized the meanings of the grammatical terms (see Figure 6.4 for the cinquain pattern and a student example).

Menu Writing

Another way to help ELLs practice using parts of speech is to help them develop menus using adjectives, nouns, and verbs (Smith & Wilhelm, 2007). Ms. Ramos, the literacy coach, used this strategy with the beginning-level English proficiency writers from Ms. Brennan's class. She showed the students menus from nearby

---

FIGURE 6.4. The cinquain pattern and a student example.

Line 1: A noun, the title of the poem

Line 2: Two adjectives that describe what the poem is about

Line 3: Three action verbs that describe something the subject of the poem does

Line 4: A phrase that indicates a feeling related to the subject of the poem

Line 5: A noun that sums up the poem, renaming it

Backpack
Purple, heavy
Holding, embracing, carrying,
My life bending my back.
Bookbag.

eating establishments and discussed the kinds of terms the owners used to describe the food. Ms. Ramos then had students develop a menu either for school lunches or for their family dinner. She encouraged the students to use adjectives and adverbs as they wrote. After the students completed the activity, Ms. Ramos developed a list of student examples such as fish taco, white rice, and chicken soup. She then explained that in English adjectives typically come before nouns. Once the students understood that concept, she showed them the adjective, noun, verb sequence and later the adjective, noun, verb, object sequence. Each of these sequences reviewed not only how parts of speech can be used but the most typical sequences of English words.

Sentence Frames

Sentence frames can be used to reinforce parts of speech while having students write a sentence. Ms. Brennan developed a chart with the parts of speech that she taught on the upper line. Since she had already taught adjectives, nouns, verbs, adverbs, and prepositional phrases, Ms. Brennan wrote those on the lines. Then she divided students into groups and asked them to brainstorm words or phrases that could fit in each of the columns of the chart. Several of her students were very familiar with these parts of speech and had no difficulty. Others listened and learned. After the students developed a short list, Ms. Brennan asked them to volunteer words that could fit in each column. In the example found in Figure 6.5, the column "Adjective" includes the words *old, cranky,* and *fluorescent.* Ms. Brennan had groups of students create sentences using one word from each column, making sure the sentences made sense even if they were silly (e.g., The cranky peacock ran quickly under the car). She then had students share their sentences, and the class discussed how each of the parts of speech was used in the sentences.

Parts-of-Speech Bingo

Playing Parts-of-Speech bingo is a fun way for students to review the parts of speech. Ms. Brennan gave her students the opportunity to play this game when they were finished with their work. First, she had students fold a piece of paper into nine squares, and had them write the parts of speech that she had taught in

FIGURE 6.5. Sentence frame.

	Adjective	Noun	Verb	Adverb	Prepositional phrase
The	Old Cranky Fluorescent	Horse Peacock Platypus	Ran Inquired Objected	Quickly Loudly Obnoxiously	In the garden On the fence Under the car

the blanks. For example, Ms. Brennan had taught nouns, verbs, and adjectives so she had students list each of these parts of speech three different times. She then provided students with several written texts: some that she had written, a few written by other students, and some that she found in children's magazines. Each student selected a piece of text and worked to find a noun in the text. Once they found a noun, they could check off one square on their bingo card. Students continued finding parts of speech and marking their cards. Once they were finished, they turned in their cards for Ms. Brennan to correct.

TEACHING USAGE AND SPELLING

English usage is a group of opinions about the way words are used or ought to be used. Brians (2003) states, "the concept of errors in English usage is a fuzzy one" (p. iv). Some language experts work from rigid rules and want to *prescribe* how English should be used. They are the ones who prefer writers to follow "rules" and judge as incorrect writing that deviates from the rules. Other language experts do not believe in prescribing usage, but *describe* the patterns of how people use language in writing or speaking. They don't put a value judgment on how writers use language.

Some rules appear rather arbitrary. For example, the "rule" that sentences should not end with a preposition stems from Robert Lowth who published an *Introduction to English Grammar* in 1792. Lowth was one of the small number of 18th-century scholars who were trying to prove that English stemmed from Latin. Lowth held the opinion that English sentences should not end with prepositions even though he realized that some sentences will have prepositions at their end. Within 100 years this became a rule (Crystal, 2004).

The rule about ending a sentence with a preposition has the problem of altering the voice and sometimes the meaning of a sentence and is an example of the kind of usage rules that needs to be used judiciously (Ehrenworth & Vinton, 2005). For example, a student might write, "What are you waiting for?" Changing this sentence so that it does not end with a preposition makes it, "For what are you waiting?" This sentence sounds formal and unlike the kind of writing we want ELLs to learn. Teachers, therefore, need to balance expectations when asking students to apply the rules of usage, and students need to realize that rules can be flexible. In the end, writers need to formulate sentences that make sense to the reader as well as apply the rules of usage.

Spelling

Spelling is a cognitive skill that requires phonological processing, syntactic awareness, working memory, and orthographic processing (Low & Siegel, 2009). There are two main theories that help us understand how ELLs learn to spell. The universalist hypothesis, or linguistic-interdependent hypothesis, proposes that the development of literacy skills is shaped by common underlying cognitive and linguistic processes (Cummins, 1979a) so skills learned in native language transfer to the second language. The script-dependent hypothesis suggests that learning to spell in a second language is influenced by the degree of differences between the languages, such as whether the language is more or less phonetic than English and whether the language uses the same orthography. Research comparing English, Persian, and Chinese found that although the spelling strategies differed, the spelling outcomes were not significantly different (Low & Siegel, 2009). This means that the same instructional practices used with native English learners can be applied with ELLs (Lesaux & Siegel, 2003). According to Low and Siegel (2009), the research base indicates that "the key to spelling success for ELL children is the quality of instruction, as opposed to differentiated instruction" (p. 304).

Correcting Spelling and Usage Errors

Teachers used to correct every error with a red pen to indicate mistakes in writing. Mina Shaughnessy (1977) questioned this practice in her classic *Errors and Expectations.* One of Shaughnessy's maxims was that errors count but not as much as most teachers think. Research supports this viewpoint. Teachers who mark every error may feel like they're doing the right thing, but research suggests that marking errors does not make a difference in student writing (Rob, Ross, & Shortreed, 1986). Most errors tend to distract readers rather then distort meaning. Although the goal of writing is to communicate meaning without distractions, errors are actually a natural part of language development and are a window into a writer's development (Schleppegrell & Go, 2007). According to Díaz-Rico (2008), "persistent errors, rather than random mistakes, provide insight into the learner's rule set" (p. 246).

Understanding the kinds of errors that ELLs make in writing is critical. According to Parker and Riley (2010), spelling errors tend to be a direct result of the phonology of English. For example, words that have unstressed syllables, such as the second syllable in the word *interest,* are often deleted. In this case, the word is spelled *intrest* by novice spellers. This example and many others cause ELLs to have difficulty spelling correctly. Furthermore, ELLs do not unlearn their first language when they learn English. ELLs develop an interlanguage (Selinker, 1972) as they move from their first language to English. This interlanguage reflects the English rules they are learning as they intersect with the rules governing the first language. The way ELLs apply the rules of English is revealed by the errors they make when they write. Analyzing errors can help teachers identify patterns that ELLs are using while learning English.

Ms. Brennan decided to try an error analysis of some of her ELLs' writings. She was especially concerned about Rosi, who was a fairly recent immigrant from Mexico. Rosi was learning English rapidly and was beginning to apply several of the grammatical and usage rules that she had been taught. Ms. Brennan used Rosi's sample writing of a biography (see Figure 6.6) to decide how to best scaffold her writing.

FIGURE 6.6. Analyzing error patterns: Student example.

Hi! My name is Rosi and I have my story like everybody my story is about my famyli my famyli is more funny and smart my siste Kelly she likes to do everybody's hair and my other sister linda she likes to cleand my room and my House and my brother edwin He likes to watch T.V. and I like to do makeup my mom likes to clean like me sister and also I like to Draw because I love art like me Friend DJ and Kourtney and also my sister Kelly.

the end

After carefully reading Rosi's paper, Ms. Brennan decided that Rosi was making sufficient progress in writing considering the time she had spent in the country. She developed a chart that detailed what she learned from Rosi's writing (see Figure 6.7) and concluded that she would have Rosi concentrate on some of the areas in which Rosi had demonstrated learning. She decided to remind Rosi to capitalize proper nouns, especially names. She also gave Rosi extra assistance in writing simple sentences. Finally, Ms. Brennan reviewed when to use *me* and when to use *my*. Ms. Brennan recognized that Rosi had additional errors in her writing, but she knew that overwhelming Rosi with too many areas to learn all at once would not be beneficial. Instead, Ms. Brennan tried to help Rosi focus on just three areas for her next piece of writing.

Teaching Punctuation

Punctuation is the use of marks to separate words into sentences, phrases, and clauses to clarify meaning. Punctuation marks are signals to readers for inflection and when to pause or stop. Speakers can make their meanings clear by changing

---

FIGURE 6.7. Rule application chart for the student whose writing is shown in Figure 6.6.

Nearing proficient	Learning	Has not yet learned
Capital I	Capital letters for names	Sentence sense
Spelling of sight words and many nouns	Additional pronoun "my sister she"	Spelling of famyli, correct letters, wrong order
	"Me" and "my" confused	Capital letters and ending marks for sentences
	Organization of paragraph is emerging, not perfect, but generally follows main idea, details, conclusion	

tone, stopping, or pausing. During writing, however, punctuation marks fulfill this role. There are rules that govern how to place punctuation marks; however, punctuation can also be a decision that is influenced by a writer's personal preferences. Punctuation marks that students need to learn are periods, question marks, commas, semicolons, colons, exclamation points, and apostrophes. Even native English-speaking students often have difficulty with punctuation.

Apostrophes are punctuation marks that deserve special attention because they can be confusing for ELLs. English uses the Latin alphabet, as discussed in Chapter 3, and it has one special punctuation mark that does more than signal a pause during writing. Apostrophes have three uses:

1. To form possessives of nouns (*Robert's, students'*).
2. To show omission of letters (*can't*).
3. To indicate plurals of lowercase letters (*p's* and *q's*).

Many novice writers, including ELLs, may overgeneralize the rules they learn, including how to use apostrophes and where to put them when making nouns plural (Ariza, Morales-Jones, Yahya, & Zainuddin, 2002). While overgeneralizing is part of the developmental process of language acquisition, students should be taught that apostrophes should not be used for possessive pronouns or for noun plurals, including acronyms.

Rosi was also developing her skill using punctuation. Since Rosi's first language was Spanish, she had to learn a partially different set of punctuation skills when writing English. Her writing indicates that she is learning punctuation but needs continued practice. After looking at Rosi's paper, Ms. Brennan decided to congratulate Rosi on her use of the exclamation point at the beginning of the paper. Even though Rosi used the exclamation point in an unusual way for English writing, it shows that she was trying to use the punctuation marks that she was learning. Rosi's writing also had one period at the end of the piece. Ms. Brennan knew that teaching Rosi how to write in sentences and punctuate those sentences could take weeks or months of teaching. She resolved to provide all of her ELLs with more instruction in writing simple sentences.

UNIQUE FEATURES OF ENGLISH

Every language has unique features, and English is no exception (Bolton, 1982). Three of the features of English that ELLs have difficulty learning are contractions, homonyms, and idioms.

Contractions

Contractions are a part of English that confuses many ELLs. Contractions are two words put together, and unlike some languages in which two or three words are slurred together in conversation but not in writing, contractions have a written form. Contractions need to be explicitly taught to ELLs. Teachers can also help ELLs understand that contractions are an informal way of speaking and writing, and that some formal writing prohibits contractions. At one time contractions were considered incorrect to use in formal essays. Now, however, contractions are often used in writing that is fairly formal. (Teachers should check with the rules for state tests to determine whether contractions are allowed.) Teachers should make it clear to ELLs which writing assignments are informal and which are formal. Teachers should also explain that contractions are often used in dialogue since they are used frequently in conversations. Figure 6.8 has a list of contractions that should be taught to ELLs.

Homonyms, Homophones, Homographs, and Frequently Confused Words

There are three kinds of homonyms. One is the words that sound and look alike such as *bank*, which could be used as the bank of a river and a bank to put money in. Another type of homonym is homophones, which are words that are pronounced alike but do not look alike (e.g., *write* and *right*). English also has words that are classified as homographs: words that look alike but do not sound alike. An example is *tear* as in the sentences: "The movie made her *tear* up," and "He

FIGURE 6.8. Common contractions.			
Two words	**Contraction**	**Two words**	**Contraction**
are not	aren't	I am	I'm
cannot	can't	I have	I've
could not	couldn't	I will	I'll
could have	could've	I would	I'd
did not	didn't	you are	you're
do not	don't	you have	you've
does not	doesn't	she is	she's
have not	haven't	she will	she'll
is not	isn't	he is	he's
let us	let's	he would	he'd
should not	shouldn't	they have	they've
were not	weren't	they would	they'd
will not	won't	we are	we're
would not	wouldn't	we will	we'll

wanted to *tear* his paper to bits." There are more than 3,000 homographs in the English language (McArthur, 1992). Homonyms, homophones, and homographs are all used differently and have different meanings (the chart in Figure 6.9 illustrates the differences). English also has words that sound similar but are spelled differently and have different meanings, such as *affect* and *effect* (see Figure 6.10 for a list of commonly confused words).

ELLs, as well as novice writers, typically find all types of homonyms confusing. These words are difficult to teach because some of them are function words that cannot be easily defined (e.g., *there*). Since these words are so often misused, they tend to be key markers that readers use to judge a writer's work. For example, a beautifully written essay may be judged as inadequate if the writer uses *it's* for *its*. It is important, therefore, that teachers spend time teaching and reviewing the words that are often misused, such as the words listed in Figure 6.10. Since it takes typical writers many years to master these words, it is important that teachers of ELLs continue to review these words several times each year and not be discouraged if the learners do not remember them.

Emphasizing Differences

When teaching homonyms, homophones, and homographs, it's important to emphasize the differences between the words. For example, Ms. Brennan wanted to teach the words *red* and *read*. She decided to write the words on a whiteboard and to draw a picture for each one under the word. For *red*, she used a red marker to draw a picture of a red dress. For the word *read*, she used a black marker to draw a picture of a student reading a book. The pictures helped the students to understand which word to use.

Using Children's Books

Children's books are another way to teach students the differences between words. One popular author, Peggy Parish, wrote books about Amelia Bedelia, a maid for a wealthy American family. In the books, Amelia Bedelia has all sorts of adventures that Parish described with homonyms, metaphors, and idioms. Parish wrote 12 books from 1963 to 1988 and her nephew has written 13 books since 1996.

FIGURE 6.9. Homonyms, homophones, and homographs.				
	Same sound	Same spelling	Different sound	Different spelling
Homonym	X	X		
Homophone	X			X
Homograph		X	X	

FIGURE 6.10. Commonly confused words.

Affect and effect
Affect means to have some influence on and is typically used as a verb.
- How much you practice will *affect* how quickly you learn.

Effect usually means the results of something or to bring about.
- We liked the special *effects* of the film.
- We saw the *effect* that the puppy had on the children.

Its and it's
Its is a possessive pronoun.
- The dog chased *its* tail.

The contraction *it's* stands for *it is*.
- *It's* warm outside today.

There, their, and they're
The word *there* shows place or is used to begin a sentence.
- We are going to play soccer over *there*.
- *There* are 10 students in my English class.

The word *their* is a plural pronoun used to show possession.
- The football players threw off *their* helmets at the end of the game.

They're is a contraction for the words *they are*.
- I asked Juan and José to go to the movies, but *they're* going fishing this weekend instead.

Than and then
The word *than* is used for comparisons.
- Marta is taller *than* Shelly is.

Then is used to refer to time.
- Sabine was here but *then* she went home to babysit for her sister.

Two, to, and too
Two is used as the number that represents one plus one.
- He was hungry so he ordered *two* hamburgers.

To is used in infinitives and prepositional phrases.
- She wanted *to* run in the cross-country meet.
- Charlie went *to* the video store.

Too is used to mean *also* and to show emphasis.
- I want a candy bar *too*.
- He ate *too* much ice cream.

Weather and whether
Weather refers to the atmospheric conditions.
- It's beautiful *weather* today so let's go to the beach.

Whether is a word that means *if* and it typically is used to compare two things.
- *Whether* or not you feel like it, you have to finish your homework.

Whose and who's
Whose is a possessive pronoun.
- I don't know *whose* purse this is, but I want to return it.

The word *who's* is a contraction for *who is*.
- *Who's* going to come to my party?

(cont.)

FIGURE 6.10. *(cont.)*

Your and you're
Your is a possessive pronoun.
 • I saw *your* brother at the movies.
You're is a contraction for the words *you are.*
 • *You're* the kind of person who can learn easily.

Idioms

An idiom is a phrase in which the words together have a different meaning from the definitions of the individual words. All languages have idioms that are commonly used in conversation and writing. Some idioms are quite similar to English ones, and others are very different. According to the *Dictionary of American Idioms* (Makkai, Belmonte, Boatner, & Gates, 2004), there are at least 8,000 English idioms. Teachers may be surprised at how often they use idioms in the classroom. A study of 18 elementary teachers found that 36% of all of the teachers' utterances were multiple-meaning words. At least one idiom occurred in 11.5% of all utterances, and idioms were used with increasing frequency as grade increased (Lazar, Warr-Leeper, & Nicholson, 1989).

Some idioms that ELLs could hear in classroom conversations are

- Barking up the wrong tree
- Bent over backwards
- Clear the air
- Couch potato
- Down in the dumps
- Get the ball rolling
- Hold your horses
- I'm all ears
- In the doghouse
- Lose your cool
- Read my mind
- Under the weather
- Work like a dog

Helping ELLs learn how to speak and write with idiomatic expressions can give their writing an authentic feel. Teachers, however, should help students understand that idioms are used more frequently in informal writing rather than in formal writing. ELLs need to experiment using idioms and will most likely make many mistakes as they learn.

Teachers can help ELLs learn idioms by encouraging them to develop lists of idioms that they hear in conversations that could be incorporated into their writing. To help students think about idioms, teachers can read children's books such as the ones that follow and have students try writing and illustrating other idioms they hear.

- Gwyne, F. (1970). *The king who rained*. New York: Scholastic.
- Gwyne, F. (1976). *A chocolate moose for dinner*. New York: Scholastic.
- Gwyne, F. (1988). *A little pigeon toad*. New York: Scholastic.
- Terban, M. (1998). *Scholastic dictionary of idioms*. New York: Scholastic.
- Terban, M., & Huffman, T. (1990). *Punching the clock: Funny action idioms*. New York: Scholastic.
- Terban, M., & Maestro, G. (2007). *In a pickle: And other funny idioms*. New York: Scholastic.
- Terban, M., & Maestro, G. (2007). *Mad as a wet hen!: And other funny idioms*. New York: Scholastic.

DEVELOPING INDIVIDUAL AND CLASSROOM GRAMMAR GOALS

Teaching grammar and usage are important components of writing instruction. As students learn English, they also need to learn how to write English so that it can be read. In this case, it's tempting to spend *too much* time teaching grammar and usage. Teachers can feel as if they have so much ground to cover that they spend more time than is warranted teaching and reinforcing grammatical rules. To stem this tide, teachers should consider helping students set individual goals and community goals for their classroom. For example, Ms. Brennan helped Rosi set three individual goals for writing:

*Grammar
Goals
Anchor Chart
Pocket Chart?*

1. Capitalize names.
2. Divide writing into sentences.
3. Learn when to use *me* and when to use *my*.

In addition to helping students set individual goals, Ms. Brennan can set classroom goals that take into account the needs of the students. These goals can focus students' attention as she decides which areas to address. As stated earlier, Ms. Brennan is a classroom teacher who had seven ELLs in her class, with a variety of backgrounds and needs in writing. Ms. Brennan, however, can set short-term goals such as helping students write sentences with punctuation. To scaffold her students' learning, Ms. Brennan could focus on capital letters and periods for her emergent learners, subject–verb agreement for her intermediate learners, and possibly sentence variety for her advanced learners.

As students make progress on their grammar and usage goals, their writing becomes more clear and readable. Learning grammar is not an end in itself, but it can lead to powerful writing.

SUMMARY

ELLs come to the classroom with different needs for grammar instruction than native speakers. Some ELLs may have learned grammar before coming to the United States whereas others have little or no knowledge of the rules that govern English. All ELLs, however, need to learn how English works, and this means teaching grammar explicitly.

Grammar, usage, punctuation, and spelling can all be taught through games and activities; they don't need to be taught through drills and worksheets. Activities such as Parts-of-Speech Bingo, menu writing, and sentence frames all reinforce grammatical terms that have been taught previously. In addition, teachers can conduct error analyses to determine how ELLs are applying the rules that they have been taught. Error analysis can help students focus on achievable goals as they learn English and how to communicate in writing.

WEB RESOURCES

English Grammar Help
esl.about.com/od/englishgrammar

Grammatical information, games, and worksheets.

Homophones
www.all-about-spelling.com/list-of-homophones.html

Lists homophones.

Idioms
www.idiomsite.com

Lists common idioms.

Interesting Things for ESL Students
www.manythings.org

Games, puzzles, slang, and proverbs.

One Stop English
www.onestopenglish.com/section.asp?docid=145114

Lesson plans on grammar and vocabulary.

Using English
www.usingenglish.com

Tools and resources for teachers including grammar glossary and references of irregular verbs, idioms, and other information.

CHAPTER 7

Assessing Writing

Spring had arrived, and teachers were busy selecting writing samples for students' portfolios. Each student in Mrs. Reece's seventh-grade class needed a formal writing sample added to the portfolio along with writing samples from other content areas. Among the students were eight ELLs. Luis and Marissa were migrant students who had just joined the class a few weeks earlier. Their English was not yet fluent, and due to their frequent moves, they had not had consistent instruction in either writing or English language development. Asha and her brother, Rajiv, had made excellent progress in English since they arrived from India last summer. They had both been well schooled in Calcutta before moving to the United States. Ivan had been in the United States for 2 years and was making progress as an intermediate-level ELL. Ana and Marisol had been born in the United States, but spoke Spanish at home and with their friends. Lien, a highly motivated immigrant from China, was the most advanced-level ELL in the class.

Mrs. Reece knew that it would not be fair to judge these students' writing samples according to the same criteria as her native English-speakers' writing. In fact, she doubted that any one set of criteria would be fair for all of her ELLs so she asked Ms. Ramos, the literacy coach, for help. Together they sat down and looked at the state English language development standards for writing. Using the standards, they were able to develop rubrics for the students at each stage of English language proficiency.

Assessment is a "process of collecting and documenting evidence of student learning and progress to make informed instructional, placement, programmatic, and/ or evaluative decisions to enhance student learning, as is the case of assessment of the monolingual or mainstream learner" (Ehlers-Zavala, 2002, pp. 8–9). Assessments are also used to determine grades. Some schools have predetermined ways of deciding what criteria are used to give students grades. If this is the case, teachers will, of course, want to follow their school's guidelines. If the school does not set criteria for determining grades, the teacher will want to consider how much weight to give to objective measures, such as tests and quizzes, as opposed to more subjective measures, such as improvement, effort, and motivation.

When assessing her ELLs, Mrs. Reece needed to remember that they are a very diverse group. Therefore, she needed to keep in mind the background of each individual student. Some of the questions she asked herself are: Is the student a newcomer or has he or she been in the United States for several years? What kind of literacy background does the student have in the home language? Is the child bilingual? (Freeman & Freeman, 2004; Rhodes, Ochoa, & Ortiz, 2005). The answers to these questions helped direct Mrs. Reece to different kinds of assessments that would, in turn, give her different information about her students' abilities and achievements. Assessments need to mirror instructional content and methodology/practice, and need to be analyzed in light of specific criteria, such as age, proficiency level, learning styles, and educational background in the home language (Teachers of English to Speakers of Other Languages [TESOL], 2001). This chapter discusses the kinds of assessments that teachers like Mrs. Reece can use to assess ELLs' writing development and what to consider when developing a comprehensive assessment program for writing.

DEVELOPING AN ASSESSMENT PROGRAM

The first step in the assessment process is planning which assessments to give and how to use them. Mrs. Reece knew that there are many purposes for assessment and wanted to identify the assessment objectives that she had for her students. Mrs. Reece's main purpose for writing assessment was to show growth over the course of the year. Some secondary purposes for assessments that she considered were to inform instruction, monitor and compare student performance, identify students eligible for special services, and evaluate programs (García, McKoon, & August, 2006a). Each of these purposes has value, and assessment tools look different and will produce different kinds of information for each one.

Categories of Assessments

Assessments fall into two categories: formative and summative. Formative assessment is usually informal, and is ongoing. Formative assessments are used to make daily decisions regarding instruction. Mrs. Reece used formative assessments regularly to determine what specific aspect of writing she needed to focus on with her seventh graders. According to Teale (2009), research supports conducting assessment for ELLs on an ongoing basis. Summative assessments, on the other hand, are usually more formal, such as annual state assessments, and are given according to a schedule. Summative assessments are generally used to make decisions about programs and for monitoring progress of individuals or groups of students over time (TESOL, 2001). Teachers tend to spend an inordinate amount of time preparing for summative assessments; however, the time it takes to prepare for high-stakes tests can take away from valuable instructional time (Cunningham & Cunningham, 2010). Figure 7.1 lists a range of formative and summative assessments that Mrs. Reece considered as she planned her assessment program.

	Formative	Summative
Features	• Focus on process • Open-ended • Scoring is subjective • Writing samples produced for authentic purposes	• Focus on product • Closed-ended • Scoring is objective • Writing samples elicit specific forms or content
Examples	• Anecdotal records • Checklists • Compositions • Conferences • Dialogue journals • Dictation • Elicitation • Grammatical transformation • Handwriting **assessments** • Open-ended response tasks • Paraphrasing • Picture-cued tasks • Portfolios • Rating scales • Self-assessments • Short-answer responses • Spelling tests • Vocabulary tests	• Cloze tests • Curriculum-based measurements • Elicitation • Grammatical transformation • Limited-response tasks • Ordering • Spelling tests • Standardized tests • Timed tests • Vocabulary tests

FIGURE 7.1. Formative and summative writing assessments.

Planning for Assessment

The first thing Mrs. Reece and the team of seventh-grade teachers did was look at both language and content-learning objectives and decide what it was that they wanted to assess. They knew it would not be possible to assess all of their objectives, so they had to choose which ones were most important. Once they knew what language objectives they wanted to assess, Mrs. Reece and her colleagues carefully crafted writing prompts in order to elicit those aspects of language. They designed their prompts to measure desired features of grammar (e.g., past or future tense, irregular verbs), spelling, vocabulary (any content vocabulary that is relevant to the writing task), and text organization, and discussed whether the assessments were formative or summative.

The teachers also considered their content objectives when designing the writing scenarios for their ELLs. They considered to what extent assessments allow ELLs to use higher-order thinking skills to complete the writing task and whether the assessments encouraged students to explore new ideas and express their thinking. They also discussed how they would modify the task for students at different language proficiency levels (see Chapter 2 for writing categories).

Mrs. Reece and her colleagues, along with Ms. Ramos, also looked at their district and state language development standards when creating their writing prompts and discussed the extent to which their assessments matched the standards. They wanted to ensure that the tasks they developed were appropriate to the students' language proficiency levels, and when assessing ELLs at the same time as native English speakers, modify the task according to the proficiency of the ELLs (Willner, Rivera, & Acosta, 2009).

Finally, the seventh-grade team planned their directions carefully so that they were explicit about what they wanted students to do and how the students should do it, how much time they would have, and what factors they wanted considered when grading the assessments. For the assessments that were graded by a rubric, the teachers aligned the categories with the objectives and activities of the lesson, and they planned to present the rubric to the students to make sure that they understood it and knew how to use it to help them with their writing.

Selecting Assessments

There were a number of factors that Mrs. Reece needed to consider when developing an assessment plan. The first thing she did was talk with Ms. Ramos about the assessment budget. When developing writing assessments for ELLs or when purchasing ready-made assessment tools, Mrs. Reece needed to consider whether the assessment was affordable and whether the tool would be worth the money that would be invested in it, in terms of student growth in writing or accountability. A second consideration was time. They considered whether the time it took the teachers to plan to design, score, and interpret the results of the assessment tools themselves was reasonable. A third consideration was reliability and validity. For composition-based assessments, the teachers needed to consider what would be the inter-rater reliability among the scorers (see below for a discussion of reliability). Finally, they discussed whether the assessments and the purposes for the assessments were acceptable to students, parents, and the community (Genesse & Upshur, 1996).

Reliability

Reliability in writing assessments has to do with consistency of evaluation of writing samples from one rater to another, from a student's work on one day to that student's work on another day, and from one student's work to another student's work. Determining test reliability is not an exact science. Reliability can only be estimated (Genesse & Upshur, 1996). To have the best chance of inter-rater reliability among the seventh-grade teachers, Ms. Ramos trained them in rating techniques and criteria. She had anchor papers available as examples so the raters could see different levels of writing (Norris, Brown, Hudson, & Yoshioka, 1998). TESOL (2001) recommends that there should be approximately 85% agreement among raters.

Validity

Writing assessment validity is concerned with how well the writing test actually measures what it is supposed to measure. Is the assessment designed to determine the extent of a student's skills in spelling, grammatical usage, vocabulary, organization of ideas, content knowledge, or other skill areas? Do the assessment activities or prompts effectively elicit the kinds of vocabulary, grammatical points, content concepts, and so on that the teacher wants to assess? Does the measurement of the student's writing skills on one assessment correlate with assessments of those skills on other assessment instruments? (Ariza, 2010). These are questions that Mrs. Reece and her colleagues considered when designing or selecting a writing assessment tool for ELLs.

Analyzing and Interpreting Assessment Data

When Mrs. Reece and the other seventh-grade teachers were almost ready to administer the writing assessments to their students, they discussed how they would analyze and interpret the work of their ELLs. They discussed what kinds of modifications needed to be made for the ELLs to ensure that their writing samples would be judged according to standards that are at the same time, rigorous and attainable. Another factor they considered was whether the information collected was under a time constraint and whether that affected the ELLs' performance.

Open-ended response tasks allow students a great deal of freedom in responding to writing prompts. There are two ways to score open-ended response tasks: holistically and analytically. A holistic score is a single score or grade that is given to the entire composition. Holistic scores reflect teachers' impression of the work as a whole and give students generalized feedback about their performance.

In analytic scoring, the teacher, or other rater, assigns separate scores to different aspects of the composition such as spelling, conventions, grammar, organization, and content. The categories that are rated in an analytical scoring system should reflect lesson objectives (Genesee & Upshur, 1996). Ms. Ramos helped the seventh-grade teachers think about their expectations for ELLs when determining performance levels for students' writing. Since she had more experience than Mrs. Reece and the other teachers in assessing the writing of ELLs, she could more easily judge what constitutes fair expectations for students at different proficiency levels. Creating rubrics for students at different language proficiency levels takes time up front, but it can save teachers time in the long run, and it is more fair for ELLs than scoring their writing according to the same proficiency standards as native English-speaking students' work is scored. Like Mrs. Reece and her colleagues, teams of teachers might want to work together to create a set of general rubrics, based on state or district standards, for ELLs at different proficiency levels in different grades. The sample rubrics that follow (Figures 7.2, 7.3, and 7.4) are based on state standards.

Very young primary students may have little concern about how their work is graded. But by the time students reach the age in which they are taking inter-

FIGURE 7.2. Writing rubric for beginning ELLs: Grade level 3–5.

Developing Application of Beginning-Level Standards	Proficient Application of Beginning-Level Standards	Exemplary Application of Beginning-Level Standards
Conventions: Student rarely uses capitalization when writing own name and at the beginning of sentences.	Conventions: Student uses capitalization inconsistently when writing own name and at the beginning of sentences.	Conventions: Student consistently uses capitalization when writing own name and at the beginning of sentences.
Conventions: Student rarely uses a period or question mark at the end of a sentence.	Conventions: Student inconsistently uses a period or question mark at the end of a sentence.	Conventions: Student consistently uses a period or question mark at the end of a sentence.
Handwriting: Student's writing of the English alphabet is illegible.	Handwriting: Student's writing of the English alphabet is partly legible.	Handwriting: Student's writing of the English alphabet is consistently legible.
Vocabulary: Student is unable to label more than a few key parts of common objects.	Vocabulary: Student is able to label some key parts of common objects.	Vocabulary: Student is able to label most or all key parts of common objects.
Structure: Student has difficulty creating simple sentences or phrases with some assistance.	Structure: Student is able to create some simple sentences or phrases with some assistance.	Structure: Student consistently creates simple sentences or phrases with some assistance.
Structure: Student has difficulty writing short narratives using models.	Structure: Student is sometimes able to write short narratives using models.	Structure: Student is consistently successful at writing short narratives using models.
Grammar: During group writing activities, student's writing of brief narratives and stories rarely follows correct usage of a few standard grammatical forms.	Grammar: During group writing activities, student is able to write brief narratives and stories with some inconsistent use of a few standard grammatical forms.	Grammar: During group writing activities, student is able to write brief narratives and stories with consistently correct use of a few standard grammatical forms.

est in how their work is being evaluated, it is important for teachers to be explicit about their criteria for scoring writing samples. Reviewing together some examples of exemplary, proficient, and developing writing samples will help students to understand their teacher's expectations for their work. This explicit explanation of expectations is especially helpful for ELLs, because it helps them to prioritize where to spend their cognitive resources and allows them to focus on the important aspects of the writing task. Ms. Ramos reminded the teachers that writing that is considered in the developing range for a student at one language acquisition level might be proficient or exemplary for a student at a lower level (Figure 7.5

FIGURE 7.3. Writing rubric for intermediate ELLs: Grade level 3–5.

Developing Application of Intermediate-Level Standards	Proficient Application of Intermediate-Level Standards	Exemplary Application of Intermediate Level Standards
Conventions: Student occasionally produces independent writing that may include some periods, correct spelling, and inconsistent capitalization.	Conventions: Student produces some independent writing that may include some periods, correct spelling, and inconsistent capitalization.	Conventions: Student regularly produces independent writing that includes periods, correct spelling, and consistent capitalization.
Structure: Student rarely uses standard word order, but may have some inconsistent grammatical forms (e.g., subject–verb agreement).	Structure: Student sometimes uses standard word order, but may have some inconsistent grammatical forms (e.g., subject–verb agreement).	Structure: Student regularly uses standard word order, but may have some inconsistent grammatical forms (e.g., subject–verb agreement).
Structure: Student has difficulty narrating with some detail a sequence of events.	Structure: Student is sometimes able to narrate with some detail a sequence of events.	Structure: Student is consistently able to narrate with some detail a sequence of events.
Organization: Student has difficulty independently creating cohesive paragraphs that develop a central idea with consistent use of standard grammatical forms (some rules may not be followed).	Organization: Student sometimes independently creates cohesive paragraphs that develop a central idea with consistent use of standard grammatical forms (some rules may not be followed).	Organization: Student regularly independently creates cohesive paragraphs that develop a central idea with consistent use of standard grammatical forms (some rules may not be followed).
Grammar: Student has difficulty producing independent writing that is understood when read, but may include inconsistent use of standard grammatical forms.	Grammar: Student is sometimes able to produce independent writing that is understood when read, but may include inconsistent use of standard grammatical forms.	Grammar: Student regularly produces independent writing that is understood when read, but may include inconsistent use of standard grammatical forms.
Genre: Student does not begin to use a variety of genres in writing (e.g., expository, narrative, poetry).	Genre: Student begins to attempt using a variety of genres in writing (e.g., expository, narrative, poetry).	Genre: Student begins to successfully use a variety of genres in writing (e.g., expository, narrative, poetry).
Vocabulary: Student has difficulty using more complex vocabulary and sentences appropriate for language arts and other content areas (e.g., math, science, social studies).	Vocabulary: Student sometimes uses more complex vocabulary and sentences appropriate for language arts and other content areas (e.g., math, science, social studies).	Vocabulary: Student regularly uses more complex vocabulary and sentences appropriate for language arts and other content areas (e.g., math, science, social studies).
Genre: Student has difficulty writing a letter independently by using detailed sentences.	Genre: Student is sometimes able to write a letter independently by using detailed sentences.	Genre: Student is consistently able to write a letter independently by using detailed sentences.

FIGURE 7.4. Writing rubric for advanced ELLs: Grade level 3–5.

Developing Application of Advanced-Level Standards	Proficient Application of Advanced-Level Standards	Exemplary Application of Advanced-Level Standards
Grammar: Student occasionally uses complete sentences and correct word order.	Grammar: Student often uses complete sentences and correct word order.	Grammar: Student consistently uses complete sentences and correct word order.
Grammar: Student has difficulty using correct parts of speech, including correct subject–verb agreement.	Grammar: Student often uses correct parts of speech, including correct subject–verb agreement.	Grammar: Student consistently uses correct parts of speech, including correct subject–verb agreement.
Conventions: Student has difficulty editing writing for punctuation, capitalization, and spelling.	Conventions: Student often edits writing for punctuation, capitalization, and spelling.	Conventions: Student consistently edits writing for punctuation, capitalization, and spelling.
Conventions: Student has difficulty producing writing that demonstrates command of the conventions of Standard English.	Conventions: Student often produces writing that demonstrates command of the conventions of Standard English.	Conventions: Student consistently produces writing that demonstrates command of the conventions of Standard English.
Genre: Student has difficulty writing narratives that describe the setting, characters, objects, and events.	Genre: Student often writes narratives that describe the setting, characters, objects, and events.	Genre: Student consistently writes narratives that describe the setting, characters, objects, and events.
Genre: Student has difficulty writing persuasive compositions by using standard grammatical forms.	Genre: Student often writes persuasive compositions by using standard grammatical forms.	Genre: Student consistently writes persuasive compositions by using standard grammatical forms.
Genre: Student has difficulty writing multiple paragraph narrative and expository compositions by using standard grammatical forms.	Genre: Student often writes multiple paragraph narrative and expository compositions by using standard grammatical forms.	Genre: Student consistently writes multiple paragraph narrative and expository compositions by using standard grammatical forms.
Process: Student has difficulty independently using all the steps of the writing process.	Process: Student often independently uses all the steps of the writing process.	Process: Student consistently independently uses all the steps of the writing process.
Genre: Student has difficulty writing short narratives that include examples of writing appropriate for language arts and other content areas (e.g., math, science, social studies).	Genre: Student often writes short narratives that include examples of writing appropriate for language arts and other content areas (e.g., math, science, social studies).	Genre: Student consistently writes short narratives that include examples of writing appropriate for language arts and other content areas (e.g., math, science, social studies).

FIGURE 7.5. Student writing sample: Intermediate-level English language proficient.

My Dream

My big sister made a swin, and I was swinging on it, and it broke, and I flew of, and landed in a pricely bush. My dad spakt me for no reesen so he carried me up and down the stairs. I was deaming that a bunch of sheeps ran over me and I really felt it. I fond my little sister homework in my backpack. I went to bleu lake park and large waves came and I was in the deep water, and I was so scared I cald for help.

---

shows an example of an intermediate-level English language proficient writer according to Mrs. Reece and her colleagues).

Limited-response tasks, unlike open-ended response tasks, elicit very specific answers. Limited-response task items will often be marked either right or wrong. As such, the scoring of these assessments is relatively straightforward. At other times, the items will be scaled; that is, they have the possibility of receiving partial credit. It is important to determine ahead of time the criteria for credit on the different test items. The final test score will be the sum of the credit given to individual test items.

For open-ended response tasks, it's best to use a scoring rubric. Mrs. Reece and her colleagues developed a set of standards-based rubrics for the seventh-grade ELLs. These rubrics allowed the teachers to consistently score each student's paper and to consider the different criteria that they had determined ahead of time. At times, teachers may want to work together to give multiple ratings to students' papers. This requires that all teachers involved be trained to ensure consistency and reliability among raters.

Interpreting the Information

Once the writing tests were scored, Mrs. Reece and her colleagues needed to return to their objectives and the purposes of the assessment in order to interpret the data. Ms. Ramos explained that when the purpose is to determine a student's strengths and weaknesses in order to plan instruction, the teacher will be able to create a class profile on the basis of how well students performed on different test items or on the different scoring criteria that the teacher set ahead of time. Mrs. Reece had noticed that many of the seventh graders had struggled with organization in their writing samples, and she mentioned that to the team. Teachers may want to use an assessment to look for students' strengths and weaknesses in a particular area of writing as a pretest, in preparation for instruction. When assessing aspects of writing such as spelling, grammar, conventions, and specific vocabulary, the same instrument can be used for both the pre- and posttest assessments.

Ms. Ramos showed the teachers that finding out how well students mastered material in a particular unit is similar to looking for students' strengths and weaknesses, except that all criteria being used to score the test is taught, usually in the lesson that the students are currently working on or have just completed. If teachers find a category on a mastery test in which many students did poorly, they may reteach that material. If only a few students did poorly on a particular strand of the test, it might be most beneficial to plan a small-group mini-lesson on that topic during a writers' workshop.

Mrs. Reece then asked whether there are assessments that predict a student's chances of doing well on a state writing assessment, so that students who are not meeting a benchmark can be provided with interventions to improve their performance. Ms. Ramos shared that in this case, a benchmark indicating the score a student needs to achieve to have a significant chance of passing the state assessment is already established. Students whose work falls below the benchmark should be given intervention instruction. An analysis of students' writing samples will usually give teachers clues about the aspects of writing for which students need additional instruction.

Ms. Ramos also clarified that if the assessment is being given for accountability purposes or to evaluate a program's effectiveness, then it is not individual scores, but a class, school, or district composite score that will be of most interest. If the composite scores reveal that a significant percentage of students are not adequately achieving, an analysis of the writing program's strengths and weaknesses is in order. This analysis gives teachers an opportunity to fill in gaps in the program and discover how they can best meet the students' needs.

PERFORMANCE-BASED ASSESSMENTS

Ms. Ramos was pleased that the teachers were interested in learning more about how to assess the writing of their ELLs. For the next meeting of the seventh-grade team, she decided to talk with the teachers about how to develop performance-based assessments. In performance-based writing assessments, the students perform a writing task. The task must be as authentic as possible; for example, writing a letter or describing a recent field trip. The writing samples should then be rated by someone who is qualified to make judgments about ELLs' writing development (Norris et al., 1998). Ms. Ramos worked with the seventh-grade team to ensure that all of the teachers understood the basics of ELLs' writing development.

As was mentioned earlier, the first step in developing a performance-based assessment is to decide the purposes of the assessment. Will the assessment focus on words, sentences, or paragraphs (Scott, 2009)? What will the results be used for? What are the teacher's instructional goals? (Instructional goals should be based on district, state, or national ESL standards.) What will the students need to know and be able to do in order to successfully complete the writing task? When developing performance-based assessments, it's important to focus on what students know and can do, not on what they don't know and can't do (Hurley & Blake,

2000). Teachers should also consider whether the writing task allows students to truly show their abilities.

The next step is to design a task that will elicit the kind of response that the teacher wants. Some language tasks (e.g., writing a business letter or analyzing character, setting, or plot in a piece of literature), are more complex than, for example, writing a friendly letter or summarizing a story that the teacher has read aloud. Teachers will want to make sure that their prompts are appropriate for their students' age and proficiency level.

Finally, teachers need to evaluate students' writing according to a carefully designed performance rubric that is standards based and allows students to know the teacher's expectations.

DIFFERENT KINDS OF WRITING ASSESSMENTS

One of the seventh-grade teachers commented that he was unsure about how to assess specific aspects of his ELLs' writing, such as grammar. Ms. Ramos replied that there are many different kinds of writing tasks to choose from for assessing ELLs' writing. Some lend themselves naturally to specific purposes for assessing. Teachers may want to try others just to add some variety to their assessments (the chart in Figure 7.6 gives a brief overview of different kinds of writing assessments).

Traditional and Alternative Writing Assessments

Ms. Ramos showed the seventh-grade team how writing assessments generally fall into one of two categories: traditional or alternative. Traditional writing assessments usually include summative test instruments such as standardized tests, timed tests, decontextualized test items, and test items that focus on one correct answer. Traditional writing assessments tend to be product oriented. On the other hand, alternative writing assessments are more formative in nature, and include writing that students have done for authentic purposes, such as letter writing or journaling. Authentic assessments are process oriented and are usually more open-ended than traditional assessments (Brown, 2003). Mrs. Reece commented that alternative assessments, such as anecdotal records, rating scales, checklists, journals, portfolios, and self-assessments, seem more fair than traditional assessments when assessing ELLs (Lenski, Ehlers-Zavala, Daniel, & Sun-Irminger, 2006).

Whether the ELLs will be working on traditional or alternative writing assessment tasks, some strategies can prove to be very helpful. First, unless the test is timed, teachers should have students work on writing assessments in several short time chunks rather than one long session. They should also allow students to use bilingual dictionaries to help them find the words to express their ideas. They can have students work in groups to complete research reports, science labs, and other kinds of written work. If possible, teachers should also model assessment

FIGURE 7.6. Different kinds of writing assessments.	
Assessment	**Purpose**
Anecdotal records	Helpful in planning instruction and as evidence of learning.
Checklists	Acknowledge the presence of targeted aspects of language in writing. Promote self-reflection.
Cloze tests	Assess specific aspects of language, such as grammar.
Compositions	Assess organization, holistic writing skills, and content knowledge.
Conferences	Promote student self-reflection.
Curriculum-based measurements	Predict success on standardized assessments; determines students in need of intervention.
Dialogue journals	Provide anecdotal evidence of students' writing strengths and needs.
Dictation	Assesses grammar, sentence structure, vocabulary, spelling, conventions, and listening comprehension. Promotes self-reflection.
Elicitation	Provides evidence of mastery and comprehension of content area vocabulary.
Grammatical transformation	Tests ability to manipulate grammatical elements.
Handwriting assessments	Assess formation of letters and writing fluency.
Limited-response tasks	Assess specific skills or aspects of written language.
Open-ended response tasks	Provide holistic assessment of writing skills.
Ordering	Assesses mastery of syntax.
Paraphrasing	Assesses comprehension and holistic writing skills.
Picture-cued tasks	Assess mastery of vocabulary, grammar, and sentence structure.
Portfolios	Provide evidence of growth over a period of time.
Rating scales	Acknowledge the degree to which targeted language aspects are present in writing. Promote self-reflection.
Self-assessments	Promote reflection on writing behaviors.
Short-answer responses	Assess holistic writing skills and content knowledge.
Spelling tests	Assess spelling mastery of specific words.
Standardized tests	Determine student achievement relative to benchmark standards; inform effectiveness of school or district writing program.
Timed tests	Test writing fluency.
Vocabulary tests	Assess recall and understanding of vocabulary words.

tasks by giving examples, simplifying directions, and giving the assessments in the student's native language (Lenski et. al., 2006). Teachers should also remember that a student's writing ability cannot be accurately assessed from a single writing assessment, whether it is traditional or alternative. Looking at multiple forms of writing assessments will give teachers a more realistic picture of a student's writing proficiency.

Limited-Response Tasks

Mrs. Reece told the team that there are times when she wants to assess specific features of language in her ELLs' writing. Ms. Ramos responded that in this case limited-response tasks would be a good choice. Limited-response writing tasks are activities in which students are asked to provide an appropriate response to some sort of prompt. They are used when teachers want to control student responses to a high degree to evaluate specific elements of language. (One exception to this is dictation, which will be discussed later in this chapter.) Limited-response tasks require students to have an active knowledge of the skill being assessed, as they must produce language in their response rather than simply select one from a list of possible responses, as in multiple-choice questions. The structure involved in limited-response tasks make them a very appropriate choice for testing students with lower proficiency levels in English (Genesee & Upshur, 1996). There are several different kinds of limited-response tasks including handwriting, spelling, and vocabulary assessments, and cloze tests, elicitation, grammatical transformation, ordering, picture-cued tasks, and dictation.

Handwriting

Teachers who work in the primary grades may want to assess ELLs' handwriting. This would be especially important if a student is already familiar with another writing system, such as those used to write in Chinese or Russian, and is just beginning to learn the Latin writing system that is used in English. A simple way to do this is to have students copy a short paragraph or a couple of sentences from the board. If specific letters are being targeted in the assessment, make sure that the prompt contains plenty of examples of those letters.

Teachers who will be using handwriting assessments for grading purposes will want to determine ahead of time what specific criteria they will use to determine what is considered acceptable or unacceptable handwriting.

Spelling

Spelling tests are another type of assessment that most of us know from school. The teacher assigned a set of words, and at the end of the week the words were dictated, usually in sentences for context. We would write the words, hopefully with the correct spelling. This kind of assessment is still useful for checking students' mastery of spelling words. Mrs. Ramos told the teachers that there are a few variations on the traditional spelling test that teachers could try. First, instead of dictating the words, show the students a picture that illustrates the meaning of the word and have them write the word. A second variation would be to give the students a multiple-choice test, with various options for spelling the word, to see whether they can recognize the correct spelling (Brown, 2004). This alternative might be especially useful when a word has several different spellings, each with a different meaning, such as *there, their,* and *they're,* or *two, to,* and *too,* in which case the teacher could assess word meaning as well as spelling.

Vocabulary

One way to assess students' knowledge of vocabulary is to ask them to define the word or use it in a sentence. It is wise to teach vocabulary words in clusters that are related to a particular unit of study (Blachowicz & Fisher, 2010). In this way, the task of defining words becomes somewhat more authentic. Ms. Ramos mentioned that giving the students a picture and asking them to define the words or write sentences about them that show the relationships among the words can be a helpful scaffold, especially for ELLs. For example, if students have been studying a science unit on a pond ecosystem, they could look at a picture of a pond labeled with several key vocabulary words. The students would then explain the meanings of the words.

Cloze Tests

In cloze tests, students are given a sentence with one or several words missing. The students fill in the correct word. One teacher who had tried cloze tests explained that he had found this kind of assessment to be especially useful in evaluating skills such as grammar. Brown (1983) found cloze tests to also be a reliable measure of oral language. In a study asking ELLs to fill in the word from a conversation in which every seventh word was deleted, Brown was able to determine how well students were able to converse in English. Another way to use a cloze test is to test grammar. For example, ELLs who are learning forms of the verb *to be* can be given a sentence in which they must fill in the blank with the correct verb form. Cloze tests can also be used to assess grammatical skills such as word order in sentences and vocabulary.

Elicitation

Another assessment that Ms. Ramos introduced to the team was elicitation. In elicitation, students are given a picture and asked to name it in writing. This can be used in ELL classrooms for newcomers, or in the regular classroom. To use this easy-to-prepare assessment, the teacher displays a picture; for example, a flower, and the students label the parts. This assessment requires ELLs to have knowledge of content area vocabulary, and is effective in determining whether students have learned both word names and meanings.

Grammatical Transformation

Grammatical transformation activities assess students' ability to manipulate specific elements of grammar, such as verb tense or pronoun use. In grammatical transformation activities, students are given a set of sentences or a paragraph and are asked to alter some grammatical feature. For example, if the paragraph is written in the present tense, students can rewrite it in the past, future, or conditional tense. Or, they might rewrite sentences, changing nouns to pronouns or inserting correct punctuation. Mrs. Reece added that she remembered doing some similar activities in her college Spanish class.

Ordering

Ordering tasks assess students' understanding of syntax in sentences. Teachers give students several sentence fragments that they must put together to create a coherent sentence. Then they have the students write out the complete, correct sentence.

Picture-Cued Tasks

There are several different kinds of picture-cued tasks. Students can simply tell what the person in the picture is doing. Or, they can write a more detailed description of the picture. Descriptions can be targeted to specific aspects of language, such as prepositions (e.g., The ball is *under* the chair; The cat is sitting *on* the chair). Alternatively, a student can be asked to put several pictures in sequence to tell a story and then write the story (Brown, 2004).

Dictation

When Ms. Ramos mentioned dictation, Mrs. Reece commented that it was the one activity that she had dreaded in her college Spanish class. Ms. Ramos nodded knowingly and added that dictation does not have to be intimidating if it is presented in the context of a safe classroom environment where it's okay to make mistakes. Dictation is a holistic language task that serves as both instruction and assessment at the same time. It can be used with both native English speakers and ELLs. She explained that dictation actively engages students with language as they write and as they self-correct their dictations (Davis & Rinvolucri, 1988). Students *listen* as the teacher reads a passage and *write* down what the teacher reads. Afterward, they *read* over their dictation papers and *talk* about any trouble areas in a class discussion. As such, dictation offers ELLs the opportunity to incorporate all four language modalities into one activity, while testing students' listening skills, spelling, grammar, vocabulary, and comprehension. Teachers who regularly use dictation with their students provide them with a model of more sophisticated sentence structure and vocabulary in the dictated passages than the students would produce on their own. They also expose their students to high-quality literature, both narrative and expository. Dictation exercises, therefore, can be linked to language arts lessons or to other content areas.

Ms. Ramos reminded the teachers that because relatively few students in U.S. classrooms are familiar with dictation, teachers will need to explain both the objectives and the procedure to their students. In traditional dictation, the teacher will usually read a passage. For younger students this could be a couple of sentences or even a few words or phrases; for older students the passage could be an entire paragraph. The first time through, teachers should read the passage at a normal speaking pace. The second time through, they read the passage in shorter chunks and give students time to write between each chunk. The third time through, the teacher reads the passage slowly, allowing students to correct mistakes and fill in parts of the passage that they might have missed.

After the students have listened and written the passage, the teacher should display it on an overhead projector so that students can self-correct any errors. They should be careful to correct spelling, grammar, and vocabulary.

Dictation activities can be differentiated for students with varying language proficiencies. Advanced-level students and native English speakers can write the entire passage, while newcomers might be given a page with the passage written and several key words or phrases to be filled in. There are many variations of the dictation activity, which can target specific aspects of language development. For a more complete discussion of dictation, see *Dictation: New Methods, New Possibilities* (Davis & Rinvolucri, 1988).

Open-Ended Response Tasks

Ms. Ramos explained to the teachers that another option for assessing ELLs' writing is the open-ended response task. In contrast to the limited-response tasks that primarily assess discrete writing skills, open-ended response tasks assess writing proficiency somewhat more holistically. Skills that are assessed using written open-ended response tasks include organization and comprehension of content material. Skills such as vocabulary usage, grammar, and spelling can also be assessed in open-ended response tasks, but the teacher will need to be very explicit about the expectations for these skills in the students' writing.

Open-ended response tasks give students more freedom in formulating their responses than closed-ended response tasks do. They include short-answer responses, paraphrasing, and compositions. Open-ended response tasks are more appropriate for ELLs who have already developed some degree of proficiency in English (Genesee & Upshur, 1996).

Because open-ended response tasks can elicit such a wide variety of responses from students, it is important for teachers to make their expectations known ahead of time regarding aspects of writing, such as spelling, vocabulary, grammar, organization, and length of response, and clearly communicate them to students. If there will be time limits set on the composition, teachers should make those explicit as well. Creating a student version of the scoring rubric can be very helpful for ELLs so they can know what aspects of the writing task are being emphasized and what they need to focus on in their compositions (see Figure 7.7 for an example of a student version of a scoring rubric).

Short-Answer Responses

Ms. Ramos told the team that there are several different kinds of open-ended response tasks. One is called short-answer response. Short-answer responses are often used to assess both writing skills and knowledge of content area concepts. Give the students a prompt that asks them to describe, explain, or otherwise demonstrate understanding of material covered in a lesson. The teacher needs to decide ahead of time how much weight to give to content and how much to language when scoring short-answer responses.

Paraphrasing

Another type of open-ended response task is paraphrasing. Paraphrasing tasks assess students' ability to comprehend the meaning of a written passage and to articulate that meaning in their own words. Paraphrasing is a challenging task for all students, but may be especially difficult for ELLs who are still limited in their ability to explain their ideas in English. For this reason, paraphrasing assessments are probably best used for more advanced-level ELLs, rather than for beginners.

Compositions

When using compositions as assessments, there are many different parts of the writing task that teachers can focus on to assess. Mrs. Reece and her colleagues, like most teachers, were interested in the students' ideas and content, as well as how they organize their thinking into coherent paragraphs with topic sentences and supporting evidence. Depending on the purpose of the assessment, teachers may want to consider grammar, vocabulary, spelling, and vocabulary usage when grading compositions. For ELLs, it will be especially important to clearly explain the criteria for the grade and to explicitly teach paragraph construction ahead of time.

Whether they use short-answer responses, paraphrasing, or compositions to assess students' writing, open-ended writing tasks give teachers a prime opportunity to provide constructive feedback to their students on their writing performance. The best feedback is specific, primarily addresses content, and points out students' writing strengths as well as areas that need correction. It is not necessary to mark every error in a student's essay. In fact, this can be overwhelming for ELLs. The kinds of errors to focus on in ELLs' writing are those that they make consistently as well as those that relate to the current or recently completed unit.

FIGURE 7.7. Student version of scoring rubric: Intermediate level, grades 3–5.

Developing	Proficient	Exemplary
When I write by myself, most of the time I don't use periods, correct spelling, or capital letters.	When I write by myself I sometimes use periods, correct spelling, and capital letters.	When I write by myself I use periods, correct spelling, and capital letters most of the time.
Most of the time I don't put words in the right order, and I make a lot of grammar mistakes.	I sometimes put words in the right order, and I make some grammar mistakes.	Most of the time, I put words in the right order, but I make a few grammar mistakes.
Most of the time it's hard for me to describe a sequence of events. I don't add many details.	Sometimes it's hard for me to describe a sequence of events. I add a few details.	Most of the time I am able to describe a sequence of events. I add some details.
Most of the time, it's hard for me to write paragraphs that have a main idea and that use correct grammar. I need help to do this.	Sometimes I can write paragraphs that have a main idea and that use correct grammar. I sometimes need help to do this.	Most of the time, I can write paragraphs that have a main idea and that use correct grammar. I can do this by myself.
Most of the time, it's hard for people to understand what I write. I make a lot of grammar mistakes.	Sometimes, people can understand what I write, even if I make a few grammar mistakes.	Most of the time, people can understand what I write, even if I make a few grammar mistakes.
Most of the time, it's hard for me to write in different genres such as expository, narrative, or poetry.	I can sometimes write in different genres such as expository, narrative, or poetry.	I can write in some different genres such as expository, narrative, or poetry.
Most of the time, it's hard for me to use vocabulary and sentences that make sense for language arts, math, science, and social studies.	Sometimes I can use vocabulary and sentences that make sense for language arts, math, science, and social studies.	Most of the time, I can use vocabulary and sentences that make sense for language arts, math, science, and social studies.
It's hard for me to write letters by myself. I don't add many details to my sentences.	I am sometimes able to write letters by myself. I add some details to my sentences.	I am able to write letters by myself. I add a lot of details to my sentences.

Curriculum-Based Measurements

Curriculum-based measurements (CBMs) in writing have the potential to enhance the writing achievement of all students by giving teachers information that they can use to plan instruction (Gunning, 2010). According to Benson and Campbell (2009), CBMs are a formative assessment that is reliable and valid, simple and efficient to use, and easily understood by all stakeholders. Ms. Ramos told the teachers that ELLs, for whom learning to write in English can be especially challenging, would benefit from a writing assessment such as the CBM in writing, because it gives teachers the data to plan more effective and more individualized writing instruction that ELLs will find helpful in developing their skills (Rhodes et al., 2005).

Identifying indicators of writing proficiency is an important step in understanding the writing development of ELLs. Another step is the development of instruments that reliably predict students' achievement on high-stakes tests and allow teachers to regularly measure students' writing progress. One measure that is being developed is the CBM in writing (Espin et al., 2008). In the study, high school students were asked to write a response to a prompt. They were given 10 minutes to write, and they marked their progress at the 3rd, 5th, and 7th minutes. The writing samples were scored according to four criteria: the number of words written, the number of words written correctly, correct word sequences, and correct word sequences minus incorrect word sequences. The researchers found that correct word sequences or correct word sequences minus incorrect word sequences had more validity and reliability than number of words written or number of words written correctly. They also found that the reliability and validity were higher for ELLs than for native English speakers.

Just as CBMs in reading allow teachers to regularly monitor student progress, develop trajectories of the growth that students need to make in order to meet grade-level benchmarks, and plan interventions that can help students succeed, CBMs in writing have the potential to enhance the writing achievement of all students.

INFORMAL ASSESSMENTS

Mrs. Reece asked whether there were other ways of assessing ELLs' writing. Ms. Ramos nodded and explained that informal assessments also give teachers valuable information about their students' writing proficiency. These informal assessments include checklists and rating scales, portfolios, dialogue journals, student–teacher conferences, and anecdotal records. While checklists, rating scales, and portfolios are appropriate places to collect data for grading purposes, dialogue journals, conferences, and anecdotal records better serve the purpose of informing instruction. Informal assessments can be especially useful for ELLs because they are often free from the cultural bias that is present in standardized tests (García, McKoon, & August, 2006b).

Checklists and Rating Scales

Writing checklists are lists of specific aspects of writing proficiency that the teacher is looking for in a student's work. For example, a checklist might have categories such as organization, ideas and content, conventions, spelling, and grammar. Checklists should describe specific, observable student behaviors that are apparent in their writing. They should also be linked to lesson objectives and standards (see Figure 7.8 for an example of a writing checklist and Figure 7.9 for an example of a rating scale).

Teachers can use checklists to help maintain consistency when grading papers. Checklists can also be shared with parents and other stakeholders as well. ELLs and other students benefit from using writing checklists to self-assess their writing. It is especially important when working with ELLs to only include categories on a checklist that have been explicitly taught. For example, if you have not yet worked with students on placing quotation marks around direct quotations, this should not be listed as an item on the checklist. It may be necessary to simplify the language on checklists and rating scales, and provide examples for ELLs at beginning proficiency levels.

A rating scale is very similar to a checklist. On a checklist, teachers or students have the option of circling *yes* or *no* to indicate whether a particular writing element is present. On a rating scale, the same categories can be listed, but instead use a number scale (e.g., 1 through 5), to describe to what extent a particular element is present within a child's writing sample (Genesse & Upshur, 1996). In this way, the rating scale provides more in-depth information than the checklist, but it is also more subjective. Teachers can update and revise checklists and rating scales according to what works or does not work for their specific situation, and to highlight specific aspects of the writing task that they want students to focus on.

Portfolios

Writing portfolios are collections of students' writing that showcase achievement over time. They show children's growth holistically and in specific aspects of writing. They can also give teachers insights into writing strategies that individual students are using (Gearhart, 2009). Portfolio entries can be stored in file folders. Each student will have a folder with his or her name on it. Teachers should be sure to have students write the date that they completed the assignment on each document that is kept in the portfolio. This way, parents, teachers, and students can all see growth through the course of the school year.

Ms. Ramos cautioned that keeping a collection of students' writing samples, while a good thing, is not sufficient to help them reflect on their progress and set goals for further growth. Teachers will need to make portfolio reviews part of regular writing conferences with students in order to encourage self-reflection and help them set goals for their writing. It may be helpful to attach student-completed writing checklists or rating scales, as well as rubrics, to each piece that is entered into the portfolio.

There are different kinds of portfolios that are used for different purposes. A working portfolio contains all of a student's written work, including first drafts, revisions, and final published pieces. A showcase portfolio contains examples of the student's very best work, and might be displayed to parents and other teachers to show the advances that a child has made over a certain time span. Teachers and students can work together to decide which writing samples would go in the

FIGURE 7.8. Writing checklist for reports: Grade level 3–5.

	Circle Yes or No.
I used periods, correct spelling, and capital letters most of the time.	Yes No
I put words in the right order, even if I made a few grammar mistakes.	Yes No
I described a sequence of events. I added some details.	Yes No
I wrote paragraphs that have a main idea and that use correct grammar.	Yes No
People can understand what I wrote.	Yes No
I can write in some different genres such as expository, narrative, or poetry.	Yes No
I used vocabulary and sentences that make sense for this content area.	Yes No
I added a lot of details to my sentences.	Yes No

From *Writing Instruction and Assessment for English Language Learners K–8* by Susan Lenski and Frances Verbruggen. Copyright 2010 by The Guilford Press. Permission to photocopy this figure is granted to purchasers of this book for personal use only (see copyright page for details).

FIGURE 7.9. Writing rating scale for reports: Grade level 3–5.

	Rate your writing in each of the following areas:
I used periods, correct spelling, and capital letters most of the time.	Never 1 2 3 4 5 Always
I put words in the right order, even if I made a few grammar mistakes.	Never 1 2 3 4 5 Always
I described a sequence of events. I added some details.	Never 1 2 3 4 5 Always
I wrote paragraphs that have a main idea and that use correct grammar.	Never 1 2 3 4 5 Always
People can understand what I wrote.	Never 1 2 3 4 5 Always
I can write in some different genres such as expository, narrative, or poetry.	Never 1 2 3 4 5 Always
I used vocabulary and sentences that make sense for this content area.	Never 1 2 3 4 5 Always
I added a lot of details to my sentences.	Never 1 2 3 4 5 Always

showcase portfolio. Teachers could have students write a short note explaining why they selected a particular piece to go in their showcase portfolio.

Either the working portfolio or the showcase portfolio can be used for grading purposes depending on the criteria for grading. Showcase portfolios emphasize the finished product and should be used for grading when this is the focus. Working portfolios, on the other hand, reveal much more about the writing process, and should be used when this is the emphasis.

Dialogue Journals

Dialogue journals, which we discussed in Chapter 5, can be used as informal writing assessments that provide teachers and students with a wealth of anecdotal evidence about students' writing strengths and needs. Dialogue journals give ELLs opportunities to share about how they see their learning progressing, aspects of the writing process that they may be struggling with, parts of the lesson that they did not understand, goals and interests, and questions that they may have that they do not want to ask in front of their peers. They can also comment on their likes and dislikes regarding assignments, which can give teachers insights into the child's dominant learning style. In addition, dialogue journals give immigrant students a safe venue for discussing their feelings about being in a new culture, learning a new language, and other issues regarding their transition to American life. Both immigrants and U.S.-born ELLs who experience racism or any other form of discrimination may choose to use dialogue journals with a teacher with whom they feel safe to express their emotions regarding these issues. Ms. Ramos reminded the teachers that it will be important for students to know whether the information that they write in their dialogue journals will be kept confidential and that teachers are required by law to report any suspected abuse or neglect.

Dialogue journals, by definition, require interaction between students and teachers. The teacher's responses can help ELLs understand how the English language works by modeling sentence structures and correct use of vocabulary words, addressing the individual needs of each student. Ms. Ramos cautioned the teachers that it is best not to grade dialogue journals, because this may cause students to become hesitant about sharing their thoughts and questions with their teacher, but the writing in students' journals can inform future instruction.

Responding to students' dialogue journals takes some organization on the part of the teacher. Some teachers read through a handful of journals on a daily basis; others devote a larger chunk of time less frequently to responding to their students. Either way, it is important to provide regular feedback to students. This way, they will know that their teachers are interested in their learning and in them as individuals.

Student–Teacher Conferences

Writing conferences are conversations between students and teachers regarding the students' writing performance. Teachers can hold conferences about writing pieces that have been completed or about work that is in various stages of the writing process. During conferences, teachers should give students the chance to talk about their writing strategies, their understanding of the writing process, ways that they are applying skills taught in recent lessons, and their goals (Gearhart, 2009). The objective of student–teacher conferences is to foster an attitude of self-reflection in students regarding their writing and to give students ownership of their own learning.

Mrs. Reece explained to the team that when she conferenced with her students, she found it helpful to keep records of what was discussed. These notes can be filed either with the anecdotal records or, when appropriate, with portfolio entries when the purpose of the conference is to discuss a specific writing sample that will be going into the portfolio. She added that she uses index cards to make notes about conferences, and that using different colors of cards helped her distinguish conference notes from other kinds of anecdotal records.

ELLs at beginning proficiency levels may be reluctant to participate in conferences because they do not feel that they can express themselves adequately (Genesse & Upshur, 1996). Teachers can help these students by encouraging them to communicate their thoughts as well as possible, by praising progress, and by focusing on only one or two areas in need of improvement at a time.

Teachers should not try to conference with all students in one day. By holding short conferences with two or three students each day, teachers will be able to get through their entire class in just a few weeks. By holding regular conferences with ELLs, teachers will gain insight into their strengths and their needs in the area of writing.

Anecdotal Records

Anecdotal record keeping, Ms. Ramos told the teachers, allows them to keep notes on what they see and hear their students doing during writing tasks, documenting the children's "aha" moments, as well as specific struggles of different children and strategies that particular students are independently using or failing to use as they write. Mrs. Reece shared that a few days earlier, when she was walking around the classroom during writers' workshop, she noticed that Olga was still not placing articles such as *a, an,* and *the* before some of her nouns. At the next table, Juan was excited and proud of himself because he had remembered to place adjectives before, instead of after, the nouns in his composition. Mrs. Reece used index cards to write about Olga's struggle and Juan's breakthrough, and included the date on each card. After class, she placed the notes in the students' files. She would use these notes, along with other anecdotal records that she had collected, to help plan mini-lessons for the next week's writing workshop. Ms. Ramos smiled, and added that anecdotal records can also be used to comment on insights gained during writing workshop conferences or when reading through journal entries. These notes can be used to help plan instruction and to document the moments when students come to a new understanding of a concept.

Teachers will need to find the method of collecting anecdotal records that works best for them. For example, some teachers like to write on index cards, whereas others may prefer to have a clipboard handy. Whatever method a teacher chooses, it is important to organize the records and to always make sure to put the date on each record. Many teachers use file boxes or folders to store records, keeping a separate file for each student.

Self-Assessment

At this point, Mrs. Reece lamented that her students often do not internalize the instruction that she gives them during student–teacher conferences. As the other teachers nodded in agreement, Ms. Ramos began to explain that self-assessment has the benefit of encouraging students to reflect on their work. When students are required to self-reflect, they learn to recognize any errors in spelling, grammar, organization, or other areas, and set specific goals for their future writing performance. This reflection and goal setting can be especially beneficial for ELLs because it gives them a measure of control over their achievement, leading to increased motivation. If the goal of self-assessment is to set goals, students can look at both short- and long-term goals for their writing. When ELLs self-assess their writing performance, it is helpful for them to use a student version of a scoring rubric that has been developed for students at their proficiency level. As they look at the different criteria, they are asked to form a judgment about their writing in relation to the standards set forth in the rubric. Self-reflection can motivate students to challenge themselves toward more proficient writing.

CONNECTING ASSESSMENT AND INSTRUCTION WITH RESPONSE TO INTERVENTION

Response to intervention (RTI) is part of the 2004 reauthorization of the federal initiative, the Individuals with Disabilities Education Act (IDEA). The RTI model is based on the idea that some students who have difficulty learning do not really have a learning disability but rather have not had sufficient opportunities for learning. Previously, students who were determined to have a measurable difference between their intelligence quotient (IQ) and their achievement were considered learning disabled. The RTI model changes that method of identification. The legislation is designed to give students multiple opportunities to learn before referring them for special education testing.

Cultural Implications of RTI

Before RTI was implemented, most policy decisions regarding special education were based on native English speakers (Vaughn, Mathes, Linan-Thompson, & Francis, 2005). As a result, there has been a disproportionate number of Latina/

Latino students in special education and an underrepresentation in gifted education (Bender & Shores, 2007; Donovan & Cross, 2002). Some educators believe that RTI has the potential to change that trend. Because identification of special education students will be based on student achievement data rather than on teacher referrals under RTI, some educators believe that the disproportionality of ELLs in special education will change (Batsche et al., 2006).

What Does RTI Look Like?

With RTI, ELLs or any other student would not be put into special education classes without first being considered general education students. After receiving assessment, interventions, and regular progress monitoring, students who do not demonstrate adequate progress are then considered for special education services (International Reading Association, 2009). At the time of this writing, there were no federal legal requirements about how to structure the assessments and interventions. Many states, however, have designed frameworks for assessment that encourage teachers to use a certain model. The three-tier model is presently the most popular way to determine which students have trouble learning and should be referred for special education testing (Fuchs, Fuchs, & Vaughn, 2008).

In the three-tier RTI model, Tier 1 focuses on providing effective classroom instruction for all students. This instruction could come from whole-class instruction or small-group instruction. In Tier 2, teachers identify students who are not responding to the instruction. If teachers find that some ELLs are not responding to instruction, they need to provide the students with intensive, small-group interventions. These interventions should be targeted to specific problems. For example, if an ELL had unusual difficulty learning letters and words, the teacher might provide that student with specific instruction focusing on letter and word learning. ELLs who do not respond to Tier 2 intervention are given individualized instruction in Tier 3. If teachers document that students have not responded to interventions at Tier 3, they will possibly be identified as having a learning disability.

Many states and districts have adopted the three-tier system for RTI. Since RTI is so new, however, there are few districts that have addressed the cultural implications of RTI. Klingner and Edwards (2006) raise the questions, though. They ask whether RTI should be different for ELLs or whether the three-tier framework will be successful in more effectively identifying ELLs with special needs. The hope is, however, that RTI will change the way teachers think about ELLs who have difficulty learning. Through wise assessment and targeted instruction, teachers will adopt a problem-solving approach to student learning.

SUMMARY

Assessments such as checklists and rating scales, portfolios, dialogue journals, student–teacher conferences, and anecdotal records provide teachers with ways to gain additional insights into their ELLs' writing development, as well as their interests, concerns, and experiences with writing and about other aspects of their lives. Some assessments can be used to determine grades, while the primary purpose of others is to inform instruction. Assessments also help to foster a self-reflective attitude in students with regard to their learning and growth in writing. In addition, assessments are used to determine whether some ELLs should be identified as needing special education.

WEB RESOURCES

Assessment Portfolios: Including English Language Learners in Large-Scale Assessments
www.ericdigests.org/2001-3/large.htm

Advantages and disadvantages of assessment portfolios for ELLs and tips on creating assessment portfolios.

ESL Standards for Pre-K-12 Students, Online Edition
www.tesol.org/s_tesol/seccss.asp?CID=113&DID=1583

National ESL standards, additional resources.

International Reading Association, RTI Policies
www.reading.org

Policies, information, and blogs on RTI and other ELL issues.

Practical Ideas on Alternative Assessment for ESL Students
www.cal.org/resources/Digest/tannen01.html

Ideas for assessing ELL's written and oral English proficiency using alternative assessments.

Resources for ESL Assessment
www.cal.org/resources/archive/rgos/eslassess.html

Links to resources on assessment of ELLs.

Rubrics
www.rubrician.com/writing.htm

Teacher and student versions of rubrics and checklists for writing in a variety of genres.

Writing Rubrics
www.rubrics4teachers.com/writing.php

Writing rubrics for different grade levels, and genres, plus 6+1 Traits rubrics.

References

Abu-Akel, A., (1997). On reading–writing relationships in first and foreign languages. *JALT Journal, 19*(2), 198–216.

Aguierrez-Muñoz, Z., & Boscardin, C. K. (2008). Opportunity to learn and English learner achievement: Is increased content exposure beneficial? *Journal of Latinos and Education, 7*(3), 186–205.

Alba, R. D., Logan, J., Lutz, A., & Stults, B. (2002). Only English by the third generation? Loss and preservation of the mother tongue among the grandchildren of contemporary immigrants. *Demography, 39*(3), 467–484.

Allington, R. L. (2009). *What really matters in fluency: Research-based practices across the curriculum*. Boston: Pearson Education.

Anderson, N. B., & Anderson, P. E. (2003). *Emotional longevity*. New York: Viking.

Anthony, A. R. B. (2008). Output strategies for English-language learners: Theory to practice. *Reading Teacher, 61*, 472–482.

Ariza, E. N. W. (2010). *Not for ESOL teachers: What every classroom teacher needs to know about the linguistically, culturally and ethnically diverse students*. Boston: Allyn & Bacon.

Ariza, E. N. W., Morales-Jones, C. A., Yahya, N., & Zainuddin, H. (2002). *Why TESOL?: Theories and issues in teaching English as a second language for K–12 teachers*. Dubuque, IA: Kendall/Hunt.

Armon, J., & Ortega, T. (2008). Autobiographical snapshots: Constructing self in Letras y Arte. *Language Arts, 86*, 108–119.

August, D., & Shanahan, T. (Eds.). (2006). *Developing literacy in second-language learners:Report of the National Literacy Panel on language-minority children and youth*. Mahwah, NJ: Erlbaum.

Bae, J. (2007). Development of English skills need not suffer as a result of immersion: Grades 1 and 2 writing assessment in a Korean/English two-way immersion program. *Language Learning, 57*(2), 299–332.

Batsche, G., Elliott, J., Graden, J. L., Grimes, J., Kovaleski, J. E., & Prasse, D. (2006). *Response to intervention: Policy considerations and implementation*. Alexandria, VA: National Association of State Directors of Special Education.

Beach, R., & Friedrich, T. (2006). Response to writing. In C. A. MacArthur, S. Graham, & J. Fitzgerald (Eds.), *Handbook of writing research* (pp. 222–234). New York: Guilford Press.

Bender, W. N., & Shores, C. (2007). *Response to intervention: A practical guide for every teacher*. Arlington, VA, and Thousand Oaks, CA: Council for Exceptional Children and Corwin Press.

Berger, L. R. (1996). Reader response journals: You make the meaning . . . and how. *Journal of Adolescent & Adult Literacy, 39*, 380–385.

Bermudez, A., & Prater, D. (1990). Using brainstorming and clustering with LEP writers to develop elaboration skills. *TESOL Quarterly, 24*, 523–528.

Berninger, V. W., Vaughan, K. B., Abbott, R. D., Abbott, S. P., Rogan, L. W., Brooks, A., et al. (1997). Treatment of handwriting problems in beginning writers: Transfer from handwriting to composition. *Journal of Educational Psychology, 89*(4), 652–666.

Besser, S. L. (2006). *What does it take to learn academic English in middle school? An investigation of the learning experiences and resultant proficiency of U.S.-born second language learners.* Unpublished dissertation, University of California, Berkeley.

Blachowicz, C., & Fisher, P. J. (2010). *Teaching vocabulary in all classrooms* (4th ed.). Boston: Allyn & Bacon.

Black, R. W. (2005). Access and affiliation: The literacy and composition practices of English-language learners in an online fanfiction community. *Journal of Adolescent and Adult Literacy, 49*, 118–128.

Bolton, W. F. (1982). *A living language: The history and structure of English.* New York: Random House.

Bouchard, D. (1995). *If you're not from the prairie.* New York: Aladdin.

Brassell, D., & Furtado, L. (2008). Enhancing English as a second language students' vocabulary knowledge. *The Reading Matrix, 8*(1), 111–116.

Brechtel, M. (1992). *Bringing it all together: Language and literacy in the multilingual classroom.* Carlsbad, CA: Dominie.

Brians, P. (2003). *Common errors in English usage.* Wilsonville, OR: William, James & Co.

Bright, R. (1995). *Writing instruction in the intermediate grades: What is said, what is done, what is understood.* Newark, DE: International Reading Association.

Brisk, M. E., & Harrington, M. M. (2000). *Literacy and bilingualism: A handbook for ALL teachers.* Mahwah, NJ: Erlbaum.

Britton, B. K. (1996). Rewriting: The arts and sciences of improving expository instructional text. In C. M. Levy & S. Ransdell (Eds.), *The science of writing: Theories, methods, individual differences, and applications* (pp. 323–345). Mahwah, NJ: Erlbaum.

Britton, J., Burgess, T., Martin, N., McLeod, A., & Rosen, H. (1975). *The development of writing abilities.* London: Macmillan.

Brown, D. (1983). Conversational cloze tests and conversational ability. *ELT Journal, 37*(2), 158–161.

Brown, H. D. (2000). *Principles of language learning and teaching* (4th ed.). White Plains, NY: Addison Wesley Longman

Brown, H. D. (2004). *Language assessment: Principles and classroom practice.* Upper Saddle River, NJ: Pearson ESL.

Browne, A. (1984). *Willy the wimp.* London: Walker Books.

Bruner, J. (1996). *The culture of education.* Cambridge, MA: Harvard University Press.

Bukiet, S. (1997). *Scripts of the world.* Lathrup Village, MI, and Cincinnati, OH: Multi-Cultural Books & Videos and AIMs International Books.

Buss, K., & Karnowski, L. (2000). *Reading and writing literary genres.* Newark, DE: International Reading Association.

Cahyono, B. Y. (2002). Maintaining process and improving grammar use in writing. *Melbourne Papers in Linguistics and Applied Linguistics, 2*(1), 57–68.

Calkins, L. M. (1994). *The art of teaching writing.* Portsmouth, NH: Heinemann.

Carlo, M. S., August, D., McLaughlin, B., Snow, C. E., Dressler, C., Lippman, D. N., et al. (2004). Closing the gap: Addressing the vocabulary needs of English-language learners in bilingual and mainstream classrooms. *Reading Research Quarterly, 39*(2), 188–215.

Carrier, K. A. (2005). Key issues for teaching English language learners in academic classrooms. *Middle School Journal, 37*(2), 4–9.

Carrier, K. A., & Tatum, A. W. (2006). Creating sentence walls to help English-language learners develop content literacy. *Reading Teacher, 60,* 285–288.

Carson, J. E., Carrell, P. L., Silberstein, S., Kroll, B., & Kuehn, P. A. (1990). Reading-writing relationships in first and second language. *TESOL Quarterly, 24*(2), 245–266.

Chomsky, N. (1975). *Reflections on language.* New York: Pantheon.

Chomsky, N., & Halle, M. (1968). *The sound pattern of English.* New York: Harper & Row.

Clay, M. M. (1975). *What did I write?* Portsmouth, NH: Heinemann.

Clay, M. M. (1985). *The early detection of reading difficulties* (3rd ed.). Portsmouth, NH: Heinemann.

Cowley, S. (2002). *Getting the buggers to write: How to motivate students to write and develop their writing skills including the basics.* London: Continuum.

Crawford, J. (2004). *Educating English learners: Language diversity in the classroom.* (5th ed.). Los Angeles: Bilingual Educational Services.

Cronnell, B. (1985). Language influences in the English writing of third- and sixth-grade Mexican-American students. *Journal of Educational Research, 78,* 168–173.

Crystal, D. (2004). *The stories of English.* Woodstock, NY: Overlook Press.

Cummins, J. (1979a). Cognitive/academic language proficiency, linguistic interdependence, the optimum age question, and some other matters. *Working Papers on Bilingualism, 19*(1), 121–129.

Cummins, J. (1979b). Linguistic interdependence and the educational development of bilingual children. *Review of Educational Research, 49,* 222–251.

Cunningham, P. W., & Cunningham, J. W. (2010). *What really matters in writing: Research-based practices across the elementary curriculum.* Boston: Allyn & Bacon.

Dahl, K. L., & Farnan, N. (1998). *Children's writing: Perspective from research.* Newark, DE: International Reading Association.

Davis, L. H., Carlisle, J. F., & Beeman, M. (1999). Hispanic children's writing in English and Spanish when English is the language of instruction. In T. Shanahan, F. V. Rodriguez-Brown, C. Worthman, J. C. Burnison, & A. Cheung (Eds.), *Yearbook of the National Reading Conference* (pp. 238–248). Oak Creek, WI: National Reading Conference.

Davis, P., & Rinvolucri, M. (1988). *Dictation: New methods, new possibilities.* New York: Cambridge University Press.

Dean, D. (2008). *Bringing grammar to life.* Newark, DE: International Reading Association.

Delpit, L. D. (1988). The silenced dialogue: Power and pedagogy in educating other people's children. *Harvard Educational Review, 58,* 280–298.

Díaz-Rico, L. T. (2008). *Strategies for teaching English learners* (2nd ed.). Boston: Allyn & Bacon.

Díaz-Rico, L. T., & Weed, K. Z. (2010). *The crosscultural, language, and academic development handbook: A complete K–12 reference guide.* Boston: Allyn & Bacon.

Donoghue, M. R. (2009). *Language arts: Integrating skills for classroom teaching.* Thousand Oaks, CA: Sage.

Donovan, C. A. (2001). Children's development and control of written story and information genres: Insights from one elementary school. *Research in the Teaching of English, 35,* 394–447.

Donovan, C. A., & Smolkin, L. B. (2006). Children's understanding of genre and writing development. In C. A. MacArthur, S. Graham, & J. Fitzgerald (Eds.), *Handbook of writing research* (pp. 131–143). New York: Guilford Press.

Donovan, M. S., & Cross, C. T. (2002). *Minority students in special and gifted education.* Washington, DC: National Research Council.

Dressler, C. A. (2002). *Inter- and intra-language influences on the English spelling development of fifth-grade, Spanish-speaking English language learners.* Unpublished dissertation, Harvard University.

Dufva, M., & Voeten, M. J. M. (1999). Native language literacy and phonological memory as prerequisites for learning English as a foreign language. *Applied Psycholinguistics, 20*(3), 329–348.

Duke, N. K. (2000). 3.6 minutes per day: The scarcity of informational texts in first grade. *Reading Research Quarterly, 35,* 202–224.

Dutro, S., & Moran, C. (2003). Rethinking English language instruction: An architectural approach. In G. G. Garcia (Ed.), *English learners: Reaching the highest levels of English literacy* (pp. 227–258). Newark, DE: International Reading Association.

Dweik, B. S., & Abu Al Hommos, M. D. (2007). *The effects of Arabic proficiency on the English writing of bilingual Jordanian students* (ERIC Document Reproductive Service No. ED497505).

Dyson, A. H. (2003). *The brothers and sister learn to write: Popular literacies in childhood and school cultures.* New York: Teachers College Press.

Echevarria, J., & Graves, A. (2003). *Sheltered content instruction: Teaching English-language learners with diverse abilities* (2nd ed.). Boston: Allyn & Bacon.

Echevarria, J., Vogt, M. E., & Short, D. J. (2010). *Making content comprehensible for elementary English learners: The SIOP model.* Boston: Allyn & Bacon.

Edelsky, C., & Jilbert, K. (1985). Bilingual children and writing: Lessons for all of us. *Volta Review, 87*(5), 57–72.

Edens, K. M., & Potter, E. F. (2001). Promoting conceptual understanding through pictorial representation. *Studies in Art Education, 42*(3), 214–233.

Ehlers-Zavala, F. (2002). *Assessment of the English-language learner: An ESL training module.* Chicago: Board of Education of the City of Chicago.

Ehlers-Zavala, F. P. (2008). Teaching adolescent English language learners. In S. Lenski & J. Lewis (Eds.), *Reading success for struggling adolescent learners* (pp. 74–89). New York: Guilford Press.

Ehrenworth, M., & Vinton, V. (2005). *The power of grammar: Unconventional approaches to the conventions of language.* Portsmouth, NH: Heinemann.

Elbow, P. (1981). *Writing with power.* New York: Oxford University Press.

Englert, C. S., Okolo, C. M., & Mariage, T. V. (2009). Informational writing across the curriculum. In G. A. Troia (Ed.), *Instruction and assessment for struggling writers: Evidence-based practices* (pp. 132–161). New York: Guilford Press.

Espin, C., Wallace, T., Campbell, H., Lembke, E. S., Long, J. D., & Ticha, R. (2008). Curriculum-based measurement in writing: Predicting the success of high-school students on state standards tests. *Exceptional Children, 74*(2), 174–193.

Evers, A. J., Lang, L. F., & Smith, S. V. (2009). An ABC literacy journey: Anchoring in texts, bridging language, and creating stories. *Reading Teacher, 62,* 461–470.

Fang, Z. (2008). Going beyond the fab five: Helping students cope with the unique linguistic challenges of expository reading in intermediate grades. *Journal of Adolescent and Adult Literacy, 51,* 476–487.

Farnan, N., & Dahl, K. (2003). Children's writing: Research and practice. In J. Flood, D. Lapp, J. R. Squire, & J. M. Jensen (Eds.), *Handbook of research on teaching the English language* (2nd ed.), (pp. 993–1007). Mahwah, NJ: Erlbaum.

Fashola, O., Drum, P., Mayer, R., & Kang, S. (1996). A cognitive theory of orthographic transitioning: Predictable errors in how Spanish speaking children spell English words. *American Educational Research Journal, 33*(4), 825–843.

Fearn, L., & Farnan, N. (2001). *Interactions: Teaching writing and the language arts.* Boston: Houghton Mifflin.

Ferris, D., & Hedgcock, J. S. (1998). Teaching ESL composition: Purpose, process, and practice. Mahwah, NJ: Erlbaum.

Filmore, L. W. (2005). *Changing times, changing schools: Articulating leadership choices in educating bilingual students.* Paper presented at the annual meeting of the National Association for Bilingual Education, San Antonio, TX.

Fisher, D., Frey, N., & Lapp, D. (2009). *In a reading state of mind: Brain research, teacher modeling, and comprehension instruction.* Newark, DE: International Reading Association.

Fleischer, C., & Andrew-Vaughan, S. (2009). *Writing outside your comfort zone: Helping students navigate unfamiliar genres.* Portsmouth, NH: Heinemann.

Flowers, L. S., & Hayes, J. R. (1980). The dynamics of composing: Making plans and juggling constraints. In L. W. Gregg & E. R. Steinberg (Eds.), *Cognitive processes in writing* (pp. 31–50). Hillsdale, NJ: Erlbaum.

Fontes, J., & Fontes, R. (2003). *A to Z China.* New York: Scholastic.

Francis, N. (2000). The shared conceptual system and language processing in bilingual children: Findings from literacy assessment in Spanish and Náhuatl. *Applied Linguistics, 21*(2), 170–204.

Freeman, D., & Freeman, Y. (2004). *Essential linguistics: What you need to know to teach reading, ESL, spelling, phonics, and grammar.* Portsmouth, NH: Heinemann.

Frodesen, J. (2001). Grammar in writing. In M. Celce-Murcia (Ed.), *Teaching English as a second or foreign language* (3rd ed., pp. 233–248). Boston: Heinle & Heinle.

Fry, E. B., Fountoukidis, D. L., & Polk, J. K. (2000). *The reading teacher's book of lists* (4th ed.). Upper Saddle River, NJ: Merrill.

Fuchs, D., Fuchs, L. S., & Vaughn, S. (Eds.). (2008). *Response to intervention: A framework for reading educators.* Newark, DE: International Reading Association.

Fulwiler, T. (1987). *The journal book.* Portsmouth, NH: Heinemann.

Furr, D. (2003). Struggling readers get hooked on writing. *Reading Teacher, 56,* 518–525.

García, G. E., McKoon, G., & August, D. (2006a). Language and literacy assessment of language-minority students. In D. August & T. Shanahan (Eds.), *Developing literacy in second-language learners* (pp. 597–626). Mahwah, NJ: Erlbaum.

García, G. E., McKoon, G., & August, D. (2006b). Synthesis: Language and literacy assessment. In D. August & T. Shanahan (Eds.), *Developing literacy in second-language learners* (pp. 583–596). Mahwah, NJ: Erlbaum.

Garland, S. (1997). *The lotus seed.* San Diego, CA: Voyager Books, Harcourt.

Gass, S. M., & Selinker, L. (2001). *Second language acquisition: An introductory course* (2nd ed.). Mahwah, NJ: Erlbaum.

Gearhart, M. (2009). Classroom portfolio assessment for writing. In G. A. Troia (Ed.), *Instruction and assessment for struggling writers: Evidence-based practices* (pp. 311–336). New York: Guilford Press.

Genesse, F., & Upshur, J. A. (1996). *Classroom-based evaluation in second language education.* New York: Cambridge University Press.

Giorgis, C. (2002). Jack Gantos—Journal keeper extraordinaire. *Language Arts, 79,* 272–276.

Gómez, R., Jr., Parker, R. I., & Lara-Alecio, R. (1996). Process versus product writing with limited English proficient students. *Bilingual Research Journal, 20,* 209–233.

Graham, S., & Harris, K. R. (2007). Helping struggling writers succeed: A self-regulated strategy instruction program. *Reading Teacher, 60*(8), 752–760.

Graves, A. W., & Rueda, R. (2009). Teaching written expression to culturally and linguistically diverse learners. In G. A. Troia (Ed.), *Instruction and assessment for struggling writers: Evidence-based practices* (pp. 213–242). New York: Guilford Press.

Graves, D. H. (1983). *Writing: Teachers and children at work.* Portsmouth, NH: Heinemann.

Graves, D. H. (1994). *A fresh look at writing.* Portsmouth, NH: Heinemann.

Graves, D. H. (2003). *Writing: Teachers and children at work* (2nd ed.). Portsmouth, NH: Heinemann.

Gunning, T. G. (2010). *Assessing and correcting reading and writing difficulties* (4th ed.). Boston: Allyn & Bacon.

Hadaway, N. L., Vardell, S. M., & Young, T. A. (2002). *Literature-based instruction with English language learners.* Boston: Allyn & Bacon.

Hadaway, N. L., & Young, T. A. (2002). Accommodating diversity in literacy instruction through interactive writing. *New England Reading Journal, 38*(3), 5–9.

Haussamen, B. (with Benjamin, A., Kolln, M., & Wheeler, R. S.). (2003). *Grammar alive! A guide for teachers*. Urbana, IL: National Council of Teachers of English.

Haynes, J. (2006). Giant steps through nonfiction writing. *Essential Teacher, 3*(2), 6–7.

Heath, S. B. (1983). *Ways with words: Language, life and work in communities and classrooms*. Cambridge, England: Cambridge University Press.

Hedgcock, J., & Atkinson, D. (1993). Differing reading–writing relationships in L1 and L2 literacy development? *TESOL Quarterly, 27*(2), 329–333.

Herman, R. L., & Flanigan, B. O. (1995). Adding grammar in a communicatively based ESL program for children: Theory in practice. *TESL Canada Journal/Revue TESL du Canada, 13*(1), 1–16.

Herrera, S. G., Perez, D. R., & Escamilla, K. (2010). *Teaching reading to English language learners: Differentiated literacies*. Boston: Allyn & Bacon.

Hickman, P., & Pollard-Durodola, S. D. (2009). *Dynamic read-aloud strategies for English learners: Building language and literacy in the primary grades*. Newark, DE: International Reading Association.

Hillocks, G., Jr., & Mavrogenes, N. (1986). Sentence combining. In G. Hillocks, Jr., Ed., *Research on written composition: New directions for teaching* (pp. 142–146). Urbana, IL: National Conference on Research in English.

Hillocks, G., Jr., & Smith, M. W. (2003). Grammars and literacy learning. In J. Flood, J. Jensen, D. Lapp, & J. Squire (Eds.), *Handbook of research on teaching the English language arts* (2nd ed., pp. 721–737). Mahwah, NJ: Erlbaum.

Hughey, J. B., & Slack, C. (2001). *Teaching children to write: Theory into practice*. Upper Saddle River, NJ: Prentice-Hall.

Hurley, S. R., & Blake, S. (2000). Assessment in the content areas for students acquiring English. In S. R. Hurley & J. V. Tinajero (Eds.), *Literacy assessment of second language learners* (pp. 84–103). Boston: Allyn & Bacon.

International Reading Association. (2009, February/March). IRA Commission on RtI: Working draft of guiding principles. *Reading Today, 26*(4), 1, 4–6.

Johns, J. L. (1981). The development of the Revised Dolch List. *Illinois School Research and Development, 17*, 15–24.

Johns, J. L., & Lenski, S. D. (2010). *Improving reading: Interventions, strategies, and resources* (5th ed.). Dubuque, IA: Kendall/Hunt.

Johnstone, B. (2001). Discourse analysis and narrative. In D. Schiffrin, D. Tannen, & H. Hamilton (Eds.), *The handbook of discourse analysis* (pp. 635–649). Malden, MA: Blackwell.

Jones, D., & Christensen, C. A. (1999). Relationship between automaticity in handwriting and students' ability to generate written text. *Journal of Educational Psychology, 91*(1), 44–49.

Kaplan, R. (2005). Contrastive rhetoric. In E. Hinkel (Ed.), *Handbook of research in second language teaching and learning* (pp. 375–391). Mahwah, NJ: Erlbaum.

Kern, D., Andre, W., Schilke, R., Barton, J., & McGuire, M. D. (2003). Less is more: Preparing students for state writing tests. *Reading Teacher, 56*, 816–826.

Kim, T. (2007). *Writing instruction for English language learners: Teacher beliefs, writing tasks, and methods*. Unpublished dissertation, University of Illinois, Urbana–Champaign.

Kletzien, S. B., & Dreher, M. J. (2004). *Informational text in K–3 classrooms: Helping children read and write*. Newark, DE: International Reading Association.

Klingner, J. K., & Edwards P. A. (2006). Cultural considerations with response to intervention models. *Reading Research Quarterly, 41*(1), 108–117.

Krashen, S. (1993). *The power of reading: Insights from the research*. Englewood, CO: Libraries Unlimited.

Krashen, S. D. (1985). *The input hypothesis: Issues and implications*. White Plains, NY: Longman.

Kucer, S. B., & Silva, C. (1999). The English literacy development of bilingual students within a transition whole-language curriculum. *Bilingual Research Journal, 23*(4), 345–371.

Labov, W. (1972). The transformation of experience in narrative syntax. In W. Labov (Ed.), *Language in the inner city* (pp. 354–396). Philadelphia: University of Pennsylvania Press.

Lanauze, M., & Snow, C. E. (1989). The relation between first- and second-language writing skills: Evidence from Puerto Rican elementary school children in bilingual programs. *Linguistics and Education, 14,* 323–339.

Lancia, P. J. (1997). Literary borrowing: The effects of literature on children's writing. *Reading Teacher, 50,* 470–475.

Lazar, R. T., Warr-Leeper, G. A., & Nicholson, C. B. (1989). Elementary school teachers' use of multiple meaning expressions. *Language, Speech, and Hearing Services in Schools, 20,* 420–430.

Lee, S. H., & Muncie, J. (2006). From receptive to productive: Improving ESL learners' use of vocabulary in a postreading composition. *TESOL Quarterly, 40*(2), 295–320.

Leki, I. (1992). *Understanding ESL writers: A guide for teachers.* Portsmouth, NH: Heinemann.

Lenski, S. D., Ehlers-Zavala, F., Daniel, M. C., & Sun-Irminger, X. (2006). Assessing English-language learners in mainstream classrooms. *Reading Teacher, 60*(1), 24–34.

Lenski, S. D., & Johns, J. L. (2004). *Improving writing: Strategies, assessments, resources* (2nd ed.). Dubuque, IA: Kendall/Hunt.

Lesaux, N., Koda, K., Siegal, L., & Shanahan, T. (2006). Development of literacy. In D. August & T. Shanahan (Eds.), *Developing literacy in second-language learners* (pp. 75–122). Mahwah, NJ: Erlbaum.

Lesaux, N., & Siegel, L. S. (2003). The development of reading in children who speak English as a second language. *Developmental Psychology, 39,* 1005–1019.

Loehr, J. (2007). *The power of story.* New York: Free Press.

Low, P. B., & Siegel, L. S. (2009). Spelling and English language learners. In G. A. Troia (Ed.), *Instruction and assessment for struggling writers: Evidence-based practices* (pp. 290–307). New York: Guilford Press.

Lyon, G. E. (1999). *Where I'm from, where poems come from.* Spring, TX: Absey & Co.

MacNeil, R., Cran, M., & McCrum, R. (2004). *Do you speak American?* New York: Random House.

Makkai, A., Belmonte, B., Boatner, M. T., & Gates, J. E. (2004). *Dictionary of American idioms* (4th ed.). Hauppauge, NY: Barron's Educational Series.

Manyak, P. E. (2008). What's your news? Portraits of a rich language and literacy activity for English-language learners. *Reading Teacher, 61,* 450–458.

Marsalis, W. (2005). *Jazz ABZ.* Cambridge, MA: Candlewick Press.

Martinez, R. A., Orellana, M. F., Pacheco, M., & Carbone, P. (2008). Found in translation: Connecting translating experiences to academic writing. *Language Arts, 85,* 421–431.

McArthur, T. (1992). *Oxford companion to the English language.* Oxford, England: Oxford University Press.

McCutchen, D. (2006). Cognitive factors in the development of children's writing. In C. A. MacArthur, S. Graham, & J. Fitzgerald (Eds.), *Handbook of writing research* (pp. 115–130). New York: Guilford Press.

McGinnis, T. (2007). Are urban middle schools leaving bright immigrant youth behind? *Voices from the Middle, 14*(4), 32–38.

Meyer, B. J. F., Brandt, D. M., & Bluth, G J. (1980). Use of top-level structure in text: Key for reading comprehension of ninth-grade students. *Reading Research Quarterly, 16,* 72–103.

Montelongo, J. A., & Hernandez, A. C. (2007). Reinforcing expository reading and writing skills: A more versatile sentence completion task. *Reading Teacher, 60,* 538–546.

Morris, L. (2001). Going through a bad spell: What the spelling errors of young ESL learners reveal about their grammatical knowledge. *Canadian Modern Language Review, 58*(2), 273–286.

Murray, D. (1982). *Learning by teaching: Selected articles on writing and teaching.* Upper Montclair, NJ: Boyton/Cook.

Murray, D. M. (1981). *The craft of revision.* Fort Worth, TX: Holt.

National Assessment of Educational Progress. (2007). The nation's report card, 2007. Retrieved June 22, 2009, from *nationsreportcard.gov/writing_2007.*

National Clearinghouse for English Language Acquisition and Language Instruction Educational Programs. (2006). Retrieved June 28, 2008, from *www.ncela.gwu.edu/expert/faq/01leps.html.*

National Commission on Writing. (2003). *The neglected "r": The need for a writing revolution.* New York: College Board.

National Council of Teachers of English. (2008). Frequently asked questions. Retrieved June 28, 2008, from *www.ncte.org/edpolicy/ell/about/122806.htm.*

Newman, J. (1983). On becoming a writer. *Language Arts, 60,* 860–870.

Noguchi, R. R. (1991). *Grammar and the teaching of writing: Limits and possibilities.* Urbana, IL: National Council of Teachers of English.

Norris, J. M., Brown, J. D., Hudson, T., & Yoshioka, J. (1998). *Designing second language performance assessments.* Honolulu, HI: Second Language Teaching and Curriculum Center.

Ochs, E., & Capps, L. (2001). *Living narrative: Creating lives in everyday storytelling.* Cambridge, MA: Harvard University Press.

Ogbu, J. U., & Matute-Bianchi, M. E. (1986). Understanding sociocultural factors: Knowledge, identity, and school adjustment. In Bilingual Education Office, Department of Education (Ed.), *Beyond language: Social and cultural factors in schooling language minority students* (pp. 73–142). Los Angeles: Evaluation, Dissemination and Assessment Center, California State University.

Ogbu, J. U., & Simons, H. D. (1998). Voluntary and involuntary minorities: A cultural–ecological theory of school performance with some implications for education. *Anthropology and Education Quarterly, 29*(2), 155–188.

Ollmann, H. E. (1991/1992). The voice behind the print: Letters to an author. *Journal of Reading, 35,* 322–324.

Olshtain, E. (2001). Functional tasks for mastering the mechanics of writing and going just beyond. In M. Celce-Murcia (Ed.), *Teaching English as a second or foreign language* (3rd ed., pp. 207–217). Boston: Heinle & Heinle.

Olson, C. B., & Land, R. (2007). A cognitive strategies approach to reading and writing instruction for English language learners in secondary school. *Research in the Teaching of English, 41*(3), 269–303.

Parker, F., & Riley, K. (2010). *Linguistics for non-linguists: A primer with exercises* (5th ed.). Boston: Allyn & Bacon.

Peregoy, S., & Boyle, O. (2008). *Reading, writing, and learning in ESL: A resource book for K–12 teachers* (5th ed.). Boston: Allyn & Bacon.

Perry, K. H. (2008). From storytelling to writing: Transforming literacy practices among Sudanese refugees. *Journal of Literacy Research, 40,* 317–358.

Persky, H. R., Daane, M. C., & Jin, Y. (2003). *The nation's report card: Writing 2002* (NCES 2003-549). Washington, DC: U.S. Department of Education, Institute of Education Sciences, National Center for Education Statistics.

Peyton, J. (1990). Beginning at the beginning: First-grade ESL students learn to write. In A. Padilla, H. Fairchild, & C. Valadez (Eds.), *Bilingual education: Issues and strategies* (pp. 195–218). Newbury Park, CA: Sage.

Phung, B. (2006). *A contrastive rhetorical study of Chinese and Mexican perceptions of their native writing instruction and its implications for ESL teaching and learning.* Unpublished dissertation, Arizona State University.

Pinnell, G. S., & McCarrier, A. (1994). Interactive writing: A transition tool for assisting children in learning to read and write. In E. Hiebert & B. Taylor (Eds.), *Getting read-*

ing right from the start: Effective early literacy interventions (pp. 149–170). Needham, MA: Allyn & Bacon.

Piper, M. (2006). *Writing to change the world*. New York: Riverhead Books.

Portes, A., & Rumbaut, R. G. (2006). *Immigrant America: A portrait* (3rd ed.). Berkeley, CA: University of California Press.

Prior, J., & Gerard, M. R. (2004). *Environmental print in the classroom: Meaningful connections for learning to read*. Newark, DE: International Reading Association.

Ranker, J. (2009). Learning nonfiction in an ESL class: The interaction of situated practice and teacher scaffolding in a genre study. *Reading Teacher, 62,* 580–589.

Ray, K. W. (with Laminack, L. L.). (2001). *The writing workshop: Working through the hard parts (and they're all hard parts.)*. Urbana, IL: National Council of Teachers of English.

Resnick, L. B., & Hampton, S. (2009). *Reading and writing grade by grade*. Newark, DE: International Reading Association.

Rhodes, R. L., Ochoa, S. H., & Ortiz, S. O. (2005). *Assessing culturally and linguistically diverse students: A practical guide*. New York: Guilford Press.

Richgels, D. J. (1995). A kindergarten sign-in procedure: A routine in support of written language learning. In K. A. Hinchman, D. J. Leu, & C. K. Kinzer (Eds.), *Forty-fourth Yearbook of the National Reading Conference* (pp. 243–254). Oak Creek, WI: National Reading Conference.

Rob, T., Ross, S., & Shortreed, I. (1986). Salience of feedback on error and its effect on EFL writing quality. *TESOL Quarterly, 20*(1), 83–93.

Rog, L. J. (2007). *Marvelous minilessons for teaching beginning writing, K–3*. Newark, DE: International Reading Association.

Rosenblatt, L. M. (1978). *The reader, the text, the poem*. Carbondale, IL: Southern Illinois University Press.

Rubin, D. L. (1998). Writing for readers: The primacy of audience in composing. In N. Nelson & R. C. Calfee (Eds.), *The reading–writing connection* (pp. 53–73). Chicago: University of Chicago Press.

Rumbaut, R. G. (1995). The new Californians: Comparative research findings on the educational progress of immigrant children. In R. G. Rumbaut & W. A. Cornelius (Eds.), *California's immigrant children: Theory, research, and implications for educational policy* (pp. 17–70). La Jolla, CA: Center for U.S.–Mexican Studies, University of California, San Diego.

Schleppegrell, M. J., & Go, A. L. (2007). Analyzing the writing of English learners: A functional approach. *Language Arts, 84,* 529–538.

Schmidt, B., & Buckley, M. (1991). Plot relationships chart. In J. M. Macon, D. Bewell, & M. Vogt (Eds.), *Responses to literature: Grades K–8* (pp. 7–8). Newark, DE: International Reading Association.

Scott, C. M. (2009). Language-based assessment of written expression. In G. A. Troia (Ed.), *Instruction and assessment for struggling writers: Evidence-based practices* (pp. 358–385). New York: Guilford Press.

Selinker, L. (1972). Interlanguage. *International Review of Applied Linguistics in Language Teaching, 10*(3), 210–231.

Shanahan, T. (2006). Relations among oral language, reading, and writing development. In C. MacArthur, S. Graham, & J. Fitzgerald (Eds.), *Handbook of writing research* (pp. 171–183). New York: Guilford Press.

Sharples, M. (1996). An account of writing as creative design. In C. M. Levy & S. Ransdell (Eds.), *The science of writing: Theories, methods, individual differences, and applications* (pp. 127–148). Mahwah, NJ: Erlbaum.

Shaughnessy, M. P. (1977). *Errors and expectations: A guide for the teacher of basic writing*. New York: Oxford University Press.

Shields, M. K., & Behrman, R. E. (2004). Children of immigrant families: Analysis and recommendations. *The future of children, 14*(2), 4–15. Retrieved June 28, 2008, from *www. futureofchildren.org/usr_doc/Children_of_Immigrant_Families.pdf*.

Shin, H. B., & Bruno, R. (2003). Language use and English-speaking ability: 2000. *Census 2000 Brief.* U.S. Census Bureau. Retrieved January 22, 2009, from *www.census.gov/ prod/2003pubs/c2kbr-29.pdf*.

Shin, S. J., & Milroy, L. (1999). Bilingual language acquisition by Korean schoolchildren in New York City. *Bilingualism, 2*(2), 147–167.

Sirin, S. R. (2005). Socioeconomic status and academic achievement: A meta-analytic review of research. *Review of Educational Research, 75*(3), 417–453.

Sjolie, D. (2006). Phrase and clause grammar tactics for the ESL/ELL writing classroom. *English Journal, 95*(5), 35–40.

Slaughter, H. (2009). *Small group writing conferences, K–5: How to use your instructional time more efficiently.* Portsmouth, NH: Heinemann.

Smith, M., & Smith, R. (2003). *B is for beaver: An Oregon alphabet.* Chelsea, MI: Sleeping Bear Press.

Smith, M. W., Cheville, J., & Hillocks, G., Jr. (2006). "I guess I'd better watch my English": Grammars and the teaching of the English language arts. In C. A. MacArthur, S. Graham, & J. Fitzgerald (Eds.), *Handbook of writing research* (pp. 263–274). New York: Guilford Press.

Smith, M. W., & Wilhelm, J. (2006). What research tells us about teaching grammar, *Voices from the Middle, 13*(4), 40–43.

Smith, M. W., & Wilhelm, J. (2007). *Getting it right: Fresh approaches to teaching grammar, usage, and correctness.* New York: Scholastic.

Spada, N., & Lightbrown, P. M. (1999). Instruction, first language influence, and developmental readiness in second language acquisition. *The Modern Language Journal, 83*(1), 1–22.

Spandel, V. (2009). *Creating writers through 6-trait writing: Assessment and instruction* (5th ed.). Boston: Allyn & Bacon.

Stein, N. L., & Glenn, C. G. (1979). An analysis of story comprehension in elementary school children. In R. O. Freedle (Ed.), *New directions in discourse processing* (pp. 53–120). Norwood, NJ: Ablex.

Stotsky, S. (1995). The uses and limitations of personal or personalized writing in writing theory, research, and instruction. *Reading Research Quarterly, 30,* 758–776.

Strunk, W., & White, E. B. (2000). *The elements of style* (4th ed.). Needham Heights, MA: Allyn & Bacon.

Suárez-Orozco, C., & Suárez-Orozco, M. M. (2001). *Children of immigration.* Cambridge, MA: Harvard University Press.

Swain, M. (2005). The output hypothesis: Theory and research. In E. Hinkel (Ed.), *Handbook of research in second language teaching and learning* (pp. 471–483). Mahwah, NJ: Erlbaum.

Teachers of English to Speakers of Other Languages. (2001). *Scenarios for ESL standards-based assessments.* Alexandria, VA: Author.

Teal, W. H., & Sulzby, E. (1989). Emerging literacy: New perspectives. In D. S. Strickland & L. M. Morrow (Eds.), *Emerging literacy: Young children learn to read and write* (pp. 1–15). Newark, DE: International Reading Association.

Teale, W. H. (2009). Students learning English and their literacy instruction in urban schools. *Reading Teacher, 62,* 699–703.

Thao, Y. J. (2006). *The Mong oral tradition: Cultural memory in the absence of written language.* Jefferson, NC: McFarland.

Torrance, M., & Galbraith, D. (2008). The processing demands of writing. In C. A. MacArthur, S. Graham, & J. Fitzgerald (Eds.), *Handbook of writing research* (pp. 67–80). New York: Guilford Press.

Tucker, G. R. (1999). *A global perspective on bilingualism and bilingual education*. ERIC Clearinghouse on Languages and Linguistics, Washington DC. (Report No. EDO-FL-99-04).

Urzua, C. (1987). "You stopped too soon": Second language children composing and revising. *TESOL Quarterly, 21*(2), 279–304.

U.S. Census Bureau. (2000). *Profile of selected demographic and social characteristics for the foreign-born population who entered the United States 1990–2000: 2000*. Retrieved February 8, 2009, from *www.census.gov/population/cen2000/stp-159/1990-2000.pdf*.

Valdés, G. (n.d.). Multilingualism. Retrieved June 28, 2008, from *www.lsadc.org/info/ling-fields-multi.cfm*.

VanPatten, B. (2003). *From input to output: A teacher's guide to second language acquisition*. Boston: McGraw-Hill.

Vaughn, S., Mathes, P. G., Linan-Thompson, S., & Francis, D. J. (2005). Teaching English language learners at risk for reading disabilities to read: Putting research into practice. *Learning Disabilities Research and Practice, 20*(1), 58–67.

Watts-Taffe, S., & Truscott, D. M. (2000). Using what we know about language and literacy development for ESL students in the mainstream classroom. *Language Arts, 77*(3), 258–265.

Weaver, C. (2007). *The grammar plan book: A guide to smart teaching*. Portsmouth, NH: Heinemann.

Wheeler, R. S., & Swords, R. (2006). *Code-switching: Teaching standard English in urban classrooms*. Urbana, IL: National Council of Teachers of English.

Willner, L. S., Rivera, C., & Acosta, B. D. (2009). Ensuring accommodations used in content assessments are responsive to English-language learners. *Reading Teacher, 62*, 696–698.

Wolf, M. (2007). *Proust and the squid: The story and science of the reading brain*. New York: HarperCollins.

Wolfram, W., Adger, C. T., & Christian, D. (1999). *Dialects in schools and communities*. Mahwah, NJ: Erlbaum.

Wortham, S. (2001). *Narratives in action: A strategy for research and analysis*. New York: Teachers College Press.

Wray, D., & Lewis, M. (1997). Teaching factual writing: Purpose and structure. *The Australian Journal of Language and Literacy, 20*, 131–138.

Wright, D. (2001). Phonetically organized spelling because—. *The Delta Kappa Gamma Bulletin, 67*(4), 30–33.

Yagoda, B. (2004). *The sound on the page: Style and voice in writing*. New York: HarperResource.

Zehler, A. M., Fleischman, H. L., Hopstock, P. J., Stephenson, T. G., Pendzick, M., & Sapru, S. (2003). *Descriptive study of services to LEP students and LEP students with disabilities*. Volume I: Research report. Rosslyn, VA: Development Associates. Retrieved June 28, 2008, from *www.ncela.gwu.edu/resabout/immigration/intro*.

Zhang, G. (2007). Multiple border crossings: Literacy practices of Chinese American bilingual families. In V. Purcell-Gates (Ed.), *Cultural practices of literacy: Case studies of language, literacy, social practice and power* (pp. 85–98). Mahwah, NJ: Erlbaum.

Zuidema, L. A. (2005). Myth education: Rationale and strategies for teaching against linguistic prejudice. *Journal of Adolescent & Adult Literacy, 48*, 666–675.

Zwiers, J. (2008). *Building academic language: Essential practices for content classrooms*. San Francisco: Jossey-Bass.

Index

Page numbers followed by an *f* or a *t* indicate figures or tables.